STANLEY JONES
and the
CURWEN STUDIO

STANLEY JONES
and the
CURWEN STUDIO

Stanley Jones

A & C BLACK • LONDON

First published in Great Britain in 2010
Herbert Press
an imprint of A&C Black Publishers Limited
36 Soho Square
London W1D 3QY
www.acblack.com

ISBN: 978-14081-02862

CIP Catalogue records for this book are available from the British Library and the U.S. Library of Congress.

Typeset in Tibere Light on 11/14pt
Typeface used by Harold Curwen at the Curwen Press

Cover and book design by Sutchinda Rangsi Thompson
Publisher: Susan James
Copyediting: Julian Beecroft
Proofreading: Lauren Simpson Publishing

Printed and bound in China by C+C Offset Printing

A&C Black uses paper produced with elemental chlorine-free pulp, harvested from managed sustainable forests.

CONTENTS

PREFACE

At a time when contemporary prints have become fashionable and most artists see printmaking as an important part of their output, it is difficult to imagine the parlous state of both printmaking and the market in the UK in the 1950s. That is not to say that prints had not been popular previously; in the 19th century, the growth of the print market mirrored the development of the middle classes. For popular artists this proved a bonanza, with Millais making more money out of the reproductions of his paintings than from the paintings themselves.

Later, in the 1920s there was not so much a boom as a bubble in the market for modern prints by artists such as McBey and Griggs, but this totally collapsed with the Wall Street crash. Although some artists continued to fly the flag, for the next two decades printmaking was in the doldrums. John Piper's attempt to popularise prints, bringing together a group of young artists under the Contemporary Lithographs banner in the late '30s, was short lived, and twenty years later he was deploring the reactionary attitude of most printmakers. However, he did note that students, admiring Picasso and Miro, recognised that printmaking could be vital and lively.

Piper could have had the young Stanley Jones in mind when he made this observation, but it needed a combination of circumstances to launch Stanley on his long career – the chance to work in an lithographic atelier in Paris, the aspiration of the Curwen Press to move into the world of fine art and Robert Erskine's proselytising desire to produce good art cheaply for the general public. The rest, as they say, is history.

Stanley's association with the Curwen Studio, as it became, has lasted over fifty years which recognises not just his loyalty, but his perseverance in overcoming the twin problems of any print studio – maintaining inventiveness and quality and financial survival. In turn artists, once they started to make lithographs with Stanley, tended to stick with him for as long as they continued to make prints – or until they died. The relationship was (usually) the ideal collaborative one – a true exchange of ideas rather than a jockeying of egos.

Over the period, Stanley has played a major part in the revival and development of lithography in the UK. The list of artists he has worked with reads like a 'Who's Who' of three generations of artists – Sutherland, Hepworth, Pasmore, Scott, Frink, Hockney, Procktor, Kitaj, Conroy, Beattie, Deacon, Paul – the list goes on, but there were three artists with whom Stanley has had a special bond – Henry Moore, John Piper and, latterly, Paula Rego.

This is the high profile side of Stanley's work – but he has been equally important as a guiding hand and mentor to his Slade students; one eminent printmaker described Stanley as a saint in his forbearance towards his wayward charges. His dedication to the traditional printmaking methods, which appeared to be slowly vanishing from art schools, also led him to push for the formation of the now well established Curwen Print Study Centre.

I was fortunate, as a print publisher, to work with Stanley for around thirty years, and it was always stimulating to visit the Curwen and discuss the latest proofs with him and the artist. There was a regular refrain when problems cropped up, whether the artist was a grand old man or a struggling youngster, which summed up their respectful view of him – 'Ask Stanley – he'll know what to do'.

David Case, 2010

FOREWORD

In November 1955 I set up St George's Gallery Prints at Number 7 Cork Street, in the West End of London. It was to be the only showroom exclusively devoted to artists' prints in the whole of Britain, largely because they had not yet become appreciated as 'proper works of art' as they had in Paris and New York. Besides, not many artists made prints (or were encouraged to do so) because the three principal types – etching, woodcut and lithography – required special skills and costly equipment, especially lithography.

Prints at that time were often amateurishly printed with dirty margins on poor quality paper by the artists themselves on their own presses, or on a friend's, or in an art school. The worst offenders were the unfortunate lithographers because there was no professional printer in Britain with a studio for an artist to work in who could pull an edition of identical prints with all the colours matching.

It was, of course, possible for an artist to visit Paris and work, like Picasso and Matisse, on the premises of one of the great artisan printers such as Mourlot or Dejoubert. But the costs were prohibitive and frequent problems with intransigent customs officials were always tiresome and time-consuming. The only practical answer was to open a similar studio in Britain.

For this very purpose, I always had my eye on the art schools, hoping to find printmaking students with the patience and potential skills to 'turn the handle' of the press as well as, or even instead of, expressing themselves in pictorial imagery. I think it was Ceri Richards, himself an accomplished lithographer, who suggested to me in his lyrical Welsh accent, that one of his students at the Slade School of Fine Art, a young man called Stanley Jones, from Wigan, Lancashire, might be just the person we were all looking for.

A trip to the Slade confirmed Ceri's premonitions. A mere glance at Stanley's work showed that he was a good artist with an exceptionally strong sense of the lithographic medium: the breadth of design, the subtle use of overprinting colours and an almost obsessive cleanliness. More importantly, he demonstrated a quiet, sympathetic and unhurried personality which would help other artists get the best out of their lithographs, calm their nerves and, if need be, flatter their egos.

In fact though, the job did not yet exist. There was light at the end of the tunnel, however, for after Stanley's graduation the Slade granted him two small scholarships in order to fund a move to Paris, and an association with the lithographic printer Patris, between 1956 and 1958. Here Stanley would find out how to run such a business, practise the skills of printing whole editions and learn how to accommodate the demands of different artists.

Then, in late 1957, while Stanley was still in Paris, I discovered that the Curwen Press in East London, already known for the high quality of its production of books and posters, was considering an expansion into fine art lithography. I immediately made contact with Herbert Simon and his son Tim, who were the prime movers in this proposition, and informed them of the imminent arrival of Stanley, who was by now not only a fully-fledged professional printer but also an ideal studio manager for their project. Persuading the other members of the board of the commercial wisdom of this step into the unknown, however, took some time and anyway, once agreed upon, the proposed 'Curwen Studio' would have to be built and equipped. These preliminaries would take several months to complete and we have to find something for Stanley to do on his return.

Some time previously I had acquired a sturdy flat-bed press which was stored (in pieces) in London. Much thought was given to where this press could be reassembled and put to work. Unexpectedly, the most obvious candidate for the lithographic printing studio turned out to be not in London after all, but in St Ives, at the very tip of Cornwall. Over the years this pretty fishing port had become a centre for painters and sculptors, largely working in the abstract mode which is ideal for the medium of lithography. Stanley and I found a small but suitable space which was rented from Bruce Taylor, a local sculptor, and with Herculean effort my mighty iron press was brought from London and set up there. The little studio soon attracted well-known names such as Barbara Hepworth, Patrick Heron and Peter Lanyon; the prints began to flow from this belt-and-braces enterprise in editions of 50 copies, and they were sent to St George's Gallery for sale.

However, it was here that Stanley's patience and calming influence received its supreme test. Despite the charm of the coastal town itself, it soon turned out that the St Ives artistic community was permanently riven by ill-feeling, both stylistic and personal, which grew into a distinctive rivalry between the clique of Barbara Hepworth and that of Peter Lanyon. For instance, a Hepworth-frequented pub was an absolutely no-go area for the Lanyon set and, of course, vice-versa; nor could there be discourse of any sort between them in the street. Gradually it became evident that the only place where these warring factions lowered their mutual hostility was in Stanley's studio. I am told that there were even occasions when both principals found themselves together in their printer's presence and got on quietly with their work as good as gold. Indeed, when the time came for Stanley to shut up shop, everybody who had made prints with him was unanimous in their praise of him as a skilled mediator between artist and stone – and, more especially, between artist and artist – a rare accolade from a society as divided as this one.

By the end of 1958 the Simons' efforts had been rewarded and the new Curwen Studio was about to open for business in Plaistow, east London. The press in St Ives was sent back to London and Stanley began his fruitful career with the Curwen Studio, which is still going strong after five decades.

I moved on to new pastures and closed St George's Gallery Prints in 1962. Looking back at the gallery's various activities, I think that the promotion of the artists' lithograph was certainly one of the most successful projects of all, and it was entirely due to that early association with Stanley Jones.

Robert Erskine, 2010

ACKNOWLEDGEMENTS

After many hours spent in conversation with Linda Sandino for the *Artist's Lives* series at the British Library, her suggestion was that I should also put down some of the material in the form of a book. It has sent me over the last eighteen months on a different kind of journey – one of words to be written, not spoken. It has also meant the distillation of a life's events to fit the pattern of a book, with the words and illustrations inevitably linked with the Curwen Studio. In this context, regrettably, much has had to be omitted that applies to significant people, places and events from every period of my life. It has been a curious balancing act. I owe a lot to the guidance of my Commissioning Editor, Susan James, who in this respect has kept a firm and knowing hand on the book's progress. With the illustrations that include the use of photography, I have had the help of Howard Anderson, whose co-operation and knowledge of computer technology has been invaluable. I also wish to acknowledge the two photographs of Wigan taken by my brother Eric, the group photographed in Atelier Patris by Norman Dilworth, and my recent portrait taken by John Claridge. The photographers of many other images included are either unknown or no longer traceable. I would, however, like to mention Julia Hedgecoe, who in the past has consistently photographed both artists and studios. For additional contributions my appreciation goes to Robert Erskine and David Case, both long-term colleagues in the world of artists' prints.

Collaborative printmaking of this kind in a workshop that has existed for over 50 years is bound to accumulate long lists of artists, printmakers and publishers who remain unmentioned but who have helped in various ways to support the studio's existence and create its character. My thanks also go to those countless individuals.

Finally, I would wish to dedicate this book to my wife Jenny, without whose participation and support it would not have been possible.

Stanley Jones, October 2010.

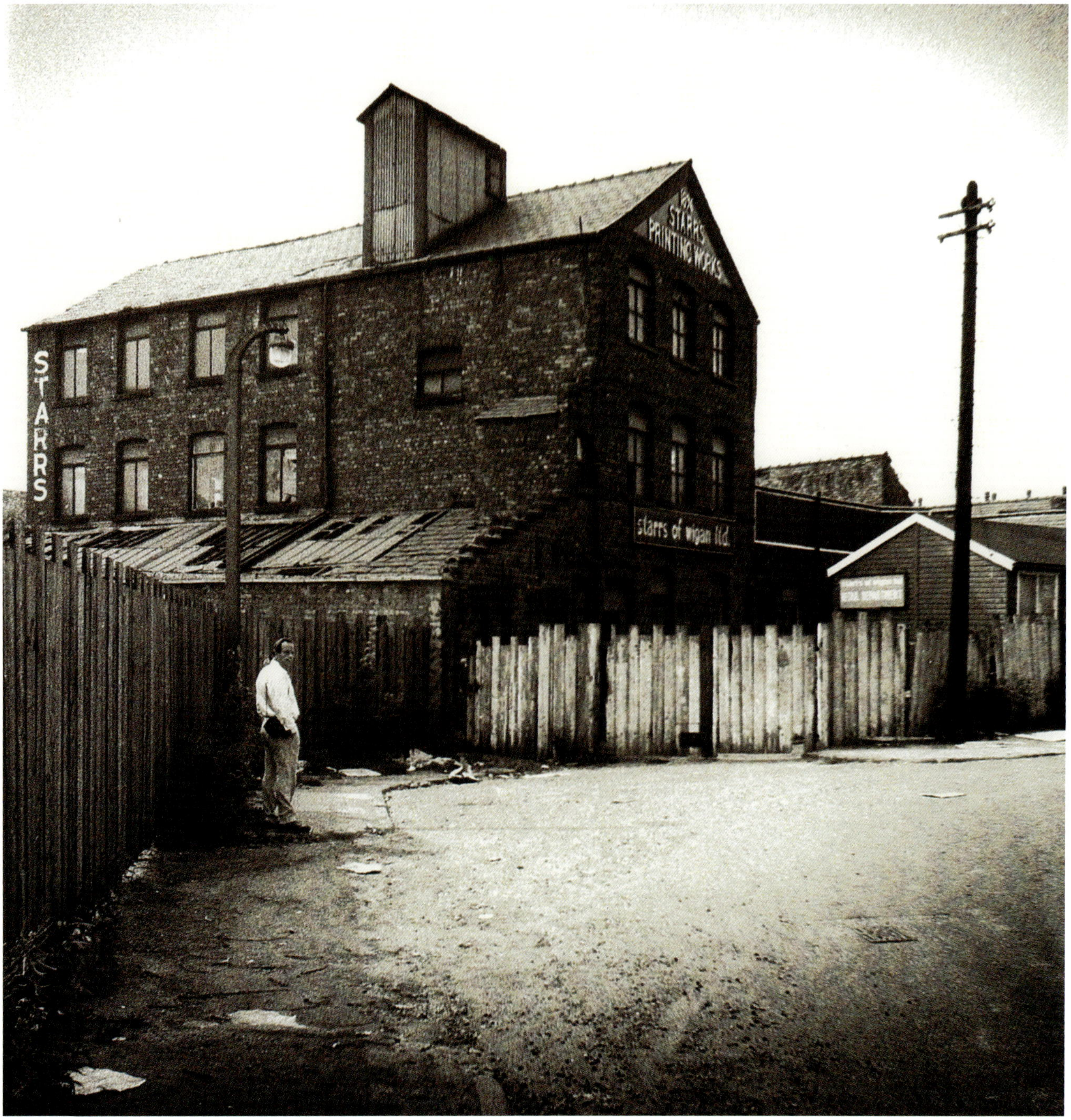
STARRS
STARRS
PRINTING WORKS
starrs of wigan ltd.

"All around was the lunar landscape of slag-heaps, and to the north, through the passes, as it were, between the mountains of slag . . ."

EARLY LIFE

Wigan: abandoned landscapes

In 1933, when I was born, Wigan was still known for its cotton mills and coal mines, peopled, as the outside world imagined, by men who wore clogs and whose womenfolk dressed in shawls. This, of course, was not the total picture. Outside the town was open countryside: to the west the agricultural Lancashire plain; to the east the Pennine moors. However, to artists such as L.S. Lowry, who worked in Manchester, what appealed was the declining industrial landscape.

Wigan shared a similar topography, formed by centuries of industrial activity. There was no escaping it; extraordinary remnants littered the land. Derelict pit tips with their lunar forms – some still smouldering in a permanently acrid atmosphere. In the years leading up to the Second World War cotton mills, surrounded by blackened streets, ceased to exist. Houses were simply hovels where inhabitants endured what must have been a dire existence. Public order could be difficult to control in the parts of Wigan which suffered from high unemployment, and areas like Scholes or Hardybutts had a reputation for deprivation and violence that would be difficult to imagine today. Housing conditions were often appalling, and drunkenness was commonplace. In Hardybutts the local priest had to help the police on Saturday nights, wielding a stout stick to maintain order if fighting got out of hand; if not quite gang warfare, this was still a constant social disturbance.

Wigan was riddled with rotting canals, declining railway sidings and recurring mining subsidence with its 'flashes' of water, collapsing buildings and the mysterious yawnings of old forgotten workings. Soot covered everything; it was part of the atmosphere, clinging like a permanent shroud to people and places alike. Since coal still drove the engines, made the gas and warmed the homes, its smog crept everywhere, only lifting occasionally (notably during Wakes Week, an annual holiday in the north of England) to reveal the underlying ravages of pollution. Such an atmosphere coloured both the inhabitants and the architecture in equal measure. The results, in many cases, were eccentric, but mostly simply depressing.

Wigan lies in a hollow to the west of the Pennines and it is said that because of this its climate was damp enough for the spinning of cotton. The coal mines, which provided the raw material for the town's power, heat and light, were first discovered in the late 16th century and gradually grew in importance as the industrial revolution progressed. Although the activities of the Lancashire coalfields have now entirely ceased, the coalfields themselves live on as part of a social legend, with the canals and railways all interdependent, moulding an environment which was fully developed largely before I was born.

Left: James Starr Printing Works *c.*1960

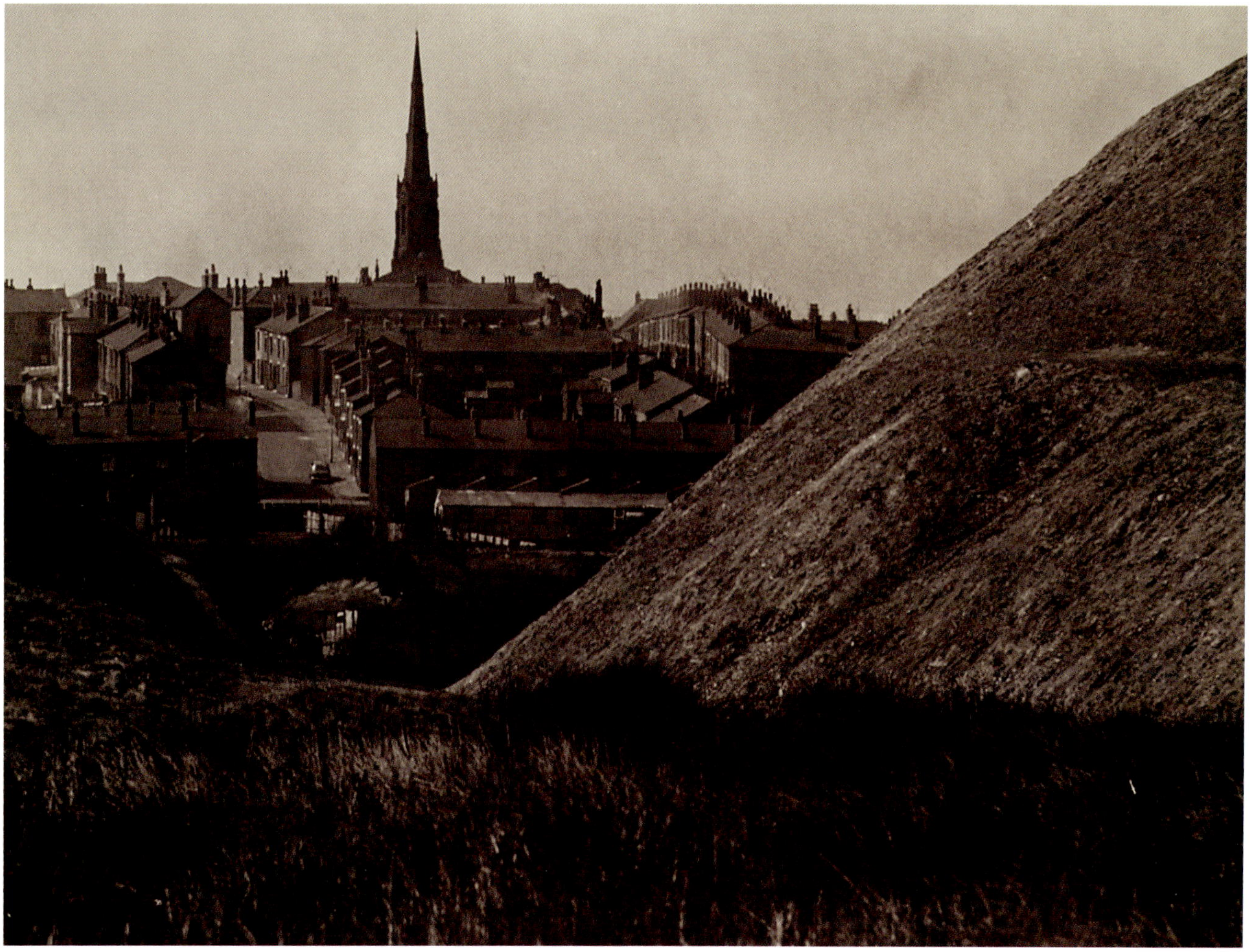

St. Katherine's Church, Wigan, 1904

In his book *The Road to Wigan Pier*, George Orwell describes his visit to Wigan in a way that has registered a certain grim image of the town in the public imagination.

> All around was the lunar landscape of slag-heaps, and to the north, through the passes, as it were, between the mountains of slag, you could see the factory chimneys sending out their plumes of smoke. The canal path was a mixture of cinders and frozen mud, criss-crossed by the imprints of innumerable clogs, and all around as far as the slag-heaps in the distance, stretched the "flashes" – pools of stagnant water that has seeped into the hollows caused by the subsidence of ancient pits. It was horribly cold.'
>
> (From *The Road to Wigan Pier* by George Orwell [London: Penguin Classics, 2001].)

Although this was written in 1937, in the 1950s the atmosphere and landscape remained the same. Of course, such living conditions must have applied to most industrialised towns and cities of the time but Orwell chose Wigan, and the icon formed from his experience has remained. In truth, though, dilapidation in Wigan occurred in curious pockets across a wide area. For instance, at the top of Shaw Street, the road where I grew up, were labourers' cottages which were little more than hovels – low-beamed and cramped for space. At the other end, a distance of some three hundred yards, lived professional people with maids in attendance. Number 15 Shaw Street, my home from birth to the age of 20, was a house halfway up the street, part of a Victorian terrace, with respectability to match. My parents were both born in Wigan. On my mother's side, an older sister,

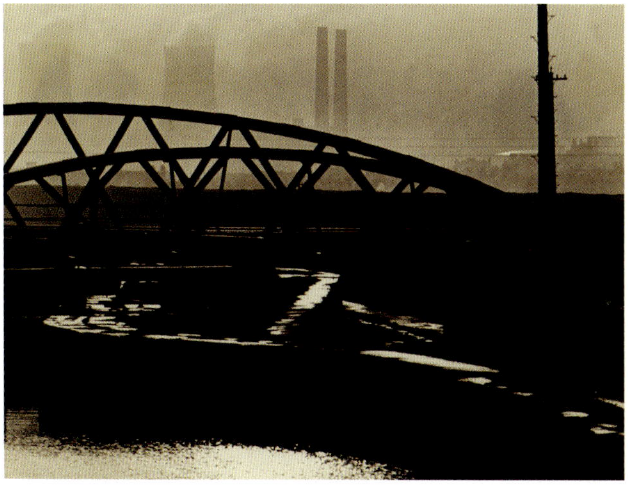

'Top Lock', Higher Ince Canal, near Wigan, 1964

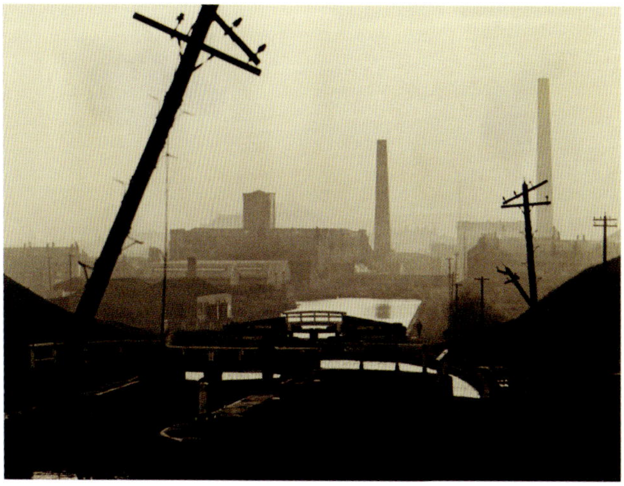

Higher Ince Canal, near Wigan, 1964

Florence, along with a younger sister, Jane, made up their family. Their mother Anne was brought up in what was a corn mill and farm property in Bottling Wood, owned by William Leather. Anne was a member of the extensive Leather family who had been in Wigan for some decades and had developed many local branches in various trades. From an early age she had a reputation as a skilled weaver. She later married John Cartwright, a cabinet maker, and the couple's three daughters were born and brought up in the shadow of Wigan Girls' High School, where their father later became caretaker.

My father's family were brought up in Poolstock, an industrialised part of Wigan with terraced back-to-back streets stretching amongst mills and mines. Their father James, an iron founder, had walked from Coalbrookdale in Shropshire to Wigan seeking work at the Wigan Coal and Iron Company. At the height of its activity this complex dominated the Wigan skyline, becoming a cauldron of flames and smoke as the furnaces disgorged their contents 24 hours a day. His occupation was the tapping of the blast furnaces – a heavy and awesome job carried out in a searing, torrid heat. Despite such a hard existence, with his wife Mary and neighbourly help (as was the custom in those days) James managed to raise a family of eight sons and a daughter. My father George was born in 1900 and he and his brothers all made a living in the railways and the mines around Wigan. Driving and understanding railway engines was to be my father's life's occupation. His work clothing always had the odour of hot oil and steam, and the rattle and clanking of rolling stock was never far away from home.

After marriage, my parents settled in Shaw Street, where my brother Eric preceded me by some four years. I am told that my birth was almost a catastrophe – a struggle between my mother and the young and (probably inexperienced) Dr Macleod, who wasn't used to babies weighing around 12 pounds. The use of forceps caused damage to my right eye and although I survived the ordeal, it took many visits to the Manchester Royal Eye Hospital before the eye took on a semblance of normality. Inevitably, its vision was impaired, but it was several years before I was able to describe this to my parents, who promptly took me back to the hospital. Mr Stirling, the chief consultant, pronounced its condition to be incurable and glasses of no use; so I began with one really good eye and the other normal to outward appearances – but virtually sightless.

Our family house in Shaw Street was well built of red pressed brick, with a slate roof, and typical of the Edwardian terraced houses found near Wigan Lane. From the front-bedroom windows you could see the tall chimneys of some of the mills and clearly hear their whistles in the early morning and at one o'clock in the afternoon. My father, bound to the railway's habits, was often summoned in emergency by the 'knocker up', who, equipped with long pole and astride a bicycle, rode around Wigan on his nightly missions sending drivers and firemen to their labours at Springs Branch loco sheds, which were lost amongst the mines and cemeteries of Ince.

At the back of the house, a flagged yard separated us from a large brick building known as Collier's. Always derelict as far as I can remember, it was formed from a fascinating series of haphazard windows, heavy wooden doors and the remains of some stables. On rare occasions workmen would invade its recesses to store building materials; otherwise it remained a monument to dilapidation. It was a constant presence during my life at number 15 – a growing source of visual fascination to me whilst growing up, as bits collapsed and others were added. As a child I delighted in exploring it, as though it were an abandoned fortification; as I grew into adulthood its qualities would remain in my mind.

Due to our Nonconformist background my elder brother and I were sent to the Wesleyan School, which stood just off Standishgate. He was four years ahead of me, and to some extent I benefited from his experiences in knowing what to expect from school. Within its sombre Victorian presence its staff had fostered generations of children into all walks of life and had an enviable reputation for feeding the local grammar and high schools with scholarship pupils. Each year had its ecstasies and depressions as we struggled with the hurdles of writing with dip pens and reciting maths tables in the stuffy atmosphere of crowded classrooms, and the excitement of being allowed to draw, if we behaved ourselves, on Friday afternoons. Guardian over all was Miss Latham: Eton-cropped and resplendent in tweeds and brogues, she could command authority at all levels, often demolishing with a firey voice anyone who wilfully opposed her. But she was not just formidable; she had an understanding of the human condition which endeared her to all sorts of people. War refugees, deprived children, the unfortunate and the desperate could always find sympathetic help or advice from her. In my class there were two lads, Stanley Connor and Eric Hutchinson, who, when I was seven years old, used to appear in an unwashed state and in clothing that was full of holes. As children we were used to it; however, once spotted by Miss Latham, her due attention in the right quarters would soon solve their predicament. In those strenuous war years she worked all sorts of miracles with the staff and her children, and her social and educational prowess never lapsed.

Childhood illness kept me from school for a considerable amount of time. but it gave me the opportunity to pursue my growing obsession with drawing, whilst in bed, on the fly leaves of books and any paper I could lay my hands on. It led to the discovery of a different world cultivated by the imagination and reading. Toys had disappeared with the war; my most treasured objects were coloured pencils found by one of my uncles who was caretaker at the local girls' high school. Outside my sickroom, the war rumbled on – the frequent air raids, the blackout, the coming and going of evacuees, with the inevitable food and clothes rationing. My family coped with all these matters – the cooperation between relatives and neighbours was often instrumental in avoiding major crises – and we all learned to live in a day-to-day state of uncertainty. Our street seemed always deserted of traffic and in those years was an ideal playground for children with homemade trolleys who were able to avoid the occasional horse-drawn carts. Older youths would play 'kick the can' and hide-and-seek through the myriad backyards. Double summer time (during WWII British Summertime was officially GMT + 2 hours) allowed for prolonged daylight during those long summer nights of the 1940s and above the noise of children's games the rumble of bombers could occasionally be heard, accompanied by ominous flashes of gunfire over Liverpool.

The war dragged on. Evacuees came and went, as did so many local men and women into the armed forces and social services; this constant flux of people, even including my school friends, became a normality. School attendance became a part-time affair and a portion of the school was transformed into an air-raid warden's post, shrouded in sandbags. As with most children, we often had time on our hands, and in the afternoons we would wander around the streets in search of adventure. One day, when I was about seven years old, two or three of us were in Swinley Road, passing the large bay window of a substantial house, when I saw a man near the window applying what looked like paint onto a white board, propped up against an easel. On it was the brightly coloured semblance of a lady who was sitting close to him. We stood watching. She turned suddenly, embarrassed by this uninvited audience of curious children and shook her fist. The painter, engrossed in his work, carried on regardless. After pulling some faces and nudging each other, my friends ran off. I remained, captivated by this activity. For me, this was a memorable revelation. I did not know it at the time but I had encountered at work the Wigan artist (and friend of L.S. Lowry) Theodore Major. I rushed home, excited, to tell my mother, describing to her what I had seen. To my mother, who had been brought up with a strict Victorian code of behaviour, the thought of my gazing into strangers' windows was a matter of some concern. She knew Mrs Major as a local neighbour and, not wanting to cause offence, she forcefully forbade me from looking into that window again. However, that studio room couldn't help but arouse my curiosity and had a direct influence on my future.

In a world bereft of visual stimulus I spent much time huddled at home over the kitchen table, drawing with anything available. In this respect I was fortunate to have an uncle who took an interest in my obsession. Peter Geary was the foreman at J. Starr and Sons, well-known locally as printers and bookbinders. On special occasions he took me on visits to the works, where the atmosphere was a curious mixture of odours: bookbinder's glue, letterpress ink and gas. The printers were crammed amongst the presses and huge stacks of paper in a manner which hadn't changed since the company began in the mid-19th century. When in full production, the building rocked and vibrated alarmingly, with the dust of ages scattered everywhere. Given its position beside the main L.M.S. line to London, the total noise was deafening. The great treat was that I normally returned home laden with offcuts of paper, having rescued them from oblivion.

I was by now approaching my ninth year, and the prospect of sitting an exam for a grammar school place loomed over me. My brother, four years ahead, was already over this hurdle. In those days, the alternative prospect of 'secondary modern' education would carry you into local employment and possibly into the nearby technical college for engineering, if that was your interest. A child's future lay at this divide, so the competition between the elementary schools for places was acute. I recall our teacher, Miss Willcock, who coached us all for these exams and had an extraordinary track record of success for scholarship awards. She gave me books to read at home and struggled with me over the maths. 'How long does it take to fill a tank which measures 20ft by 30ft?' 'With what?' I thought. 'And where was this tank?' On those long sunny afternoons, with the droning of classes reciting their tables next door my mind used to wander round these problems by reassembling the author's scenarios and forgetting his predicaments embedded in the cold print. 'What is the point of all this?' I wondered, gazing through the gothic windows across the roofs and chimneys, which on this particular day were shimmering in the spring light.

In English lessons, which were so much more exciting, we discovered poetry and a wealth of stories and books. I joined the local children's library and became a voracious reader. A different world was beginning to reveal itself, but the immediate pressure was generated by crucial examinations. First the intelligence tests, the maths and the English had to be negotiated, followed by an interview at the local education offices to face the heads of the grammar and high schools.

One morning a heavy buff envelope bearing the crest of Wigan Education Authority dropped through the letterbox. It was opened by my mother and to her relief she read that I had been offered a scholarship to the grammar school. For me a different world lay ahead; some of my friends were not so fortunate and took other directions meaning that I lost contact with them as the years progressed. By now the war in Europe was drawing to a close, and soon we had gas lamps in the streets and a gnarled old man to light them every evening.

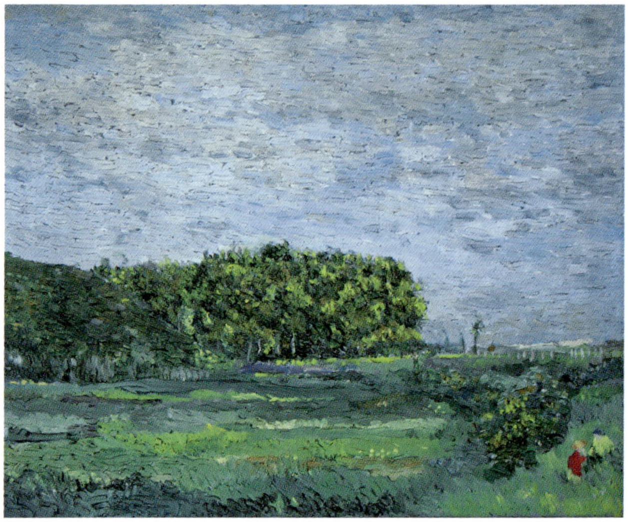

Stanley Jones, *Landscape Study*, oil painting, 1949

Wigan Grammar School

In the autumn of 1944 I started as a scholarship boy replete with a uniform (obligatory) assembled by my mother with considerable ingenuity, from various sources. Since the school's beginnings in 1597 it had provided a constant supply of students for the universities and the local trades and professions. In the mid-1930s it had been rebuilt and stood resplendent near Mesnes Park; in those days both institutions were objects of civic pride. The staff had battled through the Second World War with teacher and material shortages of all kinds, in a valiant attempt to uphold the standards of former times. Women teachers had been drafted in to fill the gaps, and the older male teachers were given an extra lease of life by virtue of the war effort. Their eccentricities had become quite pronounced, and marked them out amongst the boys – 'Pop' Skirrow, 'Pat' Lemmon, 'Old Bill' Williams and 'Teddy' Johnson come to mind as predictable performers. Was it simply a characteristic of the school system or a result of the rigours of this particular school that such idiosyncratic traits should emerge fairly commonly in teachers in late middle age? Or was it both? New to this theatre of learning we young people in Form 3 accepted it as normality, not realising that, with the presence of women teachers, there was now quite a social change taking place.

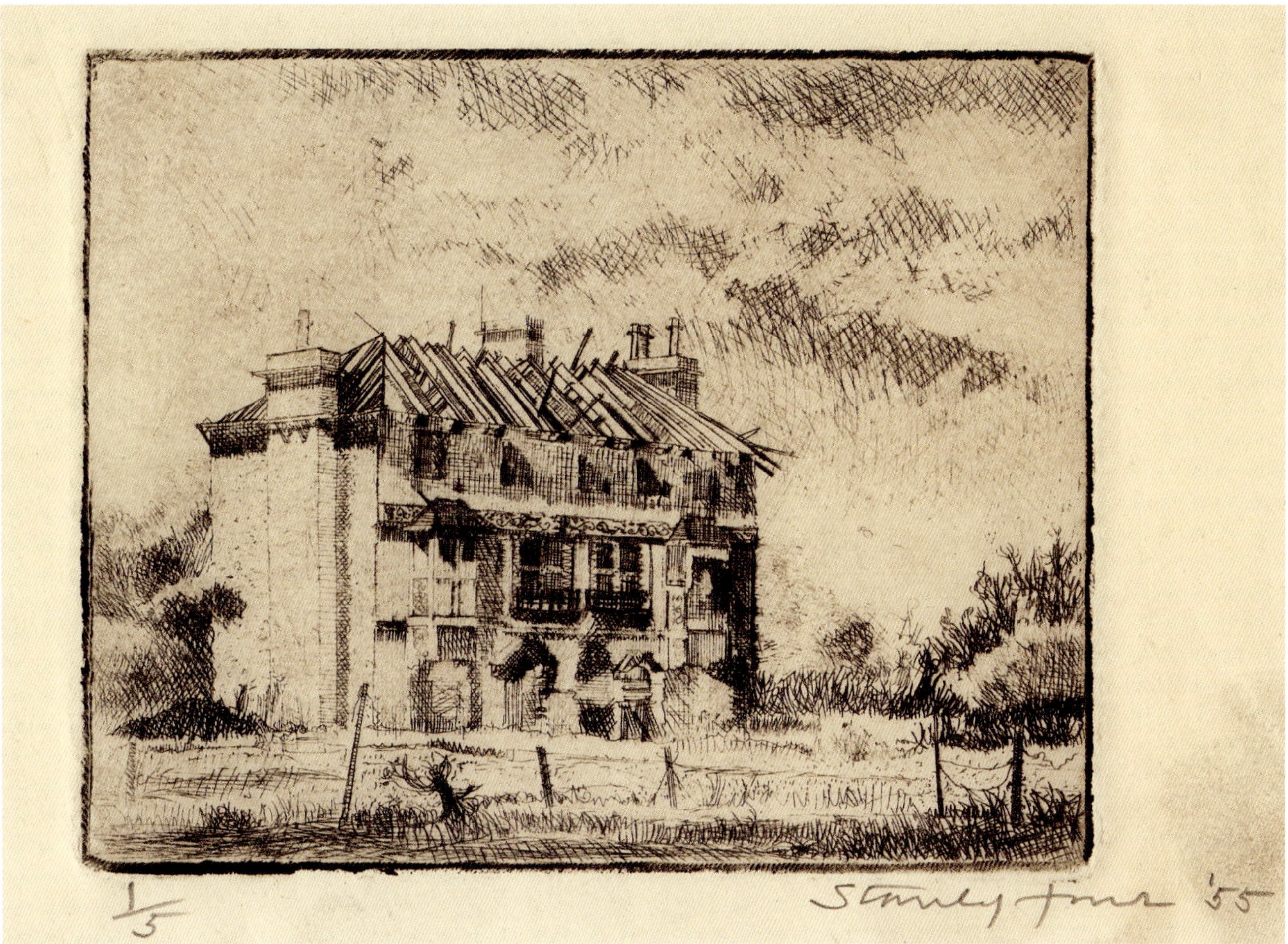

Stanley Jones' first etching, *Derelict Houses* 1953

The regime was led by the Headmaster, William Taylor, who wore the traditional mortarboard, with suitable gravitas, on all occasions. He ruled his world with a rod of iron so that discipline was not a problem in the school. Those unfortunates who ended up in his study did not forget the experience in a hurry. So it began for us, Form 3, in a classroom overlooking the quadrangle, the search for a future life in whatever form tied by the yearly obligations of study timetables and homework. Subjects such as Latin, French, chemistry and art presented me with the prospect of a School Certificate on the distant horizon. Life was beginning to broaden out in a bewildering way.

The grammar school in Wigan had been the main focus of further education for boys since its foundation in 1597, being dedicated to training its pupils for the professions and mostly linked to the arts and sciences. Part of its purpose was to provide candidates for the universities, judged by performance in Higher School Certificate exams and subsequent interviewing. As a system it was the normal academic procedure – demanding and competitive, with a high drop-out rate when the prospect of university became a family issue. The educational moulding of young and adolescent boys was an intricate balancing act dependent not only on ability, but on friendships and influences (both staff and fellow student) within the school. Parental and social backgrounds played their part. I mention this as the explanation for many of my friends who were bright stars to begin with, before slowly fading on their voyage through the school. Others proceeded on their yearly progress to university careers and whatever further horizons awaited them, unhindered by financial, social or family restrictions. In my case other events were awkwardly appearing and occupying my attention, aside from the yearly academic demands of coursework and exams. The subject of art – painting and drawing – was unheard of in my family. Of course, after my earlier experiences, I felt this a fascinating subject to practise and pursue.

To begin with, the resident art master, 'Sally' Bulmer, had a fearsome reputation. His classes were held in total silence and the only equipment allowed was a pencil, a ruler and an India rubber. In an unexpected test we were asked to draw a landscape of our choice – I produced a view of a derelict farmyard, which was duly framed by him and hung on the art room wall. Such an accolade was unheard of from him for a mere 4th-former. For me it became a curious portent. Family and friends were mystified. The possibility of a career in the art world loomed large in my imagination, although the awesome Mr Bulmer himself seemed to be a potential problem as well. Then suddenly, two terms later, he was gone, replaced by Frank Leyland, who transformed the art room and its atmosphere, opening up a totally different prospect. From then on I was set on course.

At this point I also discovered the Wigan reference library, full of books with information on watercolour, oil painting, art appreciation and the lives of artists. There was no art gallery in Wigan, so I was introduced to the historical development of painting and sculpture through books and their reproductions. I owe a debt to Mr Hawkes, the librarian, and his assistants, who sometimes allowed me to take these books out of the reference library. Nobody else seemed to be interested in Turner or Picasso in that sombre Victorian building, with its secluded and often musty atmosphere. For me, its contents were to become a growing revelation.

Academic conflict: staff disapproval

My parents, to their credit, were willing to encourage me at least for a while; my mother, with the help of Mr Leyland, managed to persuade the Headmaster, Mr Warren, that I should sit the Higher School Certificate Art exam. Very reluctantly he agreed to a compromise: that I should sacrifice the extra time allowed for my other subjects – English, history and geography. This was Mr Warren's challenge to me, a test of how serious I was about studying painting and drawing, and the persistent demands of homework and exams were to dominate my life over the next two years. As an interesting diversion Mr Leyland decided that at this time I should submit work to art schools for further study.

Other students in the 6th form had travelled this road: two years ahead of me, Kenneth Fleetwood was studying dress and stage design at St Martin's in London and became a considerable source of help and information at this formative time. He was to make a notable career with the couturier Hardy Amies.

So there were possibilities to be explored. At that time the quality of teaching staff and general art-school reputations varied a great deal – thus so much depended on choosing well. My portfolio was sent to the Slade in London, which was then headed by William Coldstream. To my surprise, I was called for an interview. It was my first meeting with Professor Coldstream and William Townsend and, in truth at the age of 15, I was somewhat overawed by the whole occasion. Nevertheless, the two men were both very encouraging and willing to offer me a place, but they also felt that I was too young to take full advantage of what the college and London had to offer. It was agreed that I should reapply after spending time in a northern art school. In anticipation of this, I had applied to the NDD courses at both Liverpool and Manchester Colleges of Art.

Meanwhile, much activity centred around the art room at school to produce work for the first local art exhibition that Wigan had ever hosted. A committee of artists and teachers had been selected to organise the event in the Grammar School assembly hall, and the exhibition we eventually staged was regarded by all and sundry as 'very progressive'. Amongst the works submitted was a large reclining nude of his wife by the artist Theodore Major, which was given a prominent place in the show. The Headmaster, on inspecting the works, absolutely refused to let the painting be hung, thinking of the complications of morning assembly each day. There was conflict and deadlock with the hanging committee, who refused to recognise the problem at all. The furore reached the local papers, and even the mayor, I believe, was consulted. Finally, when all seemed lost, a compromise was reached: a school prefect was appointed each day to unfold a portable screen, which covered the work, and remove it after assembly had finished. Everyone seemed satisfied by the compromise, though the Headmaster's view of the art world remained unimpressed. However, despite such occurrences, at this time it did seem that a broader appreciation of the arts was beginning to emerge, even in Wigan.

For me, a time of change was approaching. The conventional route to university was something I had to disregard, in favour of the art school where I first began my training. The oppressive summer of 1949 represented a formidable catharsis, with exams and college applications all crowded into a few summer months and dominating daily life. Tensions at home between myself and my parents became increasingly difficult to avoid; they could see my contemporaries choosing much more defined and predictable futures, whereas what I intended to do with an art school qualification remained a source of contention. For me, a future of full-time teaching did not appeal, so there were many questions that remained unanswered as well as constant arguments. As a diversion I took to wandering around the local woods and canals with the family dog. At this time the canals were in a state of decay, with abandoned locks and barges littering the waterways. Surrounding them, industrial buildings that had flourished in Victorian times were sinking slowly into the mud. It was all very striking and intriguing, and images such as these gradually began appearing in my sketchbooks. July drifted into August and suddenly offers of places arrived from both Liverpool and Manchester Colleges of Art. At least there were now alternative directions. The Higher School results were next to appear – all very satisfactory, particularly in art. It now remained to acquire the grant funding.

Apart from my application forms, I'd had no contact with Wigan Education Authority, so when I sat in the anteroom waiting to be interviewed I imagined that this would be a formality. It was the newly appointed Director of Education, Reese Edwards, who conducted the interviewing. He made it clear that all new art students had to study at Wigan College of Art, and that the grant offer would be solely for that opportunity. But the art master at the grammar school, who encouraged his students to apply to academically important colleges in places like London, Liverpool and Manchester, had had little contact with Wigan College of Art. So when I told Mr Edwards that I hadn't applied to Wigan College of Art and thus couldn't accept his offer, his face contorted with fury: as a newly appointed administrator he was not used to being challenged by 6th-form students. The atmosphere became very tense and the interview ended in acrimonious stalemate, putting my plans in jeopardy, with parents and the schoolteachers angry and puzzled at such unexpected treatment. Efforts to get this ruling reversed (made at such short notice) were to no avail; I was apparently the victim of a new bureaucracy. What should be done? In the worst moments I felt that this was the end of my dream, but on the other hand I resolved not to be overcome by this obstacle. I decided to go and discover what the local art school had to offer and to meet its Principal, Alec Woffenden.

Bit by bit the scattered pieces of this jigsaw were sorted out and, with his help, it was agreed that I should join their NDD course for four years and then reapply to the Slade afterwards. This idea cast a different light on matters and was eventually to prove quite salutary, unbeknownst to Reese Edwards. Needless to say, my parents were somewhat mollified that a burden had been temporarily lifted from their shoulders and they could focus their attentions for a while on my brother's career at Leicester University.

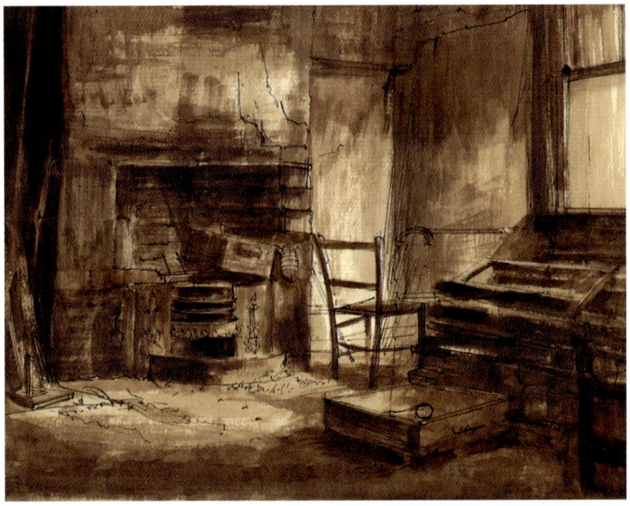

Above: *Hall's workshop studio, Wigan*, watercolour study, 1954

Right: Stanley Jones, *Local Farmhouse*, etching - two states, 1953

Wigan College of Art

Known worldwide as the Wigan Mining and Technical College, the local college had achieved a high reputation in engineering, being centrally placed among the long-established coalfields of south Lancashire. The art school occupied about half the top floor of this august institution, built to uphold the highest standards of Victorian further education. It was very common for northern towns to possess such establishments, which also tended to include an art department. As in Wigan's case, these were the only local centres where, through

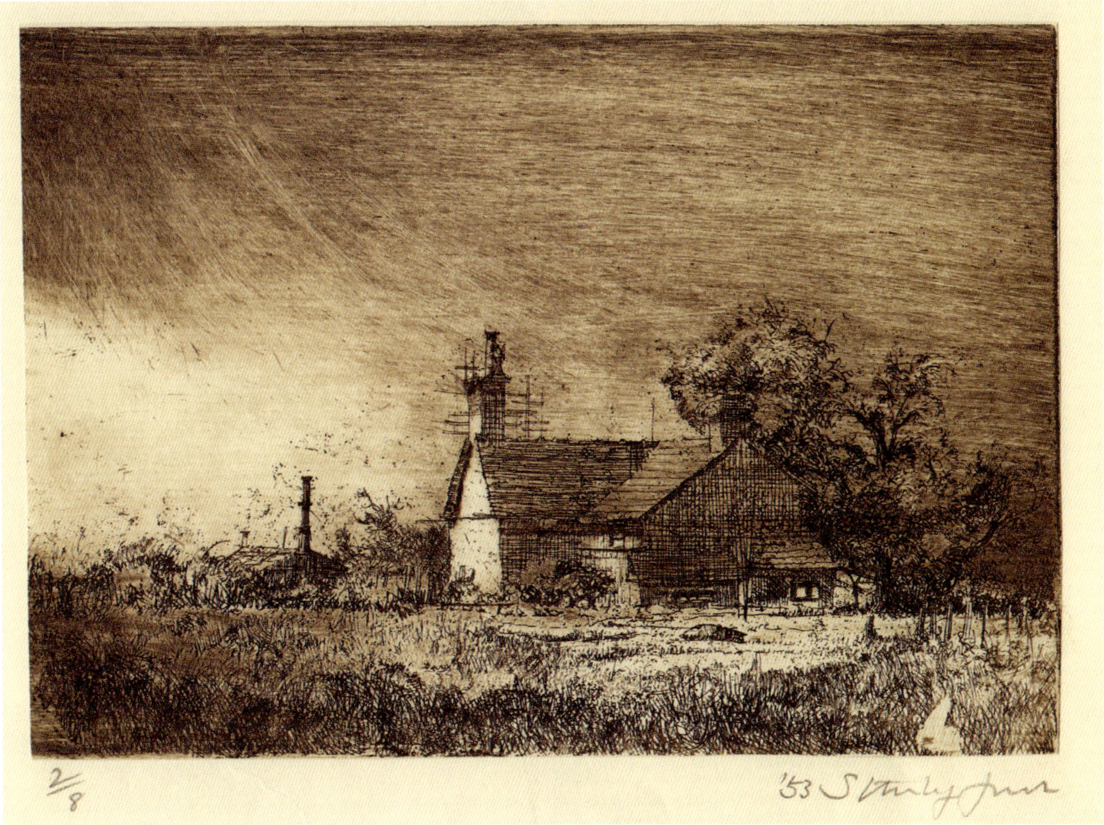
2/8
'53

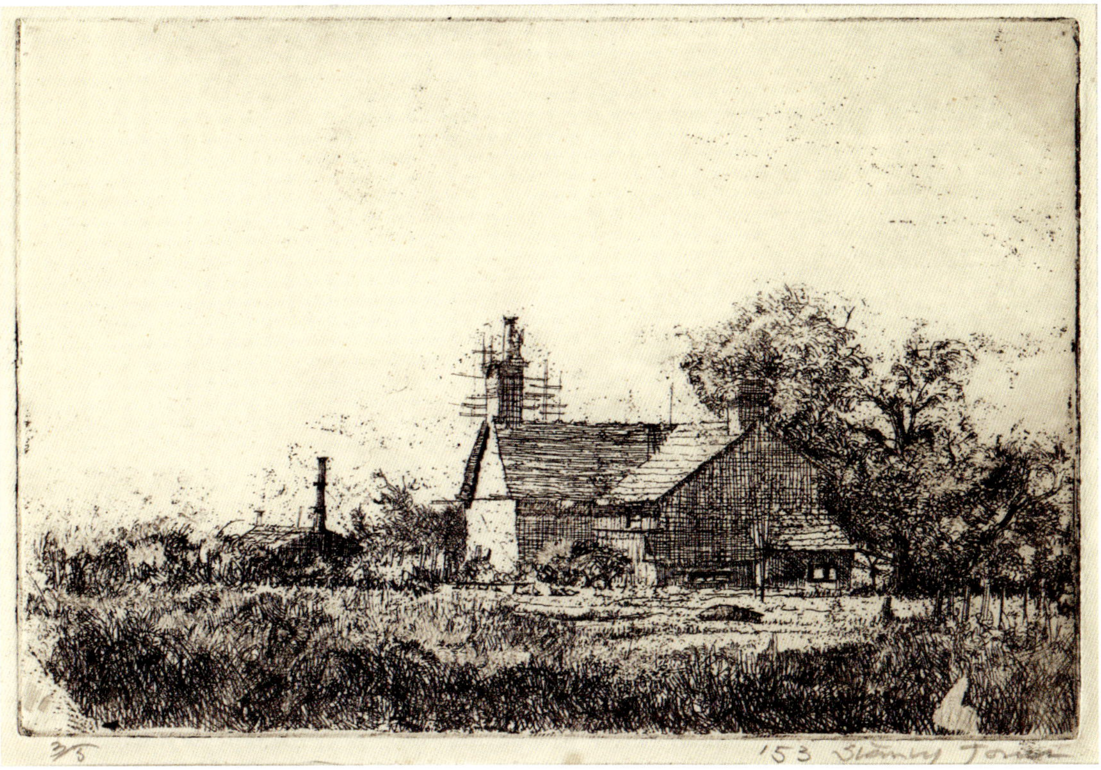
3/8
'53

day and evening classes, people interested in the arts could meet to pursue their interests. The art school, by its nature, attracted a rather odd cross section of the public and was regarded as somewhat eccentric by the rest of the inhabitants. Nevertheless, it had survived, and in these post-war years it was now attracting would-be students from the forces and new staff from London. It promised to be a heady mix.

One morning in October I arrived with fellow students from local schools, to meet the staff and the other, established students who were well-seasoned and years ahead of me. For the first time, there were mixed classes, though some of the girls I already knew from the High school. Other students, such as Bert Winstanley and Michael Goodger, were complete strangers but they would be fellow travellers, in the years to come, on this unknown voyage of discovery. It was thought by the staff to be quite a bright year – there was certainly much competition and commitment within the class. The older students, as time went on, came to look upon what our group was producing with confirmed admiration. The staff, of course, were delighted. Leonard and Margaret Penrice, Wilfred Andrews and Brian Bottomley all had their work cut out to cope with such student enthusiasm.

The teaching and training was all based on the requirement for the four-year National Diploma in Design, then the official qualification for most art schools. An intermediate exam taken in the second year was the first hurdle to be negotiated. Around this activity, individuality of approach was encouraged with all its implications. Rivalry produced competition on all levels, and it was all a healthy test of commitment. Small classes made for a personal level of tuition that would not be possible today and held considerable advantages. To obtain favourable or even derogatory comment from the staff was an added bonus that spurred us on. The value of discussion and argument was significant, as it helped to guide and develop talents along their individual paths through some bewildering times. I suppose we were often cynical about the older generation's views on contemporary movements in painting and sculpture, governed as they were by art school exam strictures. But for me they pointed out directions which I found challenging, to say the least.

The freedom to wander around Wigan with a sketchbook became a constant obsession, with its excitement and its hazards. My interest in landscape was deepened now that I had licence to spend time appreciating it. As I mentioned earlier, the smoke-stained town and its surroundings were in a picturesque state of decline, but there were still the pits and the mills, the cobblestones and the clogs. As a group we made discoveries about artists and their painting techniques in gouache and watercolour; I worked with watercolours, inks, pens, pencils of various grades and sable brushes, and made a kit in a haversack which became my constant companion for outdoor work. Sometimes cycling, at other times on foot, I explored Wigan and its outskirts in all weathers, always somehow managing to find subjects of interest. In summer the horseflies and midges made life difficult whilst winter brought rain, fog and ice, and the inevitable creeping cold.

During the summer of 1952 my continuing exploration of the environs of Wigan filled my notebooks with an unusual variety of subjects and locations; I became obsessed with the atmosphere of a collapsing industrial environment. L.S. Lowry had spent so much time walking the backstreets and alleys of Salford and Manchester to produce his individual style of work that, inevitably, his influence was apparent in most northern art schools at the time. For me, as a student, having learnt much

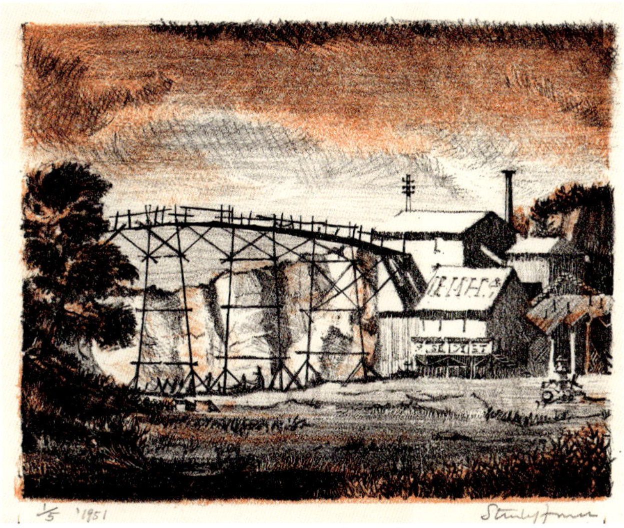

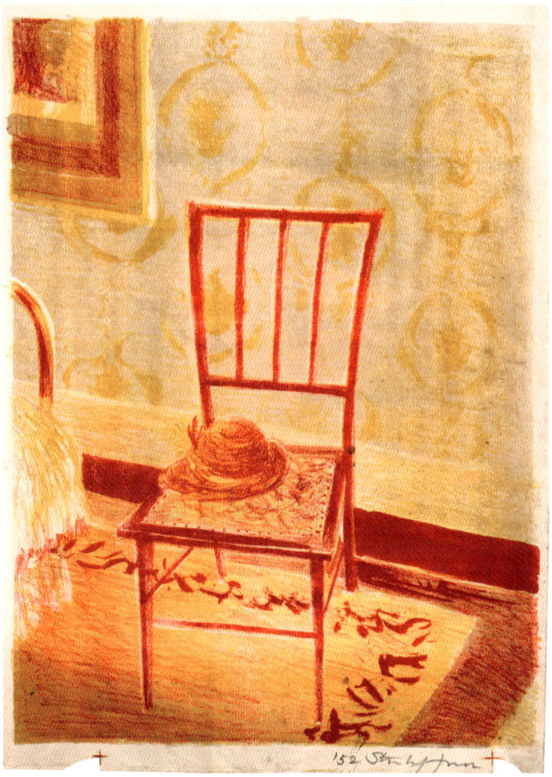

from the English landscape painters of the 19th and 20th centuries, interest lay in the direction of J.M.W. Turner, whose handling of the materials of watercolour and oil paint was a source of fascination. The world became reflected for me in studying the drawings of Rembrandt and Turner, and I was fortunate to sell some of my own landscape studies to staff members who happened to see them exhibited on the walls of the college's corridors. For other students, Walter Sickert, Victor Pasmore and Stanley Spencer were either much admired or scorned according to taste, though the current School of Paris remained unknown territory. However, experimentation was in the air and the staff were anxious to encourage it.

Leonard Penrice asked a few of us, just out of interest, to try some lithographic printmaking. For me, this was to be a significant revelation. About two years previously, a borrowed book on etching from the local library had spurred me to make a few etchings of my own and, using my mother's washing mangle and some acid from school, I was able to produce credible results from a piece of old brass plate. My mother had considerable reservations about her mangle being put to this use, but I offered in return the manpower to help wring the washing, and a deal was struck. Somehow the mangle managed to serve both purposes. Our garden shed (made from a signal box acquired by my father's brother Sam, via the Lancashire and Yorkshire Railway), where I spent many of my waking hours, became the focus of these experiments. By definition the lithographic method of printmaking was different, being much closer to the act of painting at the drawing stage and involving

Top: Stanley Jones, *Quarry at Upholland*, lithograph, 1952

Bottom: Stanley Jones, *The Red Chair*, lithograph, 1952

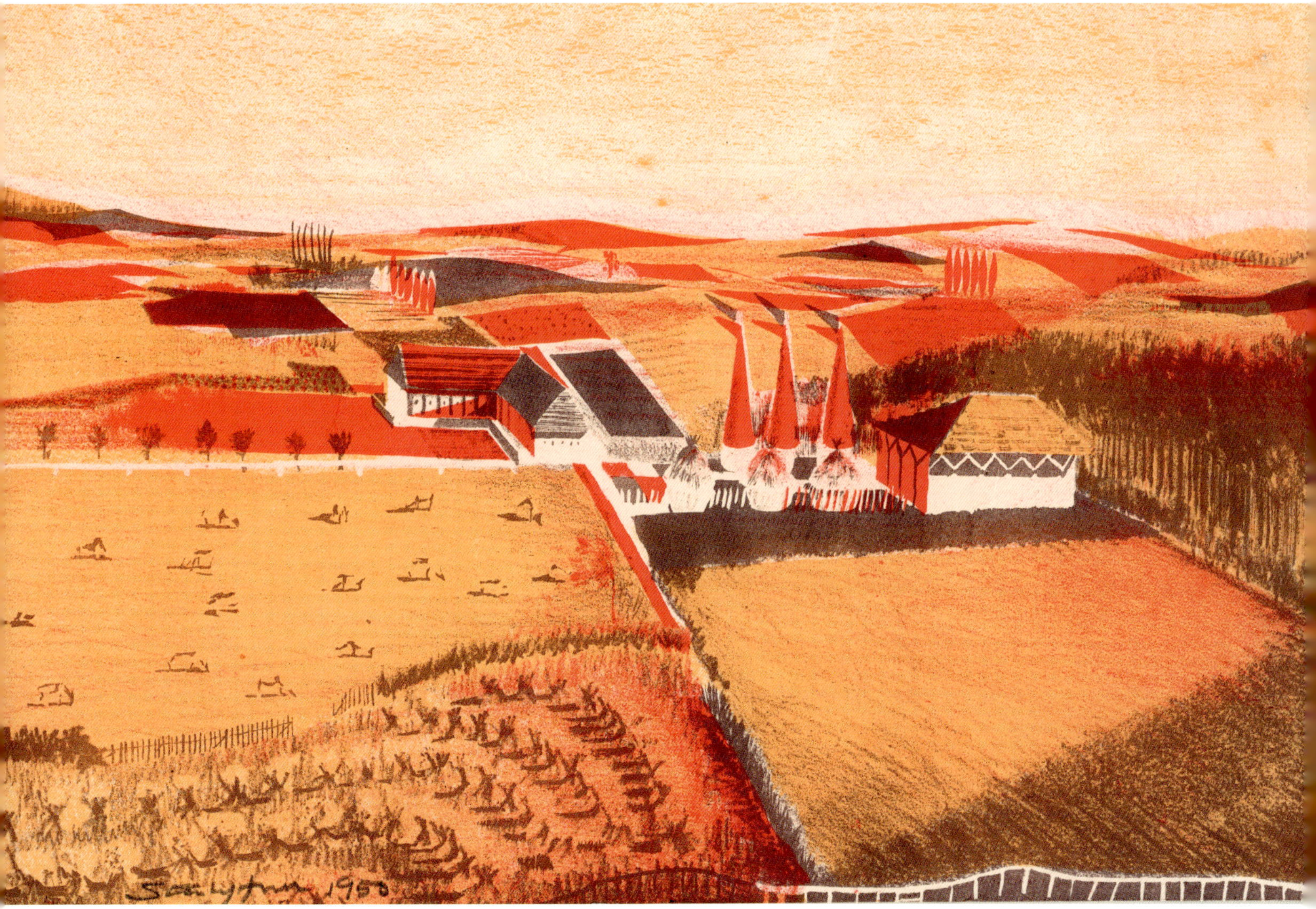

Stanley Jones' first lithograph: *Landscape Study*, 1951

infinite colour possibilities and textures. Under supervision at art college I was able to produce better results, but the original experiment was what introduced and formed the basics. It conveyed such potential that I became intrigued.

Evening classes had been a constant resource in the town for decades, and comprised a curious cross section of the Wigan community. Coal miners, office workers – all kinds of individuals took advantage of these evening gatherings to study painting and drawing and to talk amongst themselves. It had a strong social aspect, which rescued people from the boredom of their daily lives and gave them a glimpse of another world. I remember one such practitioner of many years' attendance showing his portfolio, crammed with headless life drawings, to our new member of staff, John Bailly. John did his best to help but I'm not sure how successful he was. The annual reappearance of this central core of enthusiasts must have been daunting, but was nevertheless a traditional feature of this kind of college. Others succeeded in deriving benefit from the opportunity afforded. We full-time students took advantage of any free space in the evenings, particularly if the presses were not in use.

We had the advantage of a very enthusiastic staff that was always willing to spend time and effort on any student's endeavours. The idea was to give some promising students from outside the college an opportunity to draw from a model. One afternoon in the midst of our life class a new candidate appeared from the outskirts of Wigan replete with brushes and pencils. He was set up and left to proceed. At the end of the afternoon, the staff gathered around their protégé to find on his drawing board a large drawing of a horse jumping a fence. What he thought of the lady standing in the middle of the room, we would never know, for he did not appear again. No one ever referred to the incident again.

The staff in the art school were anxious to nurture the growing reputation it was acquiring in the county, and the encouragement to work in competition with other schools was always evident. Some of our work was borrowed by inspectors and never returned; I lost many drawings and paintings in this way plus a couple of sketchbooks. At this time I discovered the direct lithographic press in the attic room of the school, and spent unofficial hours experimenting with stone and zinc plate. Studio assistant and ex-Slade student Geoffrey Currie was able to give extra guidance when members of staff were not present, but generally technical advice was limited and often inaccurate; in the context of the college's activities, what I was doing was pioneering but also often very frustrating. Gradually, however, some pieces of the process were becoming clear, and these excited me as I began to make discoveries about the possibilities of colour separation and the colour processes involved in printing methods.

By the end of the two years I sat for the intermediate examination and received a commendation. It was now necessary to choose subjects for the final National Diploma and to remember the future possibility of the Slade in London. I was now halfway through my time at Wigan College of Art and able to concentrate on painting and the experimentation with lithography. My world was beginning to open up in all sorts of ways, with a growing sense of purpose and direction. As time progressed I became more and more aware of the solitary nature of my life lived as an artist and the need for more space in which to work. I tried to work at college in the evening, but this again depended on the availability of room space. It was at this time that an old family friend, Jack Hall, offered me the use of an old workshop which had once belonged to his building company. It stood about 300 yards from our home and was empty. What a stroke of fortune! As soon as I received the key, I went to explore this relic, hoping to spend as much time there as possible.

The workshop was the remnant of two old weavers' cottages that had been knocked into one huge room that had been used to house the joinery benches; only the old cast-iron fire grates had been left. Light just about managed to penetrate the years of dust through the rickety windows. It was to be expected that cobwebs covered everything, while the silence challenged all intrusion – nothing had been disturbed for decades. Setting up an easel for painting on canvas and board, I also adapted the old workshop benches and borrowed one or two chairs from an adjoining office. It would be ideal – well, almost: the workshop had limited electric lighting, so I tended to work only in daylight, and it had no heating whatsoever. During winter it was bitterly cold and the draughts careered unhindered through gaps in the floor and roof. In the fiercest gales, the whole building shuddered and heaved; it was 'quite atmospheric', as Jack described it on one of his rare visits. Nevertheless, it became over the next few years a form of sanctuary for me – another world of solitude and possibilities that was totally different to the day-to-day domestic life of 15 Shaw Street.

After the defining nature of the intermediate exams, which tested general capability and dealt with the early steps in drawing, painting and sculpture, the next two years were a broadening experience in the exploration of painting and what was, for me, this newly-discovered medium of lithography which I found so intriguing. By chance I saw an exhibition in Liverpool devoted to Toulouse-Lautrec, which of course was a revelation; his use of colour printing and the dynamic design of the posters astonished us all. But I found the delicately drawn studies on stone to be particularly awe-inspiring – how were such qualities achieved? Their impact was to remain with me for a long time.

I was so engrossed in this new-found world that I did not realise at first that my father's health had begun to deteriorate. Always susceptible to bronchial trouble, the polluted atmosphere and extremes of temperature in which he had worked on the railway footplate began to take their toll. The signs were not good – particularly in the smog-ridden winters of the 1940s and 50s. He found attacks of bronchial asthma a particular problem, but with a family to support – my brother at Leicester University and myself hoping to continue my studies at the Slade – he had incredible determination to carry on working. At Christmas I applied for temporary postal work, trudging around the terraced streets of Scholes in the semi-darkness. This was quite an experience in seeing how some other people lived! Families were cramped in dilapidated terraced houses, back to back and with an overhanging odour of years of neglect and dampness. Instead of a letterbox, a hand would often appear from behind a door and snatch the post with a grunt of thanks. In these early hours, apart from the odd all-night party, the only sounds on the cobbles were of clog-footed miners and mill workers making their way to work. They all seemed to know each other and warned me if some families were 'sleepin' it off, like'.

With my friends at the art school, Bert Winstanley and Michael Goodger, I explored so much of Wigan and its outskirts. Equipped with paper and drawing materials, nothing seemed beyond our achievement. Sometimes the general public were curious as to what we were doing and would gather in groups offering advice and criticism, and on occasion the nuisance was

Right: Stanley Jones, book jacket design, lithograph, 1952

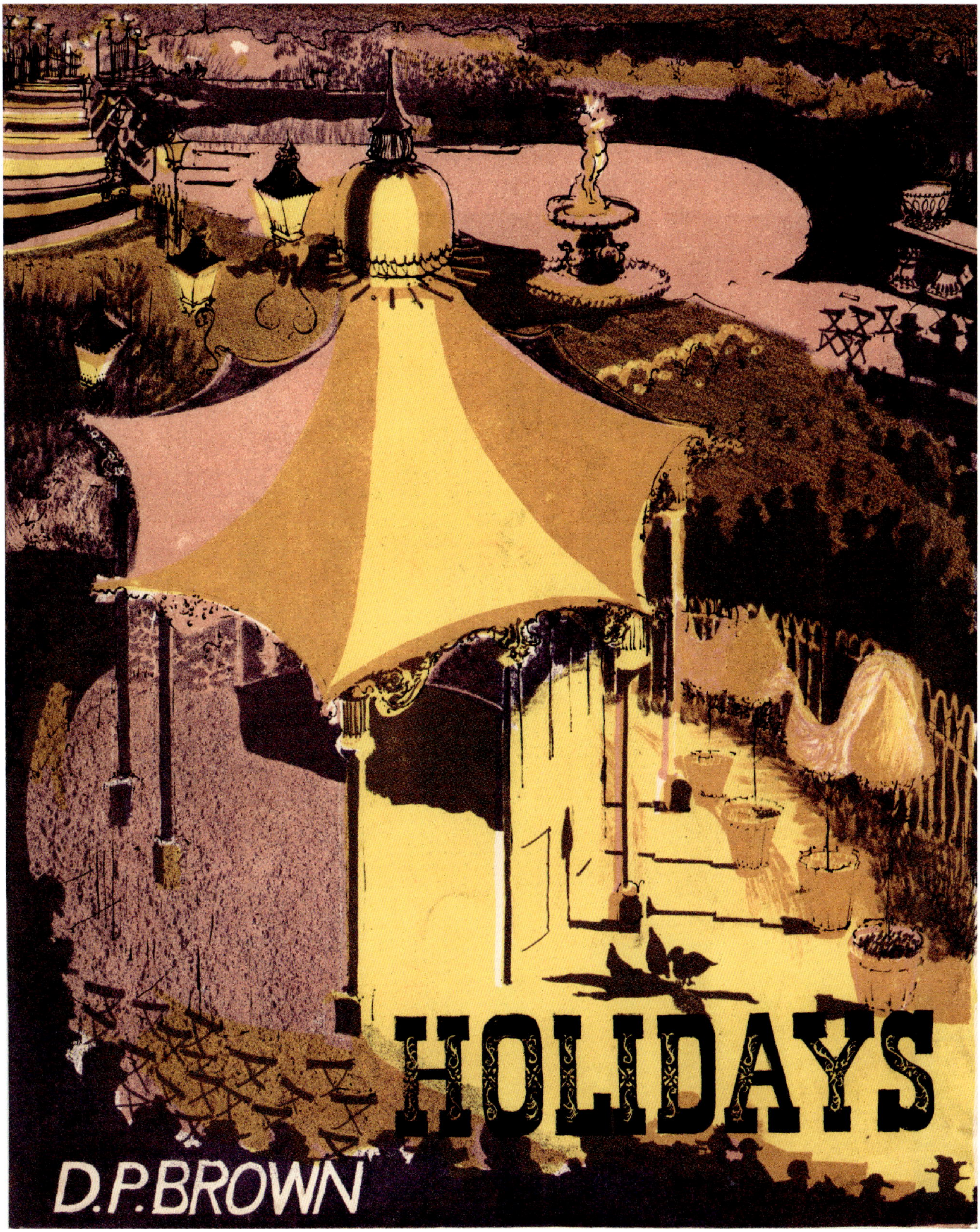
HOLIDAYS
D.P. BROWN

such that we just moved on to a new location. Even the odd newspaper reporter looking for subject matter gave us credible coverage, discovering us avidly drawing in the local barge-repair yard. I even earned money drawing pubs for enterprising landlords – it all helped to buy materials because by now, in my second year, I was preparing to reapply for a place at the Slade.

Apart from the practical work, we were obliged to write and illustrate a dissertation for the examining board on a fine-art-related subject; I was still fascinated by the work of J.M.W. Turner, who figured much in my subject – Early English 19th Century Landscape. This involved a few days in London and a trip to the British Museum. By courtesy of Mr Snelgrove (Assistant Keeper at the British Museum) I had the rare experience of examining parts of the Turner Bequest, largely untouched since its removal from his studio. I could not believe my luck! Afterwards, the sense of having handled such an extraordinary collection of unexplored work remained with me for a long time – the disturbing of such dust seemed almost sacrilegious.

Back in Wigan life circulated around applications to art schools and eternal discussions about what future lay in store. As there were no postgraduate courses at Wigan Art College, the prospect of spending time at an art school with a major reputation held out the possibility of both advancing my practice and gaining further qualifications. I was determined to reapply to the Slade, despite all the difficulties involved. Under William Coldstream it had acquired a national reputation, and John Bailly, a former Slade student, encouraged me to apply. Money was the major problem on the horizon: how was I going to fund two years in London? With my brother still studying at Leicester University and my father's health failing the position seemed impossible.

Friends and relatives shook their heads – except for the Goldsmiths, who were old family friends living in Liverpool, and who indicated that they would help me, if help were needed. More to the point, family friend Charles Goldsmith's mistrust of my relatives' influence – 'Never give up boy or you'll regret it!' – persisted in my head. For the time being I restricted knowledge of the offer and his advice to my mother and myself.

In the meantime I needed some kind of work that was well paid during the summer. The nearest solution came via the H.J. Heinz Co., which was developing its food manufacturing outside Wigan. Casual labourers were needed to work overnight on farms supplying the cannery. So began for me a nightly event from six in the evening until six in the morning, organised in military fashion with sup-ervisors and instructors all in uniform, making sure everyone conformed to company rules. It was hard physical work and, when the weather was unsuitable, we student workers spent our time in the factory crawling underneath the soup kettles placed in endlessly long rows. The intention was to scrape off the old soup, which at some time past had boiled over and set securely on the huge metal vessels. It was dark, smelly and lonely work. In the cold, small hours of the morning we devised ways of communicating amongst the square miles of piping – always keeping eyes open for the foremen on their patrols. Some hapless students occasionally got lost in this labyrinth and were duly rescued by staff, together with much cursing and swearing.

After a while I was saved from further boredom by being put in charge of the tea-making facilities provided each night at intervals. It gave me the opportunity, in any spare time I had, to draw the local landscape, and for seeing the sun set towards the coast and rise with intense colour over the Pennines. Each morning with the others, I shared a bus home from Standish with the pit-brew girls from the Victoria Colliery – bright and joking amongst themselves even after such hard manual labour on the pit surface. As the weeks wore on I could not get used to sleeping during the day and tended to feel disembodied for the last few hours of the night work. Luckily, I survived this dream state with the help of the colliery girls who, with much mocking and cajoling, made sure I got off at the right stop each morning.

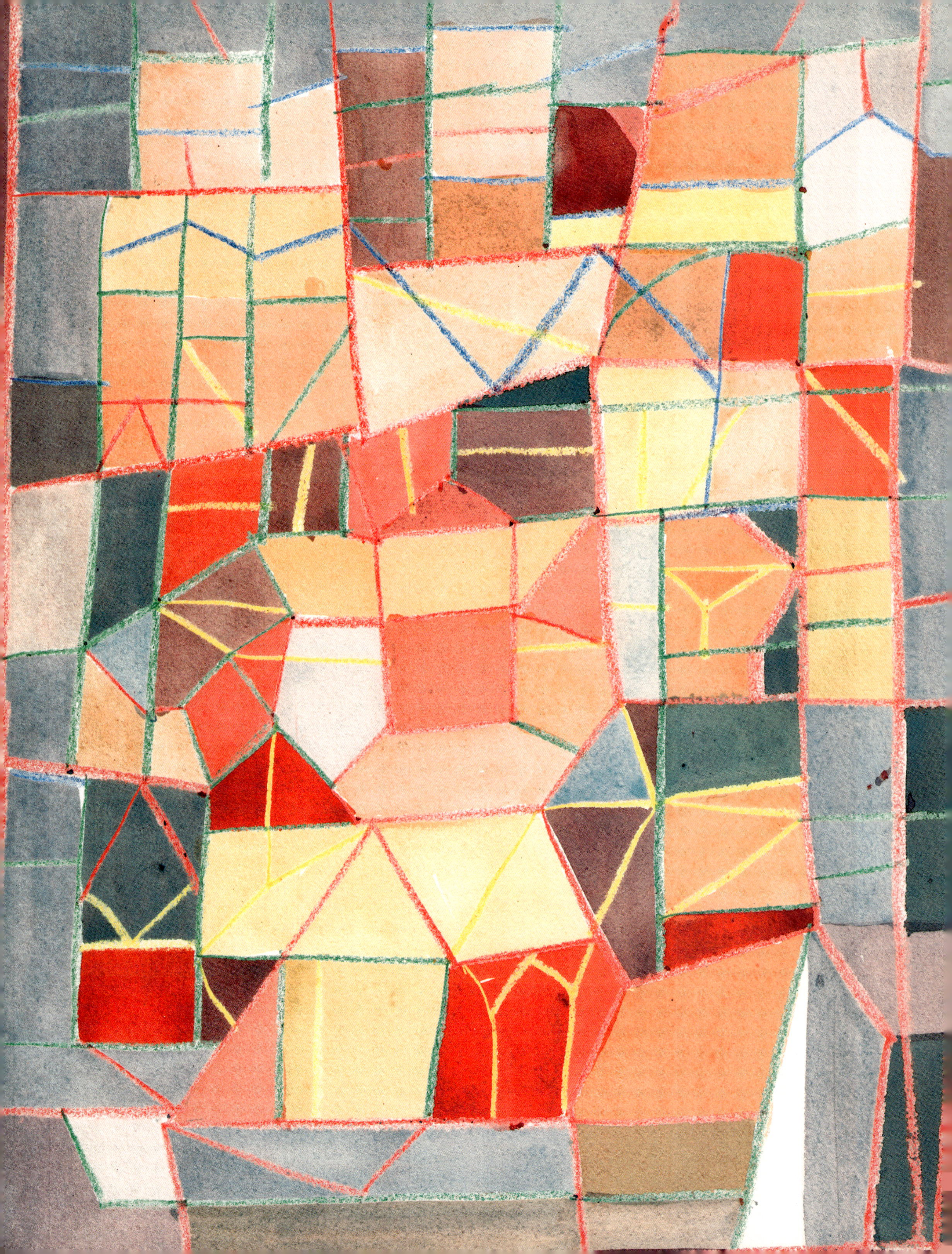

"I was soon to be thrust into a different kind of world. . ."

THE SLADE

Acceptance

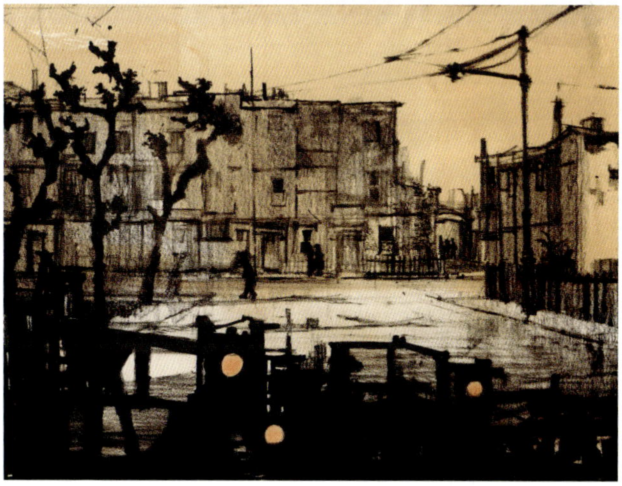

Finally, one morning an official envelope arrived with a dull thud on the doormat. With a trembling hand and great trepidation I opened it and examined its contents. I had been accepted to the Slade for the diploma course starting in the autumn. What a prospect! My friends at Wigan College of Art had begun training for teaching at Manchester or Liverpool, and in a way our lives had already begun to take separate paths; the National Diploma in Design was, curiously, the last link we had in common. Our usual banter began to have a rather hollow ring. As the prospect of the Slade advanced, I felt with increasing clarity that our worlds would soon separate. Norman Dilworth and Margaret Evans (former students at Wigan) were already at the Slade and I was now making contact with them. The term was to start in October and already instructions from University College were appearing at home with regular frequency. There was also guidance from Miss Ridley in the Slade office about college regulations, such as the necessity for drawing lots to attain a place in the life classes, etc. I was informed that my tutor would be Claude Rogers , a very well-known and respected painter. It was mentioned in the Slade handbook that there was a new department for lithographic printmaking, with artists such as Lynton Lamb, Ceri Richards and Frank Ormrod in charge. I tried to absorb all this new information in the gloomy quietude of Hall's workshop, with the usual everyday Wigan activities taking place outside in the street below. The cries of the rag-and-bone man mingling with those of Mrs Berry, selling her fish from a three-wheeled pushcart, surrounded by cats. I was soon to be thrust into a very different kind of world.

It was now September; the still skies were stained yellow-ochre from the smoke of the chimneys hanging in the streets. Art-school friends went their various

Left: Stanely Jones, Experimental Monoprint, mixed media, 1955

Above right: Stanley Jones, *Street: Camden Town*, lithograph 1954

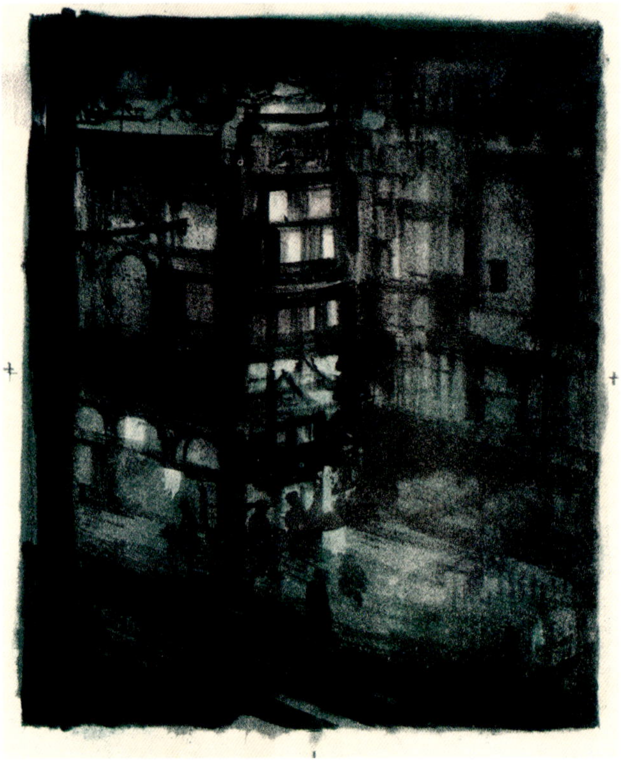

Stanley Jones, Belsize Park: variation 1, lithograph, 1954

Stanley Jones, Belsize Park: variation 2, lithograph, 1954

ways, and my own preparations had to be made for working in London. Relatives, neighbours and friends expressed their views about the wisdom of this venture; I calculated that with some help from my parents I had enough funding to last me for the first year, and that was a start. I assembled as much paper and colours as possible. By arrangement with my uncle Peter, I went on a final visit to Starr's printing works and came home loaded with offcuts for sketchbooks. The printers had never heard of the Slade but wished me luck, whilst imparting the odd ink-stained handshake. London for them was also an unknown quantity – connected only by the railway line close by, along which the expresses thundered south each day.

It was strange, as I cleared the workshop, to realise that I would only occupy this space occasionally in future; it had been of such value in enabling me to make a start. My parents took my departure very seriously, deciding to travel with me to approve the room in Belsize Park that I had been allocated by the University College lodgings bureau.

1954, the Slade

London in 1954 still bore the marks of the Blitz, from half-demolished structures to buildings pock-marked with shrapnel holes; on account of this, the surviving architecture and streets had a neglected air, awaiting the oncoming hand of development and renovation. Bloomsbury was no exception in this regard, with the area around the Slade and University College reflecting, in the dull autumn sunshine, a gentle quality of post-war austerity. There were temporary huts in available public places for all manner of purposes, and an atmosphere of

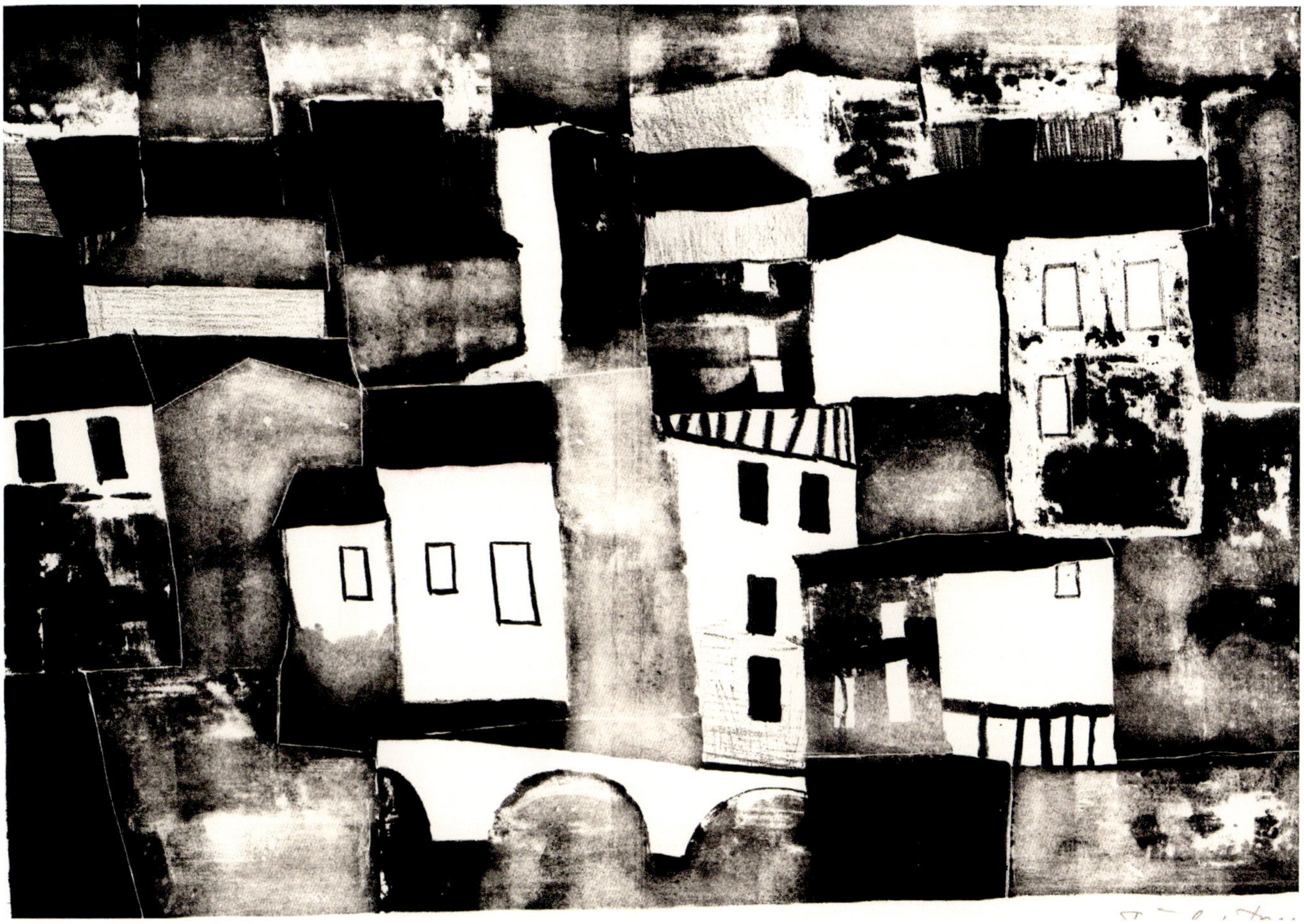

Stanley Jones, City in Winter, lithograph on stone, 1955

'make do and mend' prevailed overall; whilst 'in many of the departments at the Slade, space in particular was at a constant premium.

Since his appointment as Slade Professor of Fine Art, William Coldstream had wrought considerable changes within the school, attracting a staff of established and eminent artists, some full-time, others part-time. Its reputation was growing apace, in parallel with the emerging London art world.

So it was on a Monday morning in October that we were assembled in the library of the Slade to meet each other and to be addressed first by Professor Coldstream and then William Townsend, who was very welcoming but practical in his advice to students new to the Slade. We appeared to be a very mixed group in age, attitudes and life experience. The majority of us came from art schools up and down the country, but there were also well-to-do ladies from private schools, National Servicemen, young possibilities fresh from prep school and many from abroad anxious to sample what it was that had gained the Slade its reputation. The common room (run by the Slade Society in the basement), with its forlorn décor and furniture, would be in the short term the main source of integration, helped each day by tea and gossip between 4 and 5 p.m.

Throughout this crowded time of adjustment and discovery, I made friends with two fellow first-year students, Roy Bizley and George Wall, who had also been to previous art schools and like me were new to living in London. Our future interests were to be closely linked for the next two years. There were other groups of students from art schools up and down the country. The Bristol Boys, as they were known, were already well established in the school as a formidable group headed by Francis Hewlett and Robert Organ. Other colleges such as Newcastle were annually successful in sending students to further their studies at the Slade. The intention was to develop individuality of vision and ideas were encouraged by whatever facilities the Slade could offer. Students came from abroad, sometimes on scholarships sometimes not; and there was an indefinable intake of people of varying attributes who were admitted for reasons best known to themselves.

By tradition, the judging of the Summer Composition signalled the start of the autumn term, when staff and students assembled in what was then known as the women's life room to hear Professor Coldstream's judgement on the paintings submitted for his commendation ... or otherwise. It was a momentous time, when approbation or disapproval could mould an artist's status whilst in college – reputations were often lost and found on such an afternoon. We, as newcomers, sat and listened to Professor Coldstream's wit and wisdom, knowing that next year we also would be part of this event.

Slowly my days developed pattern. I found the lodgings in Belsize Park to be unsatisfactory: they were small and not meant for art students. Meals were provided, the landlady promising a set meal at a particular time each day, and due to the timing of some Slade lectures I could not get back to Belsize Park in time – much to the landlady's consternation. This was clearly not going to work, so I decided to look for something more practical and congenial. Roy Bizley had a similar problem, and after some fruitless investigations we knocked on the door of 5 Lady Margaret Road in Kentish Town. It was a sombre Edwardian house but with large rooms at the front. Louisa Allcock, who greeted us, was a true London cockney. She made us tea and regaled us with her life history whilst showing us the accommodation. She would do the cleaning, and we were to do our own cooking. There was to be no noise after 10.30pm because she and her husband slept next door (very little would escape Louisa). She had never had art students before but offered to do the washing and shopping for us and provide coal for the fire in winter. The deal was struck. For the next two years Roy and I were to stay here and work; this was the background that would provide us with basic essentials, plus the ubiquitous Mrs Allcock.

Days merged into weeks, and while the process of drawing and painting took on an absorbing aspect, something else had begun to occupy my interest. It was this: with the possibilities inherent in artists' graphic imagery, why was such work often undervalued in relation to painting or sculpture?

One Monday morning at the usual ceremony of drawing lots for life places, I was unlucky and did not receive a placement; this meant exploring other alternatives. I found the lithography room in the basement of the school, but at this moment, for some reason, it was devoid of any students. However, in the middle of the room, pensive over a printing plate, stood Ceri Richards, who first talked to me about the idea he was working on and then about his liking of Welsh poetry. It was a salutary beginning.

I made contact with other members of the staff – Lynton Lamb and Frank Ormrod – who were to prove very helpful in practical ways, but it was Ceri who suggested different concepts for the work I wanted to produce experimentally in lithography. Because of the requirements of the Slade diploma, the year involved not only life painting but also portrait head study, still life and landscape work. Drawing and painting had to be practised constantly; some students almost lived in the antique room which was littered with casts and plants, lost in another world. Lectures in perspective once a week with Sam Carter were obligatory as was human anatomy in the sombre medical school across Gower Street. Most significant were the history of art

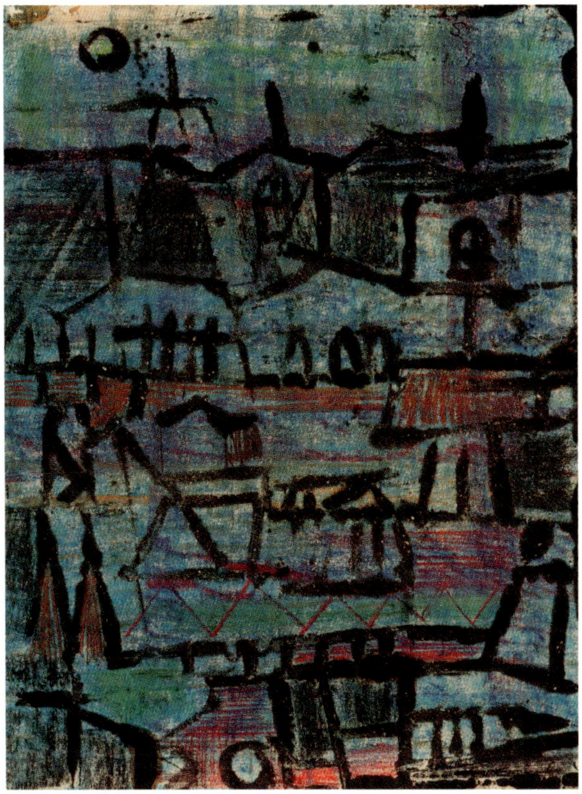

Stanley Jones, *Vista*, lithograph with added colour, 1956

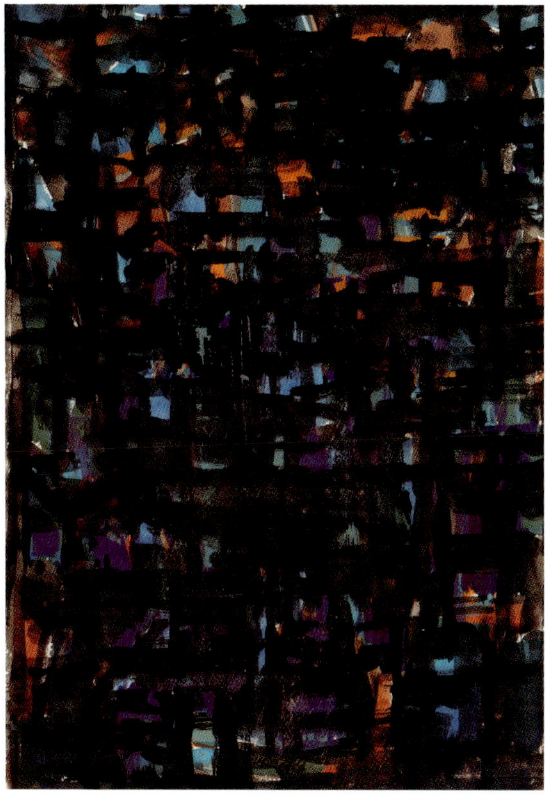

Stanley Jones, *Night Town*, lithograph, 1955

lectures given on a Friday evening by Professor Wittkover on the baroque in architecture and sculpture. Not all Slade students appreciated such erudite scholarship and, though they habitually signed the attendance book in what began as a packed lecture theatre, once the lecture began in the darkened hall, there were perceptive movements from the back row out into the corridor. At the end of the lecture when the theatre was relit, much of the audience had disappeared. I'm not sure whether Professor Coldstream was aware of this, week in, week out; but there always remained the ardent Courtauld students occupying the front rows.

Of considerable interest were the talks given by visitors: I remember in particular Georges Duthuit on Matisse, an appreciation of Van Gogh by Nicholas Pevsner, and a remarkable talk and discussion given by David Sylvester on the work of Alberto Giacometti. The issues kept us all engrossed late into the evening. At this time writers became increasingly important to us; journals such as *The Listener* and the *New Statesman* (in which Patrick Heron had made quite a contribution) were avidly scrutinised each week as we crouched around the fire in Lady Margaret Road. For a student it was difficult to evaluate the importance of the influences in the London art world at the time. The 'Kitchen Sink School' led by John Bratby, stemming mostly from the Royal College, held the interest of most of the critics and the art establishment at the time; my attention, however, was caught by what was occurring on the Continent, particularly in Paris. I was excited by the developing movements of Tachisme and Art Autre, where paint and its use played such a major part. An exhibition of the work of Nicholas de Stael at the Whitechapel Art Gallery offered new directions. It encouraged me to experiment texturally with the chemistry of lithography and the possibilities of colour printing in unexplored ways. My sessions in the lithography room were growing longer and longer, and I could work uninterruptedly with resources which were only infrequently used by most other students. Moreover, because such a pursuit

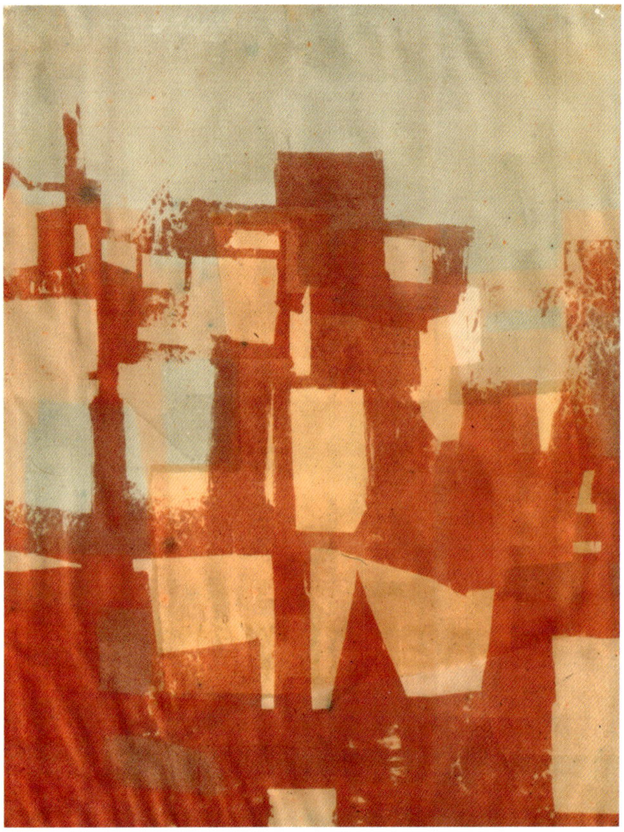

Stanley Jones, *City Destruction*, lithograph and embossing, 1955

was uncommon, the staff took an added interest in my experimental approach.

Apart from myself, there were other students at the Slade who had become involved in the development of printed images. Eric Finlay (an ex-lighthouse keeper from Northumbria) had been spending much time in the etching room, where the procedures of viscosity colour printing as developed by W.S. Hayter occupied his attention. There were other students who joined our group of printmaking enthusiasts and, as the year progressed, our ideas and intentions gradually took shape – usually around a table in a teashop called The Hall of Mirrors in the Euston Road. In a course devoted to the practice of painting and sculpture, work in etching and lithography was regarded as being of minor significance and we felt that it should be given more recognition as an important art form. There was a demonstrable separation of values not related to content. Not yet were the days when artists could specialise and make their reputation by the practice of graphic work, even though on the Continent an artist's graphic work had the full appreciation of both critics and public.

We sent work to mixed exhibitions in London and further afield and met a Swedish printmaker, Birgit Skiöld, who was to open her printing workshop at 17 Charlotte Street. Birgit brought with her a continental breath of enthusiasm for printmaking, and her basement workshop was to act as a catalyst for future printmakers in London. It was also at this time that Eric and I found the St George's Gallery in Cork Street, a newly opened space devoted to original prints, whose proprietor, the Hon. Robert Erskine, was keen to promote contemporary British printmaking. I think in retrospect he was somewhat bemused by us at the first meeting, but he still took some of our work for his stock. This was to be the beginning of a long association.

However, as the year progressed into the spring, I managed to get extra working time in the lithography room to pursue my interest in the medium, which I felt as a process was very close to the act of painting, with its use of brushes and preoccupation with colour relationships. The attraction for me was the unexpected potential of the medium, concentrating on the transformation of one's creative ideas – not tied to the academic practice of painting and drawing pursued in the life classes. It was as if another creative world could be perceived through a crack in the door of a different room. There was so much to be discovered, but the course structure demanded attention to be paid in other directions – portrait painting, landscape study and still life – with many long hours in the summer term spent figure painting in the life room. Staff would drift in and out, perhaps offering a comment or perhaps not, but in any case trying to encourage this disparate group struggling with its problems. Lucian Freud as a visiting artist was particularly revered but reluctant to enter into discussion, preferring to navigate around the easels whilst gazing intently at the model.

Despite the varied and complex work pattern of students' lives, most of us managed to strike a balance between work and time spent with friends, male or female. A group of us always made a point once a week of visiting the local cinema near the Slade, called the Tolmer, off Hampstead Road, which ran at uncertain hours and specialised in a curious variety of 'B' movies. To say it was shabby was perhaps an understatement; I only saw the interior once when the lights were switched on to quell a riot amongst some local youths. It was smoke-stained and dusty with a décor that hadn't been touched since the 1920s; somehow this seemed to complement the nature of its film programme. Nevertheless, the Tolmer remained highly popular with the varied local inhabitants, particularly in winter, because at least the central heating usually worked.

Sometimes the Slade offered its own entertainment in the form of 'hops'. These were vibrant jiving sessions inspired by the painter Michael Tyzack 'on clarinet', who had formed his group with fellow artists. Rock was in its infancy, and these events were highly sought after by students throughout the colleges. And, of course, there was the annual Christmas Ball followed in the spring by the Slade dinner (usually a riotous affair), both of which depended so much on student organisation. Most of us, however, were preoccupied with work and its implications. The summer term was approaching, and I was in the midst of experimenting with colour and zinc-plate lithography, much encouraged by Ceri Richards, who I was able to help with proofing, having learnt enough by now to be useful.

One afternoon W.S. Hayter appeared at the Slade to give a talk about his work with viscosity printing on etching plates. His enthusiasm and authority were infectious. I was being pointed toward new possibilities in printmaking, and the fact that Paris would be the centre for such further experience was to become apparent in later months. For the first time I had met someone for whom printmaking was a major preoccupation. To have met and listened to such an individual was very significant for me. I remember that Eric Finlay was similarly bowled over by this event. Afterwards in the local pub, the Orange Tree, we talked and argued enthusiastically with a group of friends, well into the night. Printmaking at the Slade was beginning to grow.

There were, however, other issues I had to consider which were becoming pressing; finances had to be coped with as living costs were tightening. Mrs Allcock helped us with our food bills, and price and quality were always a consideration when we bought our painting materials. To save on transport costs we tried walking as much as possible and in this way got to know quite a bit of central London. But the coming year was what worried me most. I would have to devote time and effort to a summer-vacation job to survive the next year. How to balance the time taken to earn money against time needed for painting and drawing was going to be a constant problem.

As the end of term approached and the diploma shows were being organised, I was fortunate to meet John Piper, who was a Slade visitor and whose work I had first discovered in a rare touring exhibition circulated by the V&A. This was, of course, my first encounter with an artist whose work I had admired for a long time. At the time I was making prints based on landscape subject matter, and he was interested to see what I was producing. He was very encouraging and particularly fond of lithography, having worked at the Curwen Press, and recently with Mourlot's printers in Paris on some experimental work. It was a fascinating encounter for me, opening up possibilities for developing my ideas in different ways. I told him of my plan to understand

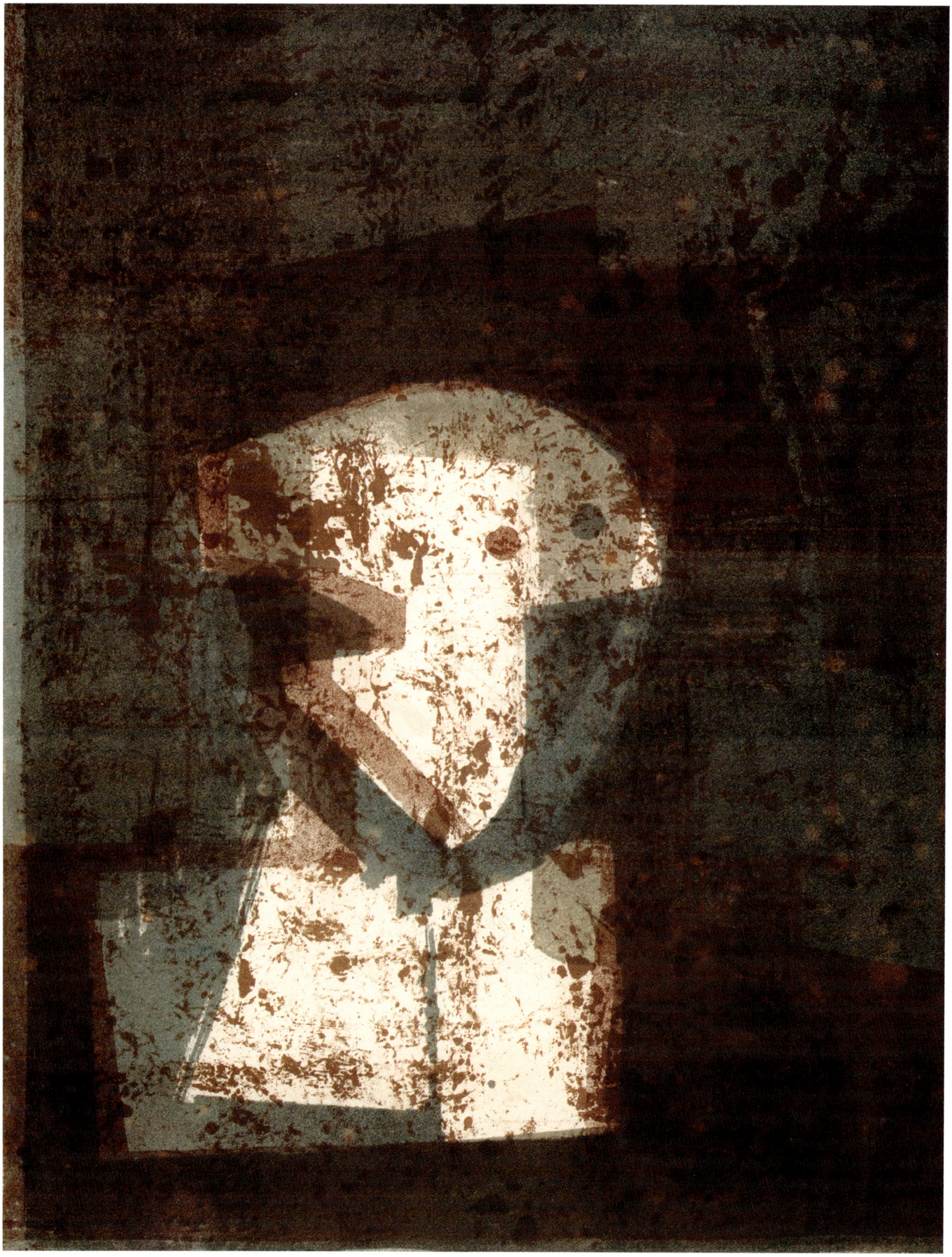

more about the craft of lithography by studying in Paris, which he felt was essential, and we agreed to discuss this the following year.

I had been making enquiries about the possibility of working for a professional lithographic printer in this country. At the time, there was no English equivalent of the French 'atelier', meaning that commissioned artists had to travel abroad if they wanted their lithographs to be printed professionally. Moreover, the printing industry at the time comprised many different union bodies, each with their own fairly strict requirements, traditions and rules. Because I was an art student wishing to specialise in a 'craft', unless I was prepared to undergo a long commercial training I could not learn the specialist processes necessary for producing the highest quality of lithography as exemplified in the work being produced in Paris or Zurich. The rules prevented artists from the free collaboration with printers in the production of their work that is so essential to the making of a limited-edition print. The fine-art printers that did exist in Britain closely guarded their craft skills both as individuals and as 'chapel' members. (In the printing industry 'chapel' is the name given to a union group within a printing company. At the Curwen Press such a description was particularly appropriate, given the company's early association with the Revd John Curwen.) It seemed an insoluble situation, and one that I would have to confront in the not-too-distant future.

My friends were already preparing for their summer breaks in various ways: some were travelling abroad, while others had the luxury of being able to spend time at home painting. How much of this I could afford to do depended on finances. I had already written to the H.J. Heinz Co. in Wigan, offering myself for night work on a temporary basis – at least the rates were good. Such a plan would also leave me sufficient time to paint.

Coming into the Slade early one morning, I met Ian Tregarthen Jenkin, the Slade Secretary, who had taken an interest in the printmaking developments happening in the lithography room. I explained to him my intentions and the problems I would have with finance in the coming year. He replied by outlining the possibility of state funding, which I had never heard of before then. Knowing little of these matters, I thought he would forget this conversation, as I subsequently did.

Some days later, I received a letter from my brother suggesting a trek around North Yorkshire using youth hostels en route. I was very taken with the idea of seeing such a landscape for the first time – especially Gordale Scar; in all it would take just over a week.

The remaining days of term saw the Slade transformed by the Diploma exhibitions and inundated by visitors – staff and students from other colleges, friends and relatives, critics and artists, all curious to see the promise of emerging talent. Apart from this, there were traditional functions such as the 'Strawberry Tea' held on the Slade lawn, and the final gathering of students in the women's life room to hear the professor speak and award prizes. This, too, attracted interest from outside, and the room was fully packed. The exhibitions were then dismantled and the rooms of the school, now emptied, had a curiously hollow ring. Fellow students began to leave and say goodbye; there was constant packing up of paintings, sculptures and possessions. It was a time for making promises and farewell parties; gradually, the frenzied activity of college ceased for a while, leaving only the beadles to anticipate the following year.

Left: Stanley Jones, *Miner's Head*, lithograph, 1956

So Roy and I said goodbye to Mrs Allcock for a few weeks and headed home, he to Swindon and myself up to Lancashire. Once there, I found an offer from H.J. Heinz for the summer awaiting me, which meant having to do night work but also part of the solution to a problem. Luckily, I could still use the workshop in Lord Street, and I also had paintings in the Northern Young Contemporaries show in Liverpool, so at least some encouraging signs were emerging.

Before all that, though, my brother and I set off for North Yorkshire, eager to see a different landscape. In the 1950s the youth hostels that did exist were in an indifferent state, with facilities varying in standard from one to another. However, they did offer board and lodging at a student rate, which suited the two of us. Equipped with basic clothing, most of the remaining space in my haversack was taken up with drawing materials. Our ex-army mackintoshes proved invaluable, for it rained liberally during most of that week. Then, arriving one evening at the Hawes hostel, I found a letter forwarded to me from Ian Jenkin to the effect that, on the recommendation of the college, I had been awarded a state scholarship for the coming year. To say I was elated would be an understatement.

We returned home having experienced for the first time the dramatic limestone landscape with its moors, dales and villages, some very bleak and isolated. It is a world carved for poets – quite unforgettable to me, even now. My invaluable sketchbook would provide copious material from this trip for graphic images that I would make later at the Slade.

At the end of this week I returned to the reality of wrestling with the painting for the Slade summer competition, only this time with less financial pressure than I'd anticipated and so less necessity to work at night for H.J. Heinz. This time I managed to limit the night work to a month by working on one of the company's farms, near Parbold. On some occasions I was able to see the brilliance of the sun setting, then the night's changing light, followed by daybreak, with the returning colour transforming the sky as the early truck rumbled us back to Wigan and the smoke.

In all, the summer passed quickly, with much effort spent on painting and drawing in the summer heat of the workshop near home, ready for the return to London. Time spent with old friends from Wigan Art School was becoming less involving than before. We were growing in different directions; my focused interest in printmaking had advanced at the Slade much more than I had realised, while my fellow students in Wigan were training for art teaching – a completely different focus. This created in me a distinct sense of isolation; I felt that my family was just as anxious about my future, and there was much intermittent discussion about it around our meal table. On top of this, my father's declining health was a constant problem for us; it seemed to be worsening with each successive winter. So when I returned to London it was with an inner sense of commitment to make the most of whichever opportunities came my way. Somehow the effort had to be made to cross the Channel.

I arrived back at my lodgings with all my luggage and painting gear, to be regaled by Mrs Allcock's often bizarre gossip about the neighbours' daughter, the resident attraction for the students lodging next door. Once this was out of the way I learned that Mrs Allcock had acquired another Slade student, a sculptor by the name of Robert Westall. He quickly gained her approval and brought a talent for cooking and conversation with which she was duly very impressed. He also had an undiscovered talent for writing, which he would go on to develop later in life by becoming a well-known children's author. Roy returned from Wiltshire with the news that he and his girlfriend planned to emigrate to Australia. It was going to be some year.

The first weeks of term were already familiar, with their exhibitions and the prizes awarded by Professor Coldstream; once over, everyone was left to concentrate on their own intentions. I resorted whenever possible to the lithography room and found experimenting with its possibilities on stone and plate to be totally absorbing. However, inevitably, work for the Slade Diploma had to take precedence. It was clear from some of the work being done at the school that influences from abroad were now appearing in the work of young British artists: Jean Dubuffet and Nicolas de Staël with the Art Autre movement from Paris had already attracted much attention, and another influence came from certain figures from the New York School who were now beginning to show in London.

The work being produced in the printmaking departments at the Slade was beginning to attract attention from members of the staff, who were somewhat bemused by the unusual nature of what etching and lithography could produce. Some felt the medium to be extreme in its presentation, its materials and the size of images produced, employing a pictorial language very foreign to English traditions. It was through William Townsend that I was able to have informal meetings with John Piper and the enigmatic L.S. Lowry, who told me that he disliked coming to London, much preferring northern 'smoke', as he expressed it. He responded positively to the subject matter of the earlier paintings and drawings that I had made in the environs of Wigan, and was intrigued by my involvement with printmaking. I got the impression that Lowry was more comfortable in discussion with students than with his peers, and we talked at length about the atmosphere and character of industrial landscapes and his difficulties as a young person developing his response to subject matter that was so unappreciated in the world of fine art. Finally, William Townsend took him, reluctantly, off to lunch, Lowry wearing his large worn raincoat, with black boots and carrying a formidable umbrella.

The year began to take on a particular form – balancing the obligations of the Diploma with the time I needed to develop my printmaking ideas, which theoretically had to be pursued whenever the studio was otherwise unoccupied. It took much persuasion to gain the odd extra hour from Mr Ansell, who was in charge of the keys. Much depended on his daily moods, which were often unpredictable and depended, I think, on the performance of Arsenal Football Club. This was a long time before the rise of open-access workshops, so press facilities were only available to students in art-school departments, and even then with strict limitations. To help matters, I discovered methods of making monoprints involving oil colours using Mrs Allcock's kitchen table, whenever the opportunity afforded itself. I found monoprinting very useful for developing ideas in colour and used basic oil colours and hand pressure to convey the marks from plate to paper. Working on a tabletop there was always a danger of spillage, and the lingering odour of turpentine was unavoidable. In retrospect I think my landlady must have been very tolerant.

The year progressed rapidly with bouts of intense working and the occasional breaks at Christmas time and Easter. My fellow students had all done compulsory National Service and knew the value of making the most of their time; I had been rejected for National Service because of my eyesight. All the while the prospect of life outside the Slade was beginning to loom over us as the final exams came closer. The search and application for potential scholarships for further study abroad became a

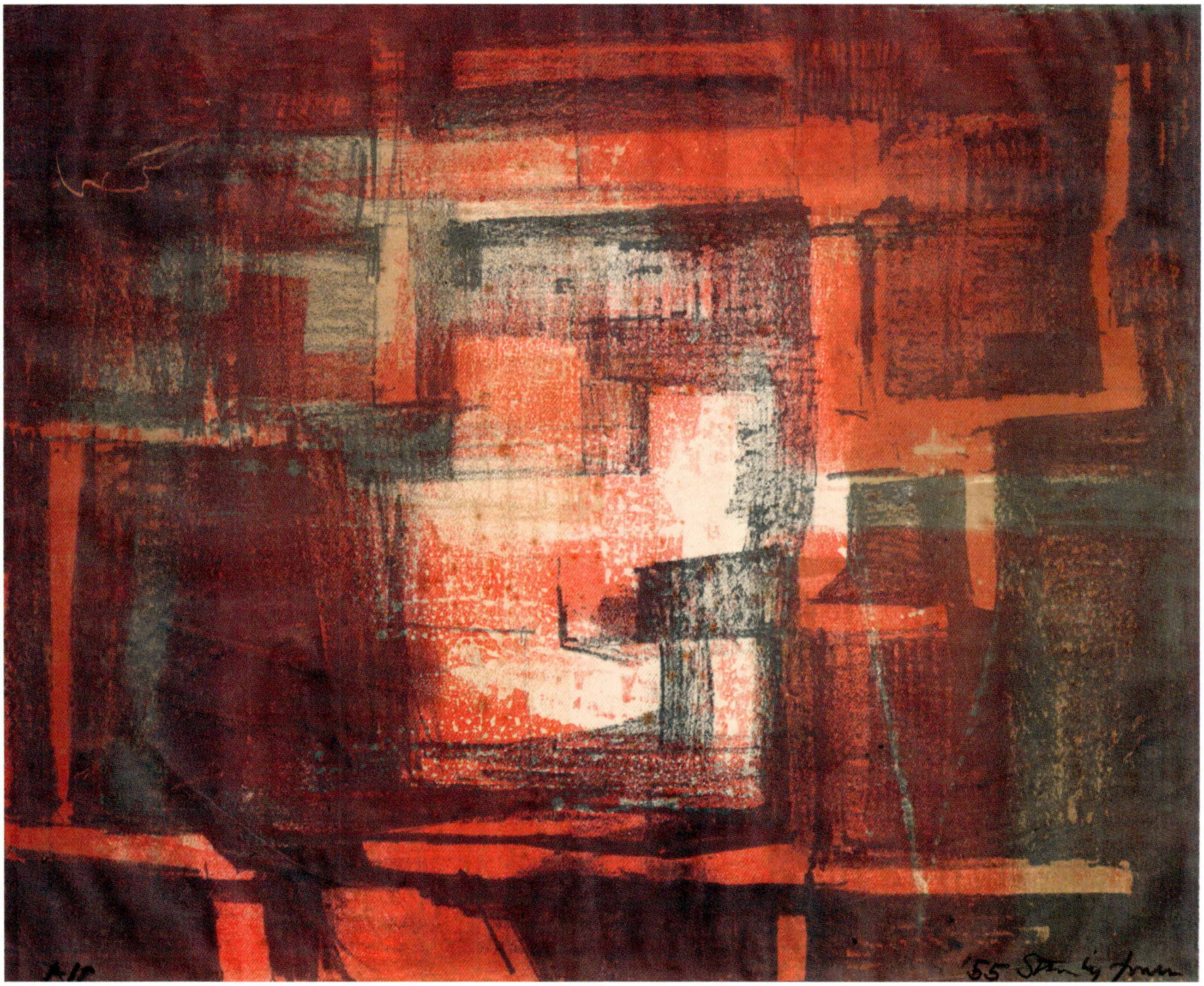

Stanley Jones, *Blast Furnace*, lithograph, 1955

constant preoccupation, adding to the already competitive atmosphere of these final months.

Because of the activity in printmaking we had several visits from the History of Art Department, who encouraged us to exhibit works in the corridor spaces near the Strang Print Room, a new venture that proved quite successful. It seemed that printed images were beginning to make their presence felt in the Slade. Meanwhile, the St George's Gallery in Cork Street was gradually establishing its reputation in the promotion of original prints, albeit mostly through the output of foreign workshops. However, it was a start, and Robert Erskine, the proprietor, was encouraged by the progress of his venture. We had many conversations in his small gallery about prints, as he already knew of my intention to work in Paris and promised to supply contacts when the time came. Ceri Richards thought I should apply for a French Government scholarship, to provide funding for at least a year; it was certainly worth trying, and so I made the application. As with all such matters, there were many other older entrants and I was asked to apply again the following year. I began to feel despondent about the prospects for my plan but in the meantime there were other urgent matters that needed my attention.

The weeks leading up to the diploma exams were grinding on, with the inevitable tensions that arose from its requirement that students should select and present their work. As with previous years, the students' reactions to the external examiners' final verdicts were as varied as ever. But it must have been a satisfactory year, as we were all duly awarded the Diploma, and in my own case there was also a special commendation for lithography. At first, the end of the summer term seemed to be marked by the usual formal occasion. There was the assembly of staff and friends of the Slade, the prize-giving and, central to it all, Professor's observations about the year and the final exhibition, delivered in his incisive but urbane manner to an appreciative audience. Despite the atmosphere of the occasion, I felt somewhat depressed at the outcome of all this effort and idealism about printmaking if it should finally lead nowhere.

On the lawn in front of the Slade, a group of us were talking about future possibilities, when suddenly William Townsend appeared, grabbed my arm and said, 'Professor would like to see you in his office at 4.30,' and vanished. Somewhat puzzled, I arrived at the office at the appointed hour to be confronted by Ian Jenkin and the Professor, who said, 'If we were to offer you two small scholarships, are you willing to use them to study lithography in Paris?' At last, an opportunity! The idea was becoming a reality, bit by bit.

On telling my parents this news, at first they were full of reservations about the prospect of me disappearing abroad but eventually became quite supportive. The remaining weeks were filled with plans and preparations for moving to France. It was also, amidst all this activity, a time for farewells amongst friends of all kinds, from college and elsewhere. Amongst many others, we invited Mrs Allcock to our final party at 5 Lady Margaret Road, where she had survived us for two years. Now, with regrets we realised things would be very different. As artists, we vowed to keep in contact by whatever means, which we did; gradually the passage of time and events were to change all our intentions. But before going our separate ways, Roy and I went to have tea with Ceri Richards and his wife Frances. He had been inspirational to us both. I promised to keep him informed, for I knew he would be keen to hear all about Paris.

PARIS

Towards Paris, 1956

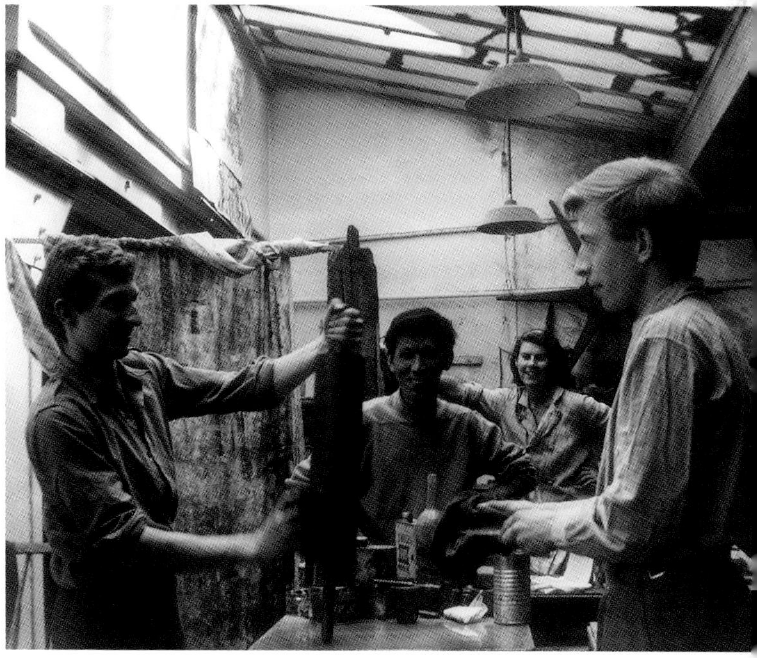

All kinds of friends sent information and advice, and by the time the departure date arrived I was reasonably well equipped with various addresses. Nonnan Dilworth from the Slade was also planning to live in Paris, and I had discovered a suitable hotel in the Cour du Commerce near the Odéon Métro. I was ready to make the crossing. The voyage from Newhaven is the longest sea route to Dieppe, taking 9–10 hours depending on the weather in the Channel but was the cheapest for student travel. There were many of us going to France that day, and I managed to pick up from one or two information about living on the Left Bank. As we approached the French coast I could see some of the remnants of the Second World War, both in the water and along the shoreline, wrecks and relics from the D-Day landings – a stark reminder of the recent conflict. From the boat, the train waited to convey passengers to Paris. By now the light was beginning to fade, so for the rest of the journey I was lost in trying to read a copy of Paris Match. From the Gare de L'Est, I found the Hôtel de Rouen – a somewhat sombre establishment – with the help of a gendarme who, luckily, was anxious to practise his English conversation. He kindly walked me down the Boulevard to an alleyway in which the hotel stood. It was by then almost eight o'clock, almost dark, and the Latin Quarter was just beginning to liven up for the evening.

There was still a lot of post-war austerity in Paris but at this time the Quartier St Germain des Près was the centre of a growing club nightlife centred around the personality of Juliette Gréco. Jazz throbbed for the jivers into the small hours each night, so I had to move from my hotel, which was right at the heart of all this

Left: Stanley Jones, *Rue Daguerre*, lithograph, 1956

Above right: Atelier Patris, photograph. L to R: Gerard Patris, Sugai, Nono Rheinhold, Stanley Jones nocturnal activity. But as the days went on, I managed to get my bearings by means of the local restaurant, named Jean, which provided soup and was popular amongst students. With sawdust on the floor and an atmosphere blue with the smoke of Gauloises, the din of intense conversation and argument dominated. The wearing of dark glasses and, in the case of some women, white makeup was part of the current existentialist uniform; Sartre and Simone de Beauvoir reigned supreme. I had been advised to register at the École des Beaux Arts to study lithography, which, as a part-time student, I duly did under the watchful eye of a Mme Moutarde (Chef d'Atelier). She also directed me to the Collège Franco-Britannique in the 14th arondissement, which would provide me with bed and breakfast. The location was handy, because from there I could walk to find Bill Hayter at Atelier 17 in Montparnasse.

A day or so later I knocked on the door of his apartment. He was very welcoming and over strong black coffee we discussed the problem of getting me into a lithographic studio to learn the craft of lithography. The French printers were loath to divulge the secrets of their métier, he felt, but he knew of a young artisan printmaker called Gérard Patris who was making his reputation in lithographic printing with artists, and who by temperament would be more sympathetic to my intentions. His studio was just round the corner in the Rue Boularde and stood at the foot of a flight of stone steps occupying the whole of the courtyard.

I walked down the passageway of Number 26, and was met by M. Patris. We shook hands and in very basic French I explained who I was and why I had come. Bill had given me a curiously typed introduction, which seemed to appeal to Patris. We agreed that I should learn the processes and practices of the studio one day a week at the École des Beaux-Arts, and in any spare time would do my own work. It was a beginning; we were both pleased and willing to make an effort, and with the Australian painter Stashak Halpern, who was working there that day, we then all adjourned to the local bistro to further our friendship.

Stashak was to be a constant help in those early months, through his capability of speaking both English and near-fluent French. Having lived in Montparnasse, with some struggles, for several years, he now knew a lot of people in the Parisian art world and was gradually making his life as a painter whilst working at Atelier Patris. He had become a part-time member of the staff and introduced many School of Paris painters to the studio. Under his guidance I grew accustomed to the everyday French language (sometimes in its most surreal expressions), as well as learning all the technical terms that related to studio life. It took some time and was often quite embarrassing.

Another member of the staff was Dado Miodrag Djuric, who, as legend had it, came to Paris from Montenegro by accompanying a football team, with whom he failed to return home. Patris had given him shelter and trained him as a highly skilled printmaker, but described him as 'a bit maverick'. There was also another staff member, nominally an assistant, also Yugoslav, whose tasks were confined to basic studio necessities such as stone grinding, looking after the machines and helping Patris with the pulling of impressions. For some reason he was nicknamed 'Ug-Dag' and was quite proud of it. There were several other part-time helpers who came according to Patris's requirements to help with the progress of editions.

Patris had his living quarters behind the studio, while the studio office was within the open-plan area of the atelier. All the printing machines were the classic star-wheel type, strongly constructed of wood and steel

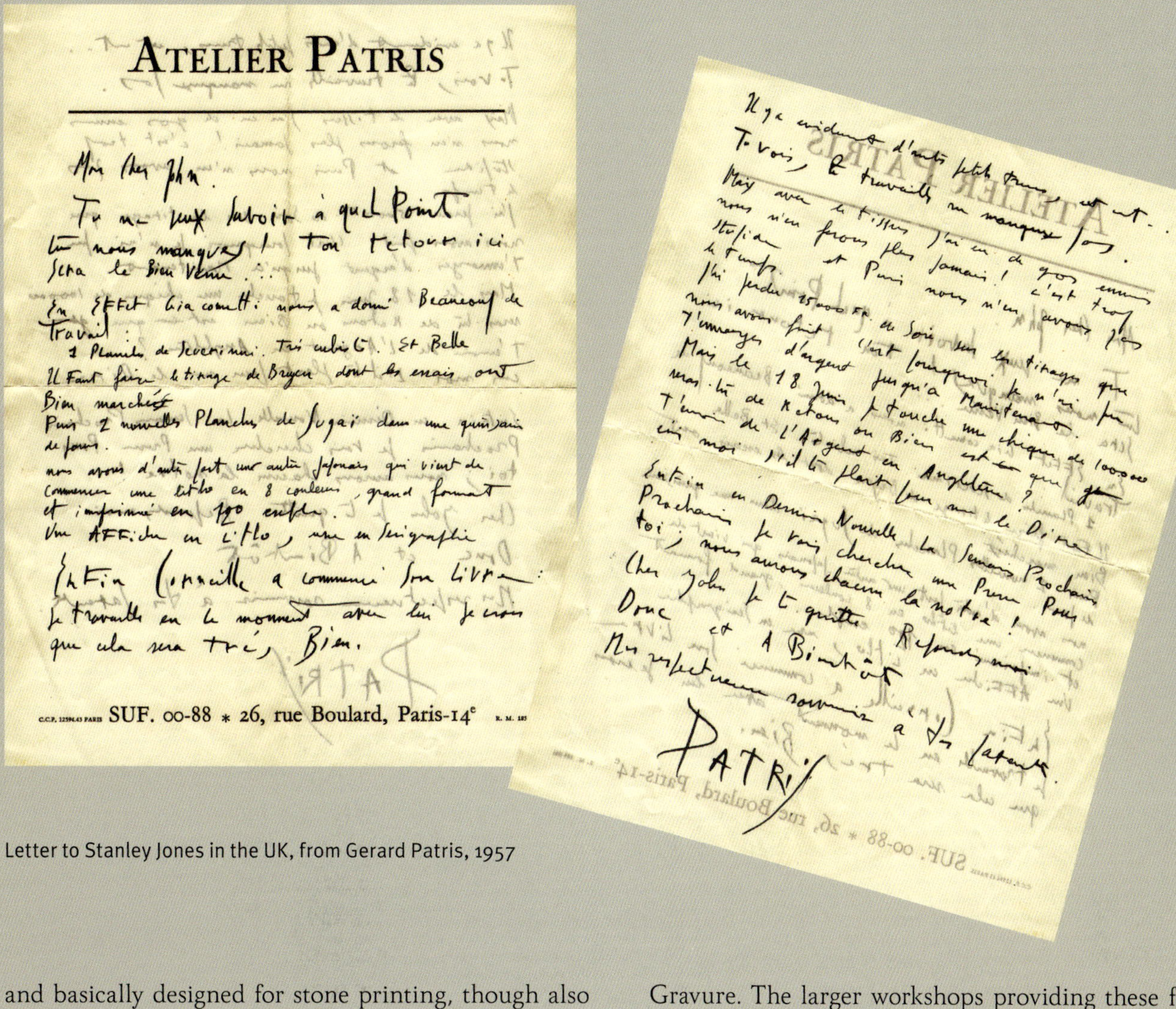

Letter to Stanley Jones in the UK, from Gerard Patris, 1957

and basically designed for stone printing, though also adaptable for work on grained zinc plate. They were cumbersome to operate (their design hadn't changed since the 19th century), but it was part of my practice to learn how to proof and edition work on these formidable presses. There were also facilities for etchers, who could rent a large intaglio press and the space to do their own printing in a separate part of the workshop. This was organised by Nono Rheinhold, a Dutch artist who like me had been introduced by Bill Hayter. It took some months for me to become accustomed to the muscular exercise involved in the daily studio tasks of stone preparation, mixing ink in quantity, and printing long editions, sometimes five to six hundred copies in ten or twelve colours. This was the only way to learn.

We were directly competing with other workshops to produce artists' lithographs for Continental print publishers such as L'Oeuvre Gravé and La Guild de la Gravure. The larger workshops providing these facilities, such as Mourlot Frères or Desjoubert et Cie., often employed 10, even 20, printers and had long-established reputations. Such was the artistic activity of the time, there was enough work from artists of all kinds to support a large number of ateliers in the centre of Paris. Patris was well aware of the competition and made sure that he kept in favour with the publishers. We grew to know particularly well M. Pillon, an agent who acted on behalf of L'Oeuvre Gravé and who also originated from Yugoslavia. He was well versed in the politics of his trade and knew how to manipulate and coerce to his own advantage both artists and printers. Nevertheless, because we were a relatively young company, he provided us with constant work; in spite of the ribbing he received from Patris and the irascible Dado, he was quite an ally and was anxious for us to succeed.

Gradually, my days and weeks began to take shape. Each morning I would walk to the studio from the Franco-Britannique, sometimes with the lines of clochards pushing their battered perambulators along the boulevard, aiming to spend the day, if the weather was cold, on the pavement grills of the Métro. That particular autumn was rich in colour, with what seemed to be constant sunlight percolating through the trees, contrasting vividly with the monochrome buildings, many of which still bore marks of neglect from the Occupation.

I attended regular classes at the École des Beaux Arts, making images on stone and learning the French procedures current at the time in lithography. Sometimes the professor would appear to give advice to students. Most of the students ignored him, and I was told later that he had collaborated with the German authorities. However, I was able to make use of the department, producing my own work on stone; their library proved very useful with what it offered on lithography.

I was, in fact, beginning to learn much more at Atelier Patris, and being able to work there at weekends helped a great deal. I became aware, inevitably, of Patris's turbulent private life, which would cause increasing problems for him as time progressed. When I met him in 1958, Patris was a talented craftsman making his reputation in Montparnasse as a lithographic printmaker. He had been married several years to his wife Brigitte but their living accommodation was next door to the atelier and the activities related to it were always present. Patris had a wide circle of friends and acquaintances and by temperament liked to be the centre of attention, enjoying flirtations with women friends that were the cause of frustration for his wife. Finally, she sought out her own lifestyle, forming associations with several artists that caused Patris to rely increasingly on Dado and myself for daily support.

To begin with, however, it was Dado who was our main concern. When out with his friends, he often had to be rescued from the prefecture, being unable to produce his papers during police raids. This was a time when Algerian activists were appearing on the streets of Paris, so police of all types were constantly in operation around the cafes and bistros. Patris seemed obliged to look after Dado's welfare as he relied on him for edition printing. On one occasion we spent an afternoon cleaning his living quarters and his clothes of fleas, acquired after a wild weekend with some friends outside Paris. Gradually, as the weeks went by, we all began to work as a team and the daily involvement in work took its course. I learned the techniques of stone printing, in particular the use of dilute nitric-acid washes to preserve the most delicate work and the mixing of colour followed by the cleaning of the hand rollers for proofing or edition printing, to be practised every day. These were disciplined and often laborious tasks but essential to the nature of the work. Until my command of French had improved (of necessity, it did) I had to work under Patris's instruction but we did make good progress. Those who came to create prints seemed to like the working atmosphere of the atelier with its young cosmopolitan staff, who were very willing to experiment, if allowed to, with the artists' ideas. At that time the studio was attracting painters of the calibre of as Sugai, Corneille and Bryen, who had strong reputations around Europe with both galleries and publishers.

Christmas came and I was allowed to return to England, feeling a somewhat different person. It was curious to leave the Gare St-Lazare on the boat train early in the morning and arrive in Wigan late the same evening. This was an unbelievable contrast in all respects and it took several days for me to adjust to such stark differences. Relations and friends were inquisitive about my life in Paris and the days spent at home with them went by very quickly. However, I had a distinct sense of disorientation about an environment that had once meant so much to me. The mills and the mines were being pulled down and dereliction was spreading once again. I was very anxious to get back across the Channel, even with all its difficulties.

My involvement with Atelier Patris began to deepen as the weeks went by, and I decided that from a learning and practice point of view my days would be better spent in the workshop. So I duly left the École des Beaux-Arts, which meant relinquishing student status and searching for other accommodation near the studio. This pleased Patris, who could now rely on my daily presence as a constant arrangement. He allowed me space in the studio where I could do my own work, particularly at weekends. I could then afford a small room in the Hôtel Descartes, in which I could eat and sleep away from the studio and have a change of space, with a different kind of lifestyle and other friends. My new accommodation was in an indescribably old building that was said to be a remnant of the old wall of Paris. The room was triangular in shape and overlooked a large courtyard which seemed to be constantly inhabited by North Africans of all kinds. Since I wouldn't be there during the day, the noise levels didn't seem to matter. I got used to the overall gloom within the building and the constant smell of oriental cooking. An ancient door opened onto Boulevard Raspail, which then led directly to the Rue Boularde and Atelier Patris – a fairly easy walking distance.

With the gradual build-up of work in the studio, a widening range of artists appeared on the doorstep and I took on more responsibility for proofing images and giving advice if asked. Unlike many of the larger ateliers, which employed '*chromistes*' (professional lithographic draughtsmen), we preferred to allow the artists to draw up the work themselves, unless there were difficulties. However, this was a time when Art Autre and Tachisme were current modes of expression and it took a certain amount of technical invention to translate these ideas into lithography. The painter Camille Bryen was a leader in this field and enjoyed his visits to the studio, being very satisfied with the results we obtained with him using stone. He had the unusual practice of bringing his wife along to convey his ideas to us, beginning each sentence with, 'M. Bryen wishes you to know'. We learned to accept this as part of his working method. It was customary for those of us who could to attend private views (*vernissages*) each week. Nowadays such activities would be labelled as 'networking', and there was no doubt it helped to introduce new artists, as well as publishers, to the workshop.

There was also an active social life of parties in artists' studios, held for all manner of reasons – often including the latest craze for jiving. Patris had a wide circle of friends including many avant-garde artists and musicians, one of whom was Luc Ferrari, a pioneer of musique concrète. He was a frequent visitor to the studio and took much interest in its activities. If invited out at all, we were usually taken in Patris's open tourer, a Fiat of uncertain pre-war vintage, which was normally employed to carry paper or inks. It had survived the Occupation, Patris's driving and the French traffic for many years and bore all the marks of such encounters. On occasion, we used it for transporting lithographic stones to artists who were unable to come to the workshop. Gino Severini, advanced in years, was living on the top floor of a tenement in Montparnasse, and had been commissioned by a publisher to make an image on stone based on a still life. It turned out that there would be eight large stones involved. The struggle was considerable, involving three or four helpers each time, as there was no lift and minimal lighting on the stairs. We had to provide him with each stone ready to be drawn, when required, in his studio. It was an awesome task. However, he was very grateful and invited us each time to have coffee and talk about the work. Through the window of his studio one had a remarkable rooftop view of the quartier, and the room itself was bedecked on all sides with Futurist pictures in various states of completion. This was one of several images that we eventually made with him, which involved spending concentrated hours adjusting to the detail of his work.

The approach of members of the Jeune École de Paris (young school of painters) resulted in a greater intricacy of colour separations. In contrast to the traditional use of accepted lithographical materials (inks, crayons, etc.), the avant-garde School of Paris painters were generally more vigorous and experimental in expressing pictorial qualities, using large brushes with admixtures of water, petrol and lithographic ink. John Levee, an American artist resident in Paris, brought just such a concept to the lithographs that we produced with him.

There were painters of all nationalities gathering in post-war Paris at this time, particularly those associated with the emerging New York School, who were establishing their own aesthetic identity. On visits from America, Robert Motherwell, Jackson Pollock and David Smith had been frequent workers at Hayter's Atelier 17. Painters from the East such as Zao Wou-Ki and Kumi Sugai were enriching their reputations by experimenting with printmaking. For two weeks or so, Sugai and I ground and reworked stones until the right textures were achieved – finally by using an unusual mix of sand and washing detergent – but we had also discovered something new about how to corrode textures. During the long autumn and winter months of 1956, we were beginning to attract more of the younger School of Paris painters such as Roberto Matta, Gianni Bertini and Robert-Edgar Gillet. Overall, there was a growing interest from publishers and artists in the nature of the studio; the fact that we had a young and enthusiastic staff probably counted in our favour.

We were also attempting to meet the demands of the new School of Paris artists, whose attitudes to lithography were experimental. The new styles of painting developing amongst this group had spread into printmaking, particularly etching and lithography. They did not as yet involve photo-process techniques but in the case of lithography were concerned with using grease-containing substances. The use of fluids such as petrol, MEK (methyl ethyl ketone) and oleic acid was common practice. The idea seemed to promote a broadening of the materials used in lithography from the conventional ones into the more unorthodox, which lend a more unnatural quality to the artist's image. Jean Dubuffet was a clear example of this practice. He eventually set up his own litho workshop so that he could experiment without interruption.

In early January 1957, on my return from England, I found Patris anxious to stabilise my position in the studio and come to some financial arrangement with me, given that my scholarships were due to finish a month or so later. We agreed that I would work at the studio indefinitely and become a permanent member of his staff. The finances, though highly unofficial, would improve my quality of life somewhat and it would be possible to improve on my diet, which until then had

Right: Stanley Jones, *Variations on Parisian Street*, four studies for lithographs, 1956

centred around horsemeat and vegetables from the street market. We did, whenever possible, dine in the studio as a group – Patris was very generous in sharing his wife's cooking and sometimes a girlfriend of his would cook a meal in the kitchen. But this was always a bit haphazard. I think we all had secret stashes of bread and cheese hidden away for emergencies. On our perambulations around Montparnasse we would sometimes gaze in wonderment through the windows of La Coupole. Such centres of French cuisine were common and famous in Montparnasse, with a great variety of dishes on offer. To us they were an unobtainable luxury, existing as we did on a day-to-day diet based on whatever we could afford. In the winter months we would start work early at about 8am and a breakfast of a croissant and a small cognac would suffice until lunchtime; both Dado and I had to keep to agreed schedules each day in order to deal with the increasing workload. Nevertheless, we had to guard any spare time for our own work – usually in the evenings and at weekends. Overall, this was a beneficial and disciplined learning curve for us both.

It was also interesting to occasionally make contact with other lithographic printers engaged in similar activities. One such was M. André Clot, whose workshop was at 106 Rue du Cherche-Midi. I was introduced to him by Anthony Gross who taught etching at the Slade whom he had known for some years. One afternoon, given the opportunity, I knocked on the door of 106, with its ornate Art Nouveau portal. M. Clot, by then an elderly gentleman, listened to me with interest as I explained who I was and my reason for being in Paris. We spent a fascinating afternoon discussing printmaking while he continued to work at his press. He showed me the examples of work by his father Auguste Clot, done in collaboration with Rodin, Renoir, Redon and Cézanne, which demonstrated his remarkable lithographic skill. Realising that I was resident in Paris, he invited me to visit the studio again, which I subsequently did, learning much from his conversation about the family's association with artists and their pioneering of the medium of lithography. I was intrigued on one visit to watch him grind his own lithographic ink, which he preferred to do according to the nature of the work in hand.

Through February and March the weather began to warm a little and on some days I could dispense with my much-envied Crombie overcoat. This garment was a standby which had been crucial in the Parisian winter, *sans chaufage*, as well as those occasions when I shivered with *la grippe*, the flu, for several days. I sometimes loaned it to Dado for special 'social' occasions, even though it didn't quite fit.

During the spring I continued my search for a more permanent place to live, since Patris was anxious to stabilise the staffing of the studio. The room I lodged in at the Hôtel Descartes had always been a somewhat temporary situation, although I had by now acclimatised to the odorous, dank corridors and the shadowy inhabitants who shuffled up and down at all hours. Occasionally, there were commotions and screaming – eventually the police would arrive, accompanied by a remonstrating concierge, anxious about his licence. The progress of my own work was becoming more important and I needed more space, so I made up my mind to find another place. Friends promised to search around, which seemed to be the best way of locating accommodation but times were hard and an influx of refugees from Hungary, fleeing the Soviet invasion of that country, had reduced the available housing stock. However, I was lucky one morning to meet Stashak Halpern in the local bistro, who told me he had decided to move from his current studio in the Rue Maurice Rouvier to one in a more central location near Raspail. Was I interested in his old place?

We walked there that evening from the atelier; apart from Stashak's assemblage of paintings and bizarre furniture, it seemed ideal. Two rooms in a building with no concierge and plenty of light, where I could work, sleep and cook if necessary, and in peace and quiet. Stashak had been there several years undisturbed but needed more space, for he now had the prospect of one or two dealer's contracts; my moving would save us both trouble if his landlord would agree, though this in itself might take a little time. Finally, after considerable haggling, I was given the go-ahead to move in. Unfortunately, however, Stashak's plan to move out had had to be put back a bit and, given that I had already quit my previous digs, I accepted Patris's offer of temporary accommodation. This turned out to have complications; I was aware of the complicated domestic private life in which Patris was embroiled after workshop hours. I also now realised that there were liaisons involving other women; the noise generated by their lovemaking often woke me up – sleeping, as I was, on an insubstantial camp bed in the next room.

After some weeks of disturbed sleep I moved gratefully into my own place. I was able to reorganise the accommodation and the landlord allowed me to furnish it with a table, chairs and other odds and ends from the flea market; at least it was a beginning. I could walk to the studio down the Avenue Alesia and on these occasions I would sometimes meet Alberto Giacometti on his way to and from his studio in the Rue Hyppolite Maindron. We had first met when a sculptor friend, Norman Dilworth, took me to visit him in 1956. He was familiar with London and the Slade, having paid several visits in the 1950s. I mentioned a print he had made of the red trolleybuses and the interplay of the overhead wires, which he recalled with a broad smile. On hearing that I was working at Atelier Patris he promised to call in and look at the workshop.

I was intrigued by Giacometti's working studio, the smallness of the two or three rooms and the fusion of ageless dust and plaster chippings that covered every surface. From the floor, through this accretion of meaningful rubble, rose an assemblage of haggard, sculptural figures in various stages of progress or decay. On the darkened walls were the myriad brush marks of years of alteration and reconsideration – the artist's frenetic calligraphic language mixed with figures and portrait notes, all gazing out at their companions. In the gloom of the corners, dust-laden canvases lay cluttered but undisturbed on chairs and boxes. Some frail tables, half-hidden under sacking, supported strange semi-human forms covered in hacked plaster. Occasionally, standing forlornly on the floor, metal armatures awaited his unpredictable attention. The scene amounted to a bewildering landscape of ideas and relics that the artist had worked with throughout his daily life, reflecting an obsession with the attempt to capture and render his elusive ideas through such basic materials. His visits to the Atelier Patris were unpredictable and depended on whether we were working later than usual. He would wander in to sit and watch the activity; even on occasion picking up a piece of litho crayon to work out an idea, which he seemed to do with unusual ease.

The flow of artists through the workshop continued to increase, and with it the pressures on time for my own work. Somehow I managed to find time enough to produce work for mixed exhibitions at several galleries in the 5th arrondissement, around the Rue de Seine, and I was also sending work back to London for exhibitions; but it was an uphill task, time being the major factor. However, there was sufficient studio time available for

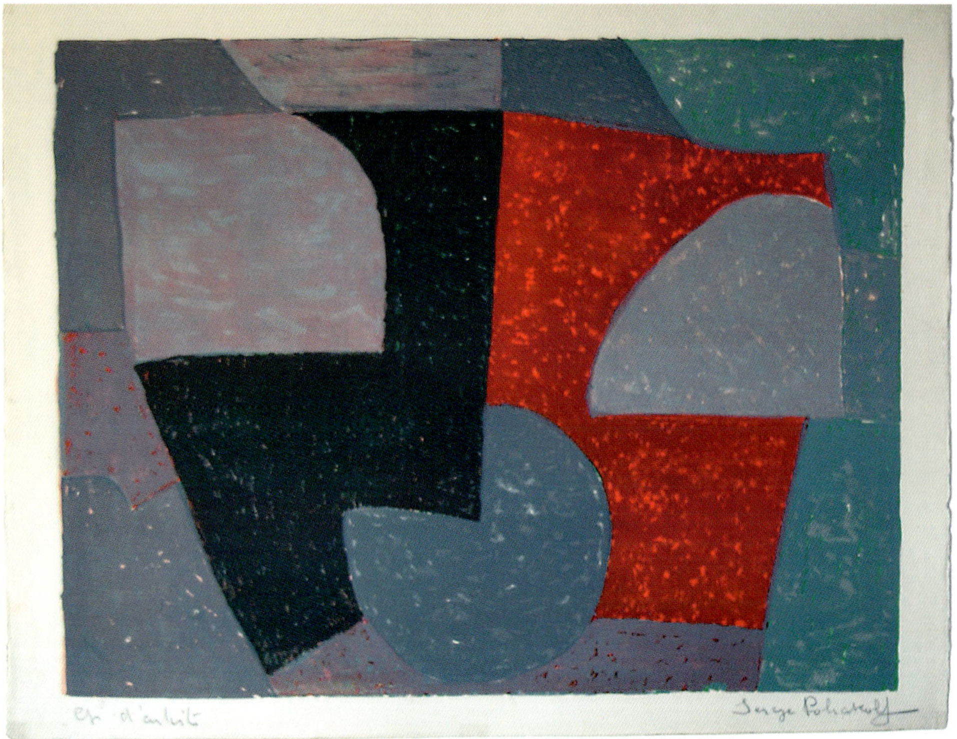

Above: Poliakoff, lithograph, 1957

Right: Stanley Jones, *Alesia*, lithograph, 1957

me to do this, mostly at weekends, as in the evenings during the week we frequently had to work with Patris.

We were becoming part of the competitive print world in Montparnasse but at the same time we had to be aware of the demanding nature of making prints. The work was often arduous, as none of the presses were mechanised, and a considerable amount of physical effort was required for each impression. We would exchange positions during printing to alleviate the strain and concentration required; in this way Dado and I became quite skilled in editioning, particularly in the realm of colour mixing and hand rolling. It was proving to be an invaluable experience, if also exhausting on occasions. Moreover, when publishers were slow to pay Patris for the work, we were obliged to tighten our belts. This would mean eating in the studio and often living on a frugal diet based on the aforementioned horsemeat. Dado and I used to invent the most unusual meals based on what we could discover in the street market of the Rue Daguerre. This situation helped to nurture a strong camaraderie amongst us, which helped the studio to function harmoniously from one month to the next. Meanwhile, M. Pillon tried to keep a fatherly eye on us and with this in mind sent the painters Gillet and Jean Le Moal to begin work with us.

During the normal course of events for a studio of this kind, all sorts of things happen, for whatever reason, which affect its existence and have to be endured. In the early summer of 1957, Dado received a letter from his girlfriend in Yugoslavia announcing that she would be coming to visit him in Paris. He was delighted at this news and spent much time describing her virtues to us; Patris and I were duly impressed. One morning, she appeared on Dado's arm and their happiness seemed complete; Patris granted them holiday time and they went off to enjoy Paris together. We applied ourselves to the studio work for a fortnight without a sign or word from Dado. Increasingly concerned, we sent out search parties, which revealed no sign of our friend. Suddenly, at the end of the third week he arrived in the studio,

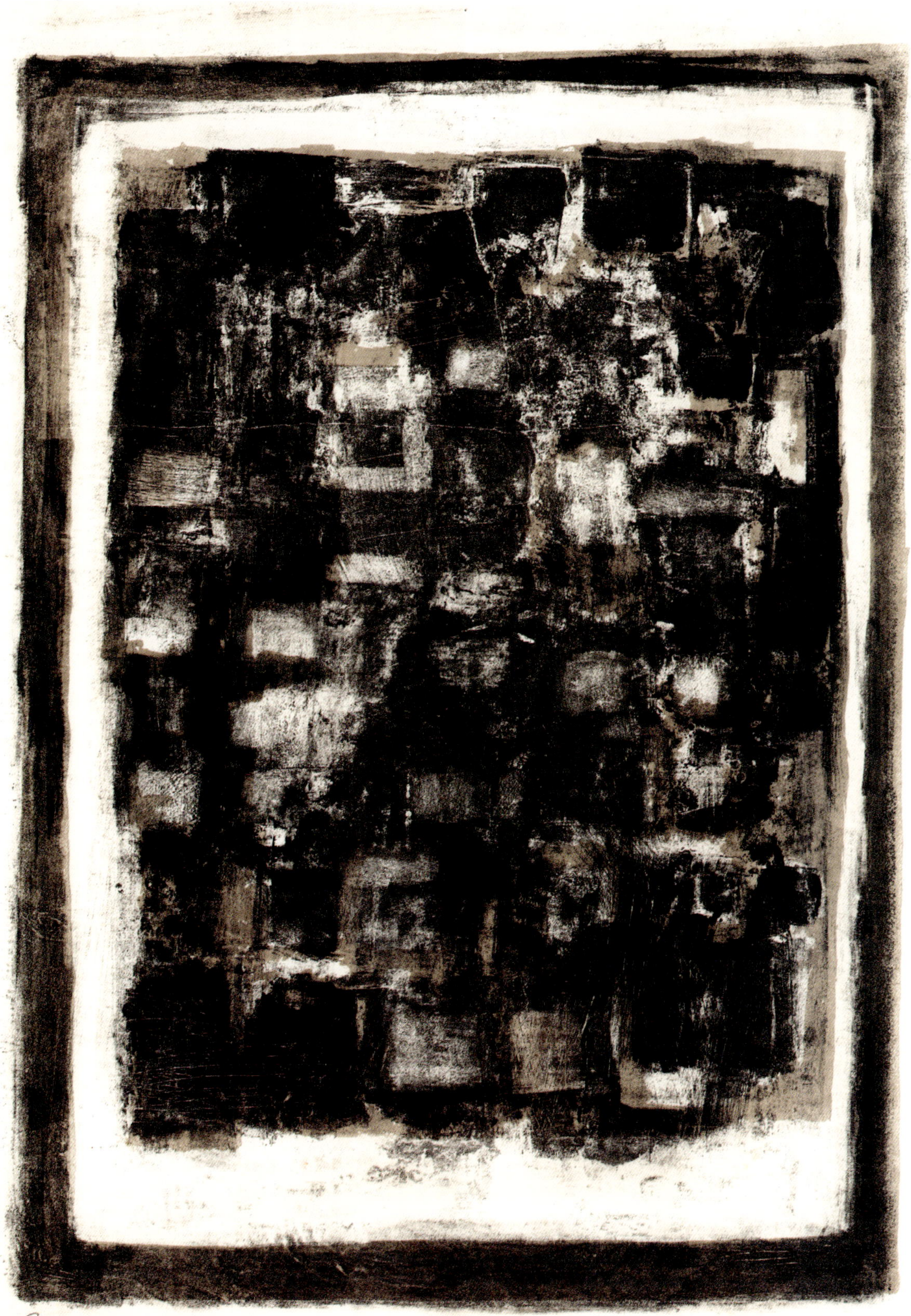

Essaye ① A/P

[illegible] '57

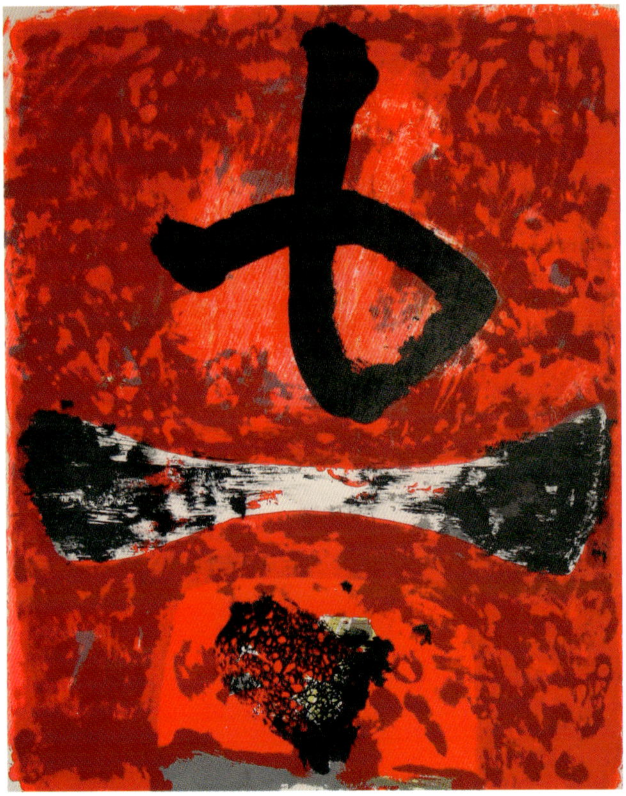
Sugai, *Summer*, lithograph, 1957

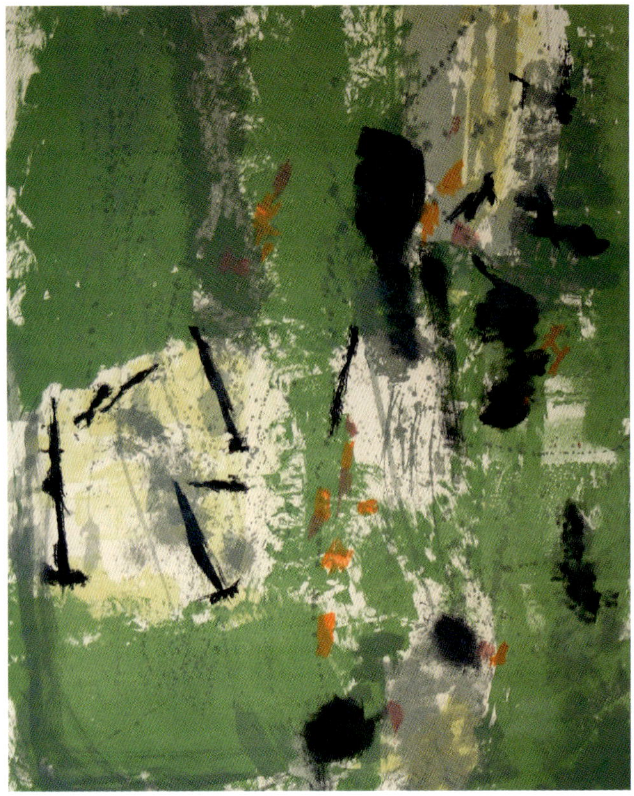
Camille Bryen, *Springtime*, lithograph, 1957

looking somewhat dishevelled, glum and minus his beloved. It seemed that she had been so overwhelmed by her Parisian life that she had abandoned Dado for someone else. *Déçu de la vie*, he had decided to drown his sorrows. Of course, he was forgiven by Patris and welcomed back, and soon the whole event became a distant legend, almost beyond recall.

It was during Dado's absence that Patris talked with me about future plans for the studio, since it was now developing into an active atelier for lithographic print-making and appeared to have a promising future. We decided to work together for the foreseeable future; I was now domiciled in Montparnasse, with working colleagues and an income that would enable me to produce my own work and absorb the practice of lithography. Patris and I got on well, and my command of French had improved beyond all recognition; it seemed a satisfactory proposition for both of us.

Meanwhile, around the studio had grown an assortment of friends from many countries and occupations: poets, musicians and writers, as well as the constant traffic of painters and sculptors. There were oddities amongst them, such as the Australian cartoonist Will Marshall, who earned a lucrative living from the newspaper *France Soir* through illustrating the adventures of the American gangster John Dillinger. By this means he had acquired a small chateau outside Paris and ran several sports cars too; in those austere times that was quite an ac-complishment. During the summer we were often invited to spend weekends at the chateau, an isolated rambling mansion with a wild garden full of ripening fruit trees – a very enjoyable wilderness for summer picnicking. Returning to Montparnasse in the cold of early Monday morning for the day's work in the studio, clinging to the back of the open-top MG as it careered across Paris, was exhilarating. We were often stopped by suspicious police demanding explanations. We were wary of them after one of our friends, Will Wills, an American architect, had been mistakenly apprehended and then beaten up by police as they cleared a student demonstration. He ended up in hospital for several weeks and was somehow never quite the same again.

During the succeeding summer months Paris became quite hot but the studio managed to remain cool for lithographic printing, aided by the old wine we used to dampen the stones when editioning prints. I was starting to show my work locally and with the help of Bill Hayter began to acquaint myself with some of the galleries on the Left Bank. There was increasing activity in the printmaking world, and the Guilde de Gravure and the L'Oeuvre Gravé were both very active in supplying us with artists to be published. During those summer months Corneille, Gillet, Maryan and Bertini came to us with their various methods for creating graphic images; it was a demanding but invaluable experience depending much upon the studio's collaborative abilities.

In those days August was a time when a lot of Parisians left the city for holidays and the streets became relatively quiet. Shopkeepers and tradespeople of all kinds closed for a week or so, leaving only the tourists, it seemed, to pursue their interests. In the studio we were able to catch up on work promised for the autumn. We were all occupied with these tasks one Friday morning when there was a loud knock on the studio door. As was the custom, everyone seemed too preoccupied to answer, and it was only after repeated knocking that one of us went to open the door. In walked the familiar figure of Robert Erskine.

Since this was his first visit we made him feel very welcome. He seemed quite intrigued by Atelier Patris, the people and its working atmosphere. After looking at the work in progress, he suggested that he and I should have lunch to discuss printmaking matters. I thought he was interested in using the atelier for future work, but that was not what he wanted. It appeared that the Curwen Press in London wished to renew its connexions with working artists through the formation of a new studio in which original limited-edition work would be produced – ideal for Robert and his publishing needs. Gazing out into the bustling Rue Daguerre that I had grown so familiar with, I asked where this was to be situated, to which Robert replied, 'Near the company, in the East End of London. Would you consider coming back to run this venture, with their support?' After a long pause, I replied, 'Not really, Robert. As you can see, we have a very good studio working here, full of promise, just beginning to make its way.' There was another pause while he thoughtfully scratched his beard, then said, 'What if you would consider just setting it up – say, for a year – and then returning to Paris?' 'I'll talk with Gérard and see what we can agree on,' I said, feeling the whole idea to be vague and unreal. Robert promised to write with more information but I felt that the project was

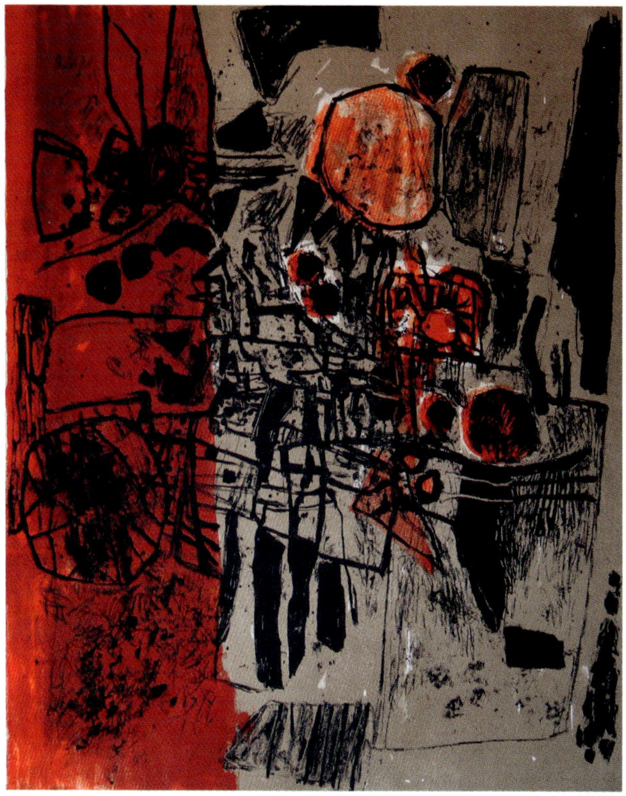

Corneille, *Summer Games* , proof, 1958

highly improbable and would somehow soon be just a lost memory. However, it did seem significant that he still had plans and enthusiasm for printmaking.

I discussed this proposal with Patris and like me he was very sceptical about its probability, being naturally more interested in the development of Atelier Patris. So we focused our attention on other matters, such as the poster for his next exhibition that we were helping Bill Hayter to make, and more or less forgetting this issue. Nevertheless, some weeks later I received a letter from Robert with yet another set of ideas, proposing that I should meet with a Mr Herbert Simon (Head of the Curwen Press) on my next visit to England and at the same time discuss with Robert a possible printmaking project involving artists in St Ives. Much, it appeared, depended on the Curwen Press and the seriousness of its' intentions.

The start of Curwen

I was due to come home in November and decided to break my return journey in London to discuss these possibilities en route to Paris. Back in Wigan, I was surprised to see how far my father's health had deteriorated during the previous year; his condition was still causing great concern to the family. I turned these matters over in my mind, journeying back to London with the aim of meeting Herbert Simon at the Curwen Press in Plaistow. The East End of London was still recovering from the ravages of the war; here more than anywhere was dereliction, mixed with what had survived of the industrial docklands. Autumnal fog left me with only a vague impression of the area but this was in total contrast to the ambience of Montparnasse.

Amidst all this, in his office on the corner of North Street, H.S., as I came to know him, and I sat facing each other. I knew something of the past history of this eminent company and of its standards and impressive achievements in the field of printing and graphic design; Herbert and his brother Oliver (who had died in 1954) had helped to build the firm's contemporary reputation. Our conversation focused on the possibility of building a small experimental studio by converting some redundant stables situated further down the road and separate from the main company. This was the idea of Oliver's son Timothy and Herbert's son Robert, who was active in the production of work at Curwen. Herbert himself, although supportive of the idea generally, felt that a two-year trial would be 'a fair period of time' in which to judge progress either way. If it succeeded, all well and good; if not I could return to Paris and resume my career in Montparnasse. Would I be willing to consider this? I gathered that he had yet to convince his fellow directors about the wisdom of such a venture into the world of fine art; collaborative printmaking with artists when there was no obvious market in this country, we agreed, was an undoubted gamble, to put it mildly. I said I would give it some thought and we parted, agreeing that there was much else to ponder over; I felt that in the background were other problems that he had not mentioned. But we had got on well; he was certainly in full command, judging by the deference shown him by his staff. I had yet to meet the younger generation, Timothy and Robert, whose ideas would be different and surely more crucial to Robert Erskine's aims. But even if all went well, the new studio would take some time, perhaps a year in preparation, to become a reality.

Back in Paris, Patris was anxious to hear about my trip and the contact I had made with Curwen; he felt intrigued but unconvinced of the plan's probability.

Unknown to me, Erskine was already exploring people and places in St Ives to set up his publishing project, so as to fill the time while the stables were converted into a studio. A week or so later I received from him an invitation to start this pre-Curwen venture as soon as early January, which would leave enough time for him to have proofs ready by the autumn. A second letter indicated that he had also made contact with several well-known St Ives artists who were interested in participating. In addition, a sculptor, Bruce Taylor, was keen to cooperate in this publishing scheme. He possessed a lithographic proofing press with stones, plus the necessary studio space. After much weighing up of the complexities of the situation, I decided to accept the offer made by Herbert Simon, in truth because of the future possibilities inherent at Curwen. In the long term, the foundation of a more permanent professional atelier in England would be a pioneering and long-overdue venture. Such a studio could provide facilities for artists and publishers that were not previously not available. There was a quality of adventure about the idea and the timing seemed curiously appropriate. I felt that Patris understood my reasons; we had worked very satisfactorily together, and his studio by now had trained artisans to help its continued growth. These were the kinds of thoughts that crossed my mind as I reread Erskine's letter to grasp fully its implications. It would mean leaving so much I had learned to appreciate – the atelier, the work, fellow artists, all the friends and the quality of life in a Montparnasse which could still, occasionally, possess some of the magic of the famous pre-war years. There were, however, intimations that the balance of influence in the European art world was beginning to change. American artists were striving for their own recognition and the New York School was coming to the fore, and with it printmakers and studios ready to accommodate their new graphic ideas. Perhaps London would be in a similar position in the near future.

Bidding farewell was difficult; everyone felt it was a temporary arrangement and that I would soon reappear and continue as usual. I almost began to believe this myself as the time drew near to depart. Bill Hayter was very enthusiastic about the idea – at least to try it out, he counselled – and promised to visit this new pioneering project in London. Anyway, as Patris said, it was a good excuse for one of our studio parties.

I arranged to leave around mid-December to make preparations in London with Robert Erskine and to visit my family in the North, who were keen to know all about this new prospect in Cornwall and London. Robert and I decided that we would need a larger press than the one in Bruce Taylor's studio and we were lucky enough to find a Winstone proofing machine, supplied by a firm of printing engineers, Thomas E. Knight of London. As a gesture Mr. Knight gave us some 'nap' leather hand-rollers and several large lithographic stones. This was a fortunate stroke of luck, since these materials were not easy to find at short notice. Hunter Penrose supplied the majority of the other necessary equipment, which was sent in advance to St Ives. Robert's attention was now focused on organising arrangements with Bruce Taylor and his wife Jenny concerning finance and my accommodation in their premises, as part of the temporary agreement. It was understood by all that when the new studio was ready at Curwen, the project in all its aspects, myself included, would be transferred to London.

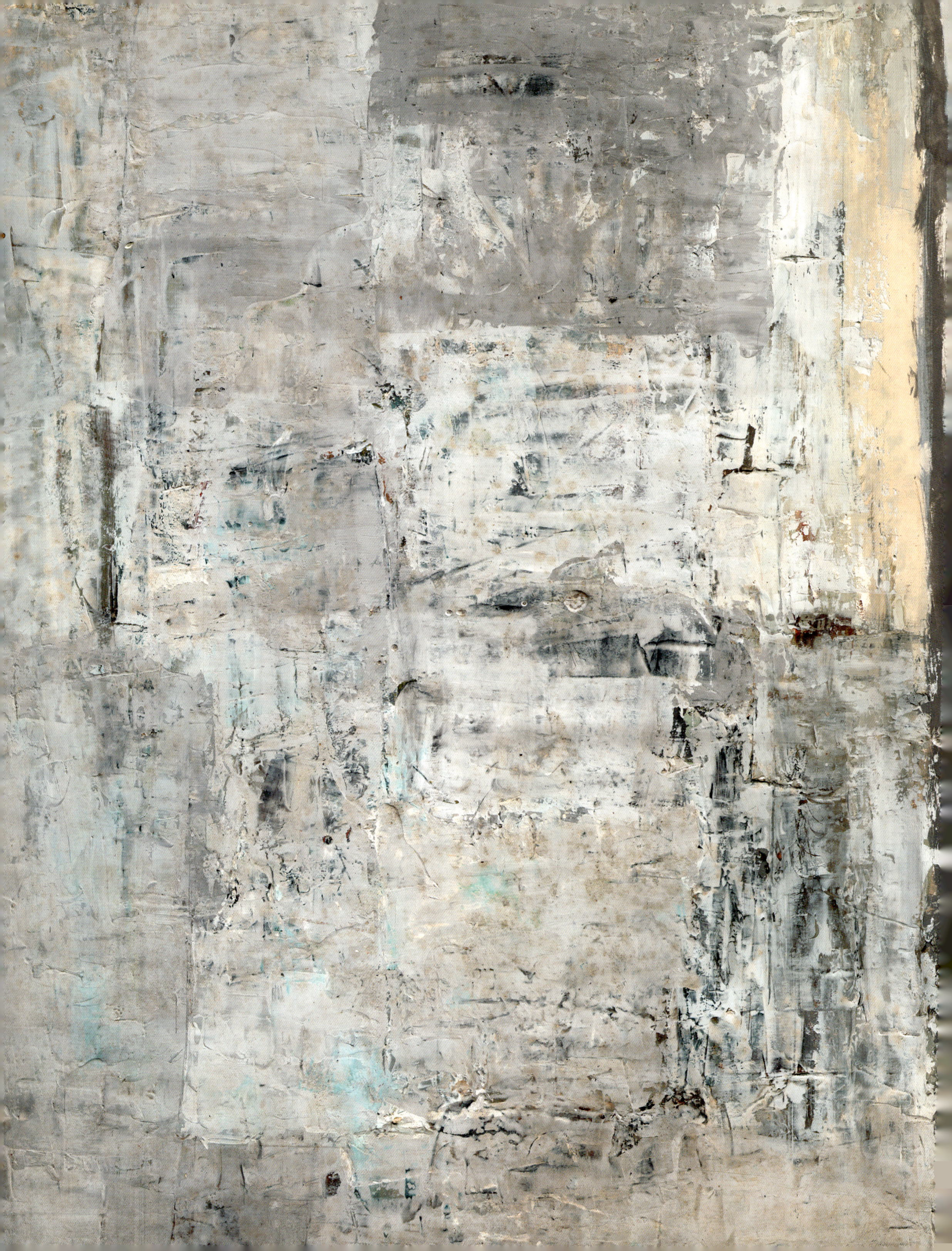

"... no one has ever tried such a project in this country before."

ST IVES

To me, St Ives was an unknown quantity. I had never visited the area and did not know anyone who lived there. Its reputation as a focus for the *avant-garde* art movement in this country was well established, centred largely around the work and activities of Ben Nicholson and Barbara Hepworth, who had moved to Cornwall in 1939, and Bernard Leach. Since then it had attracted innumerable painters, sculptors and potters; by 1958 it was probably at the height of its national and international aesthetic importance. It was a focus of attention for critics, dealers and artists from abroad who came to investigate its atmosphere and sample the qualities which had drawn fellow artists from other parts of the country, year after year. But 50 years ago, apart from this core of recognised individuals, there was also a population of aspiring amateur artists with varying means of support, whose social lives blossomed mainly during the summer months amongst the growing number of holidaymakers. Fishing was still practised by certain local families but by 1958 it was a declining occupation; more and more reliance was being placed on income from annual visitors. The presence of artists of all kinds helped to foster the unique attraction of St Ives to the outside world, encouraging an influx of the curious that was not always welcomed or understood by some of the local inhabitants. To complicate matters there were, apparently, divisions within the artists' community itself, centred around the Penwith Society, which encompassed most of the established *avant-garde*. This was the overall view given to me by Robert's secretary, Anne Lane, at the St George's Gallery before my departure to Cornwall.

Any problems would certainly be of a very different order to those of the 1950s Paris that I had just left. Adjusting to this new environment would take time, even though the duration of my sojourn there would be fairly short. On my arrival in St Ives, Robert intended to come down on a visit to help me settle in and to make contact with artists whose work he wished to publish. Their response held the key to the progress of his idea; no one had ever tried such a project in this country before.

A date was fixed for me to make the initial journey down in early January and to stay with Bruce and Jenny Taylor in their newly established gallery and workshops on Fore Street, facing the harbour. They had settled in St Ives with their family, both being former students of the art school at Corsham Court, at which many of the St Ives artists had taught. Their home had become quite a centre of communication for the artists' and writers' community as well as housing the Penwith Society Gallery; such enterprise had made them well known in the locality to a wide range of people.

In those days, the journey to St Ives from Paddington by steam train could take most of the day, with darkness

Left: Stanley Jones, *Rocks: Portleven*, gouache, 1958.

setting in by four in the afternoon at this time of year. My initial view of Cornwall was shrouded through an obscuring half-light and drizzle, which grew more intense as the train approached St Ives. Finally, in the wet cobbled street, I was welcomed at number 36 by Jenny's mother, Mrs Martin-Jones, Bruce and Jenny being on their way from London as well.

The following morning I was awakened early by the screeching of seagulls outside my window in Academy Place; that day Bruce and I would start the planning of the studio and the solving of practical problems to make this scheme work, some of which would remain with us in the months ahead. Overall, it was a temporary solution, demanding all kinds of unusual expertise in this remote place, until the premises at Curwen were ready. But lithography takes no prisoners so preparations had to be thorough and carefully controlled and included considerations such as: the organisation of the artists working in the studio; the recording of detail, particularly proofs and prints; and the ordering of materials.

The evenings and weekends would be the time available to me to do my own work but the remainder of the time would involve the running of the studio. Robert and his wife were due at the weekend to make final arrangements and to talk to the assembled artists in Bruce's living quarters. In the meantime, shelves and benches were erected, lighting installed and stones made ready for drawing. Bruce's press – which we would be obliged to use until the larger proofing machine arrived from London – needed all manner of adjustments; luckily in an old workshop we discovered sufficient nuts and bolts with which to repair it. I found Bruce and Jenny to be very helpful and they made me welcome in their home, even as they endeavoured to cope with their two daughters and the visitors who thronged the house at various times. Bruce seemed to have a problem finding time for his own sculpture work and he was also teaching in Penzance. Because of this, we agreed to respect each other's obligations, a solution that worked quite well.

Robert arrived on the Friday and we made the arrangements for the Taylors' living room to be available for his film, *Artist's Proof*, and the meeting with prospective printmakers. Seven o'clock on Saturday evening came and there was quite a gathering of artists – some seriously interested, others merely curious. It was all quite informal and amicable – several of the gathering had visited the Sloop Inn before arriving – but there was also genuine interest. At the end of the evening I had a list of people to contact plus a possible assistant, Monica Harman, who hoped to learn the technology and carry on the project when I had departed for London. I was willing to cooperate with this idea in theory but felt intuitively that there would be too little time for her to accomplish such an intention. 'Give it a try anyway,' I thought.

Robert organised a preparatory list of artists to start work with me; Patrick Heron, Barbara Hepworth, Trevor Bell, Bryan Wynter, Peter Lanyon, John Wells, Alex Mackenzie and Karl Weschke were among the first names chosen; Willie Barns Graham and Sandra Blow were to follow with others at a later date. Ben Nicholson, who had separated from Barbara Hepworth and was now living in his own house, was planning to leave and live in Switzerland. Before he left he would call in to see developments and talk about the differences between etching and hand-drawn lithography, which he had never tried.

First the studio had to be completed. A schedule that suited both the individual artists and Robert Erskine's publishing plans had been agreed upon and everyone was keen to start. In those days, with no mobile phones or e-mail to turn to, arranging a schedule of this kind

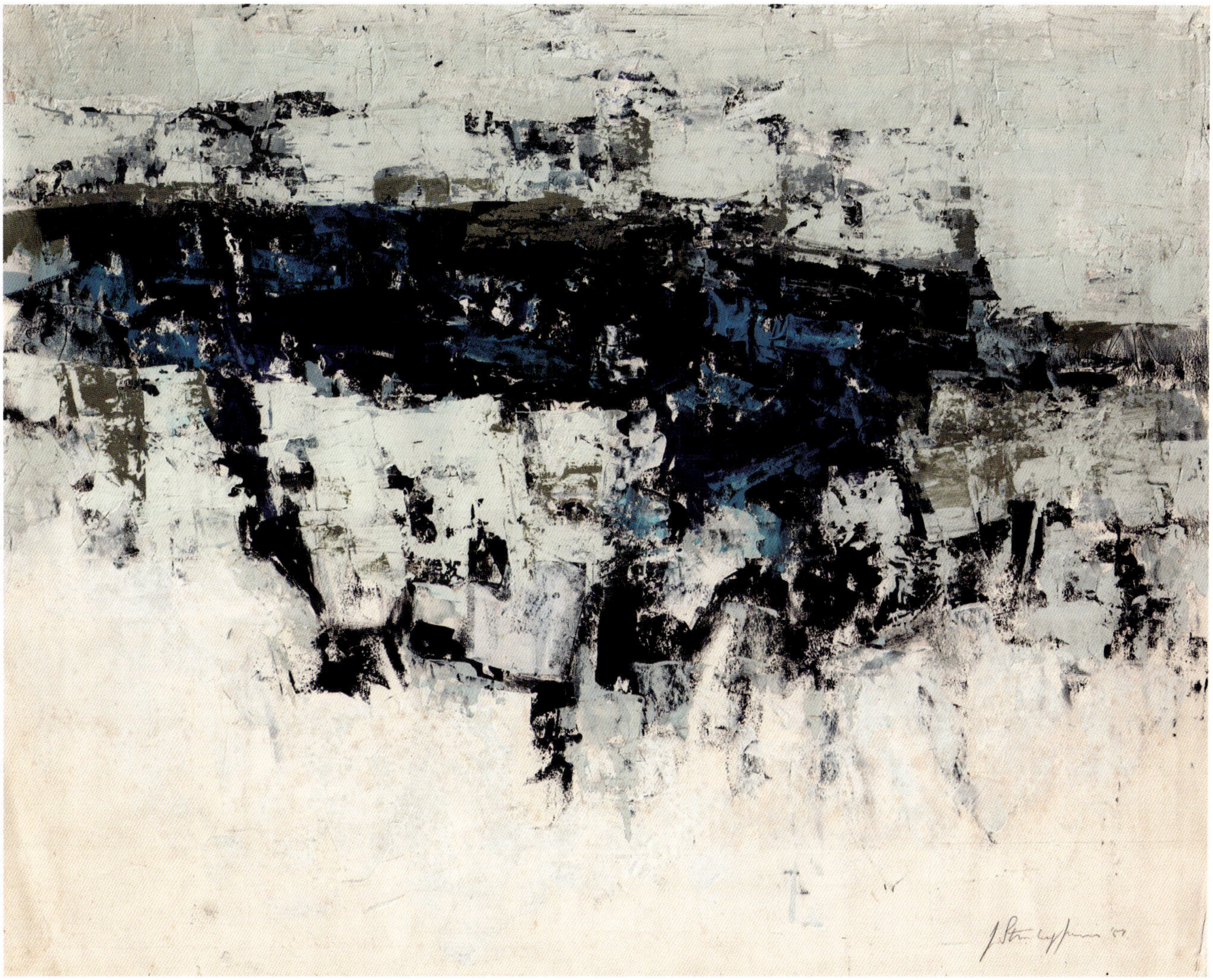

Stanley Jones, *Porthmeor* study, gouache, 1958.

with people living in isolated cottages, for example, could be difficult. So a strong element of trust was involved, so that a day-to-day activity could be planned for the studio without too much disruption. Ultimately, as there was no alternative, we had to rely on each artist's individual professionalism.

One absentee from the Saturday evening meeting was John Wells, who had expressed interest in Robert's idea but was notorious for not wishing to communicate with the outside world.

Alex Mackenzie, a close friend, was the only person seemingly able to elicit a response from John and suggested that we travel in his car to visit him at his studio in Newlyn. Robert was due to return to London in the afternoon, so we set off for Newlyn in a rainstorm with quite a gale blowing. Arriving at John's studio, Alex valiantly tried by banging on the door to rouse the artist, but without success. We trooped round the back of the building and hidden in dense undergrowth we located the back door and again banged heavily on it. This time, from within, we heard John's voice saying: 'Go away Alex, I'm working. **** off!' We stood huddled in the howling wind in the overgrown garden, and Alex apologised for the reception saying that this behaviour was 'not unusual'. Curiously, the following day in St Ives, the studio door opened and there stood John, somewhat sheepish but anxious to begin. Once he got started, he worked with great interest and dedication.

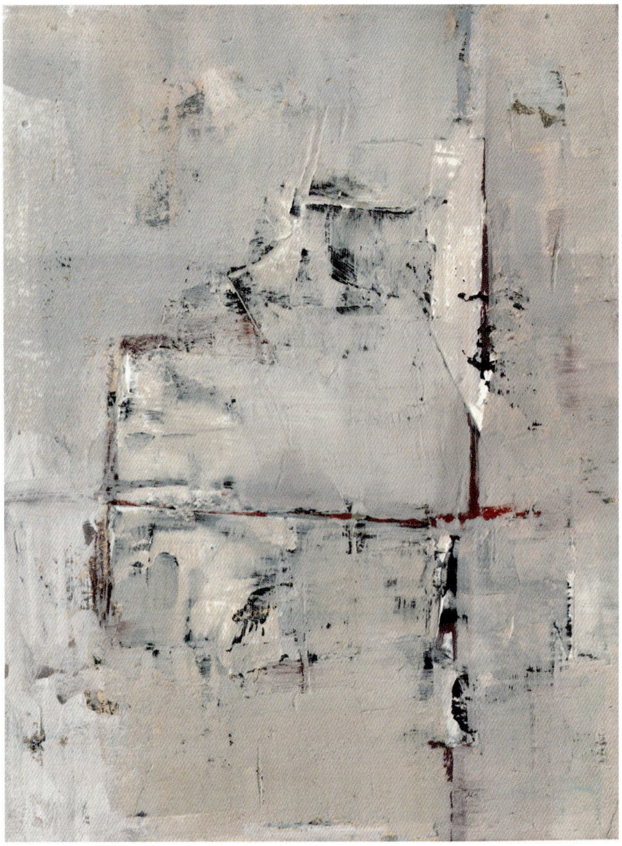

Left: Stanley Jones, *Coast Forms*, gouache, 1958.

Top right: Stanley Jones, *Porthmeor II*, gouache, 1958.

Bottom right: Stanley Jones, *Porthmeor III*, gouache, 1958.

Gradually, as the weeks went by and artists began to frequent the studio, much to Robert's relief all this activity began to bear fruit in the form of trials and proofs. Being new to St Ives I was unaware of the local liaisons and politics that were an inevitable part of such a community. However, I was often kept informed by artists' gossip as heard in the studio and in this way managed to avoid unnecessary embarrassment. It was important to know, for instance, that Peter Lanyon and Barbara Hepworth were not on speaking terms – for reasons unknown. So I had to make sure they did not meet in the studio. Somehow this was achieved, though in such a small place it wasn't easy and required careful diary arrangements. The studio generated its own atmosphere of purpose and the artists who came liked to spend time on their images both on a daily basis and for shorter durations as part of an excursion into St Ives for other reasons. There developed also a social aspect to the studio whereby other artists and dealers or collectors from London, for instance, would use it as a meeting place. This is how I first met Allan Davie and Peter Gimpel (the latter initially in Barbara Hepworth's studio in the spring of 1958) who were visitors to St Ives on occasion.

Generally, the appointments system seemed to work successfully, and on those occasions when it didn't we were able to proceed with work on someone else's images, so the time wasn't wasted. There were artists who were not part of Robert's venture, such as Brian Wall and Roger Leigh, both of whom were employed by Barbara Hepworth as assistants but spent much of their own spare time watching the processes involved in making a lithograph. Had the project remained in St Ives, they would certainly have made their own graphic images. Barbara herself was keen to make prints, never having tried such a process before. I spent some time with her in the studio explaining the basic technology of lithography, in which she could see many possibilities. Eventually she departed, full of enthusiasm, with several newly grained plates, only to reappear a few days later having removed the printing grain before starting her drawing! Luckily, she did not mind remaking the work, having a great determination to succeed, and after considerable effort she produced two very successful proofs for Robert Erskine.

The large Winstone press ordered by Robert was due to arrive in February and had become necessary to the progress of the scheme. We had managed to procure locally a suitable electric motor necessary for its operation; the challenge was finding an engineer capable of making it drive the machine. Local enquiries did not help and the mention of a printing machine seemed to make them shy away from such a problem. One day, as I was exploring a spot near the harbour called 'the Island', I discovered a large battered shed full of rusty tools of all shapes and sizes. The weathered signboard revealed that it belonged to Tressider and Co., boat engineers.

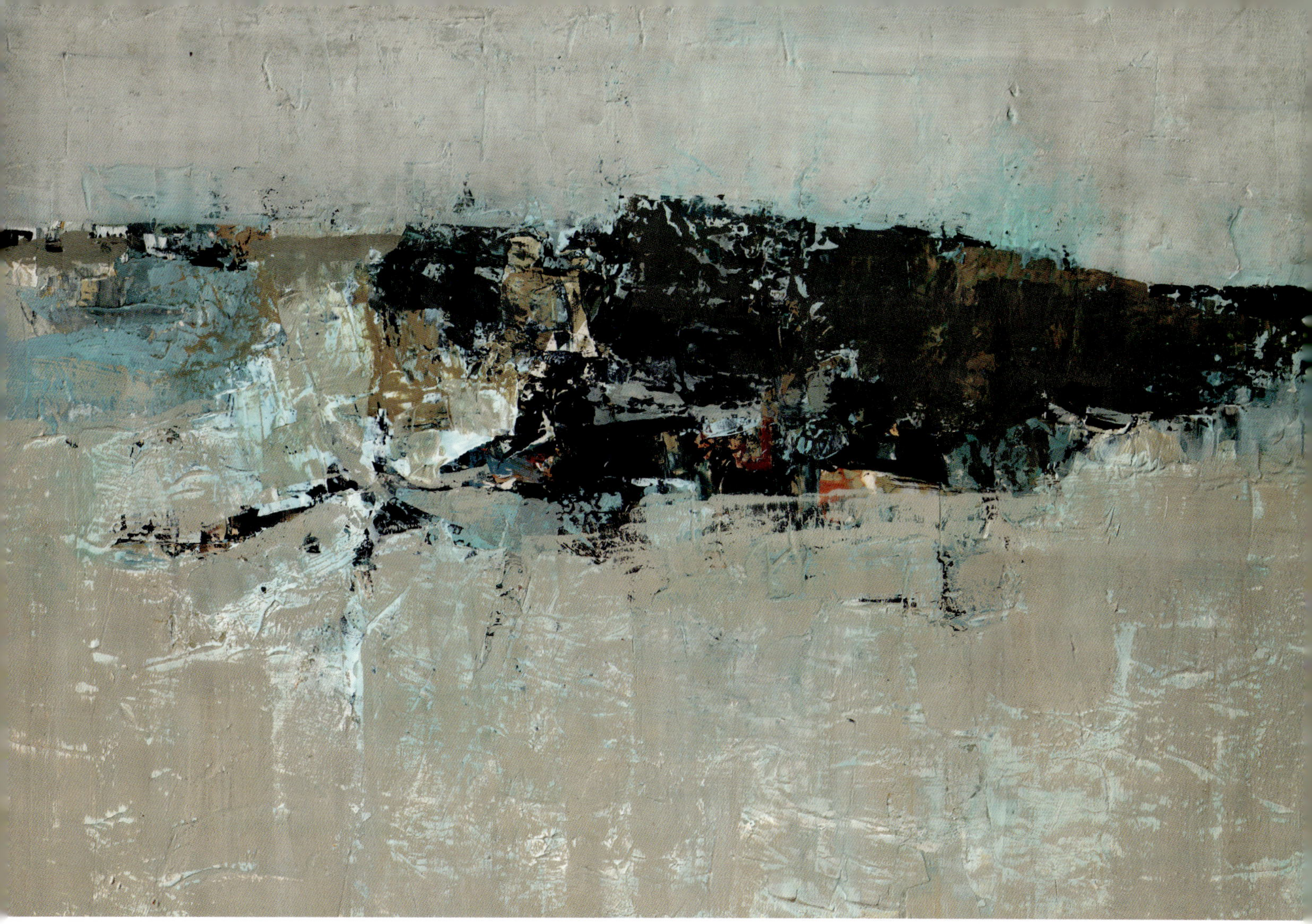

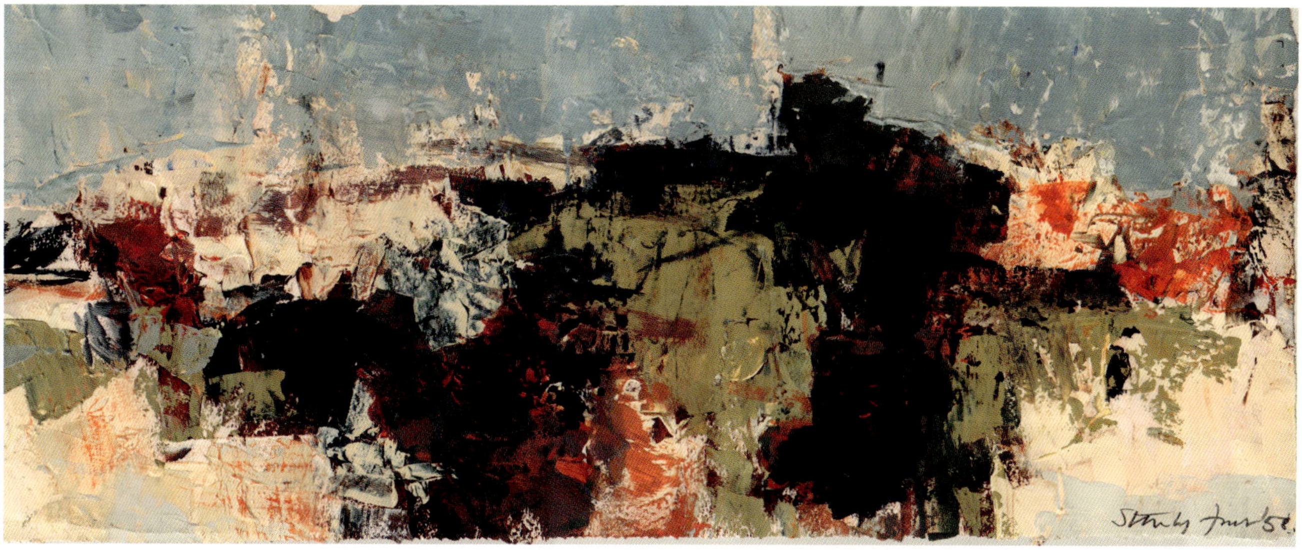

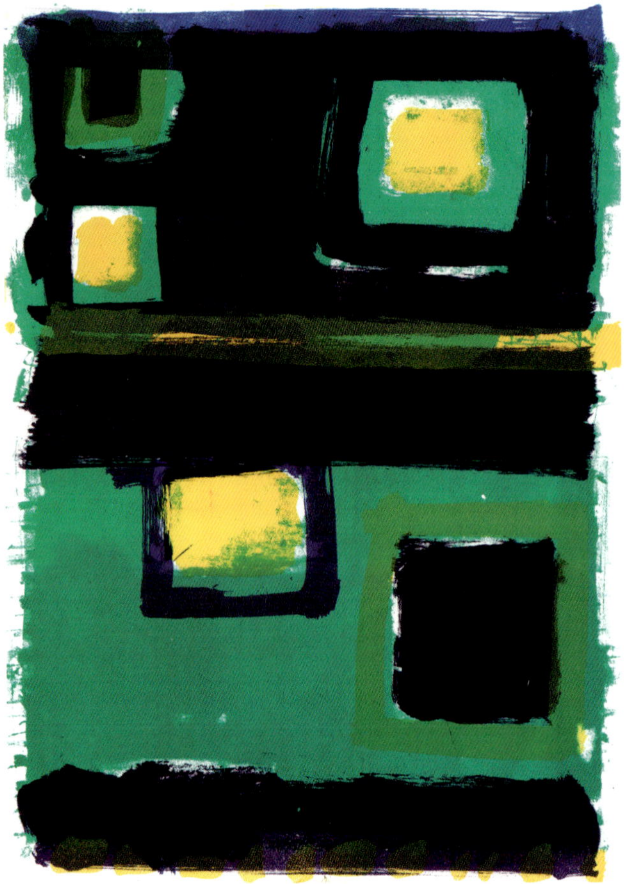

Patrick Heron, *Abstract Forms*, lithograph, 1959.

Trevor Bell, *Experimental proof*, lithograph, 1958.

Noting down their telephone number on a scrap of paper, I called them and, after several attempts, spoke to one of the Tressider brothers. I explained to him the nature of my problem. He was nonplussed but said they were willing to think about it.

The following week, a large lorry arrived from Thomas Knight carrying the proofing press. It completely blocked Fore Street for several hours as we struggled to manhandle the pieces up the slippery, cobbled alleyway. In this venture we were generously helped by the poet W.S. Graham and friends, fresh from a visit to the Sloop; their muscle and enthusiasm were much appreciated and fortunately no one was injured.

The Tressider brothers duly arrived one afternoon from Newlyn, and stood for some time in their grease-coated overalls, engrossed in their calculations with tape measures and lengths of string. After considerable intense conversation between them, involving much head-scratching and polishing of wire-framed glasses, it was decided that they would tackle the work forthwith. About a week later, they duly appeared in the studio with an array of gears and pulleys and set to work. In the meantime, I had to postpone Peter Lanyon's visit until the press was ready but he was so keen to start that he insisted on coming to help prepare the lithographic stones for his work. The engineers had calculated well and, to my relief, when the start button was pressed we were able to start edition printing. However, it became immediately apparent that the wooden floor made vibration a problem – one that could really only be solved by major alterations. As there were children and other residents who could be disturbed by the noise as well as the vibration, we had to be careful how and when the machine was operated, and thus it was agreed

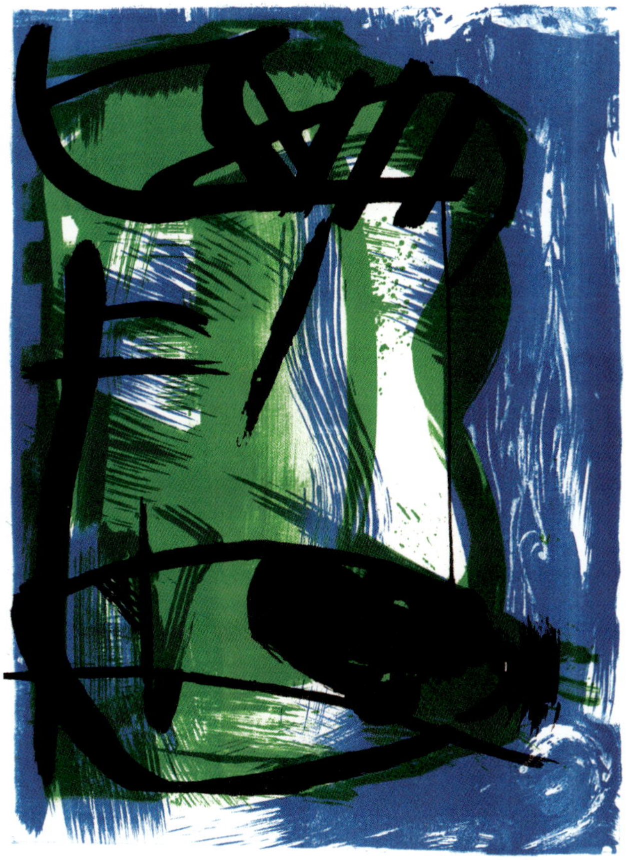

Peter Lanyon, *Coastal image*, lithograph, 1958.

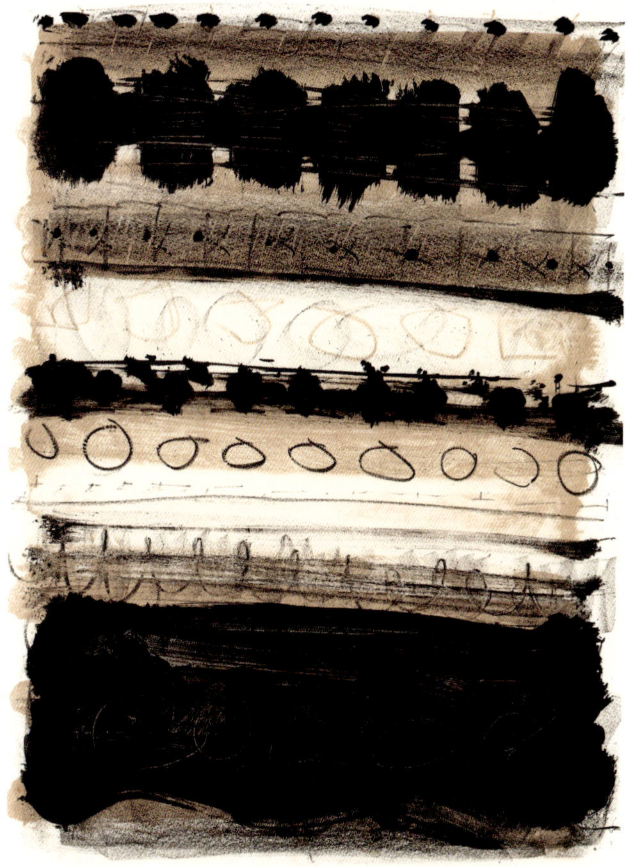

Patrick Heron, *Grey and brown stripes*, lithograph, 1958.

that we should only run it between the hours of 10am and 5pm.

From then on, the running of the workshop became more rational, with artists coming and going under the watchful eye of Robert in London, who was anxious now to get work on exhibition there as soon as possible. The work began to intensify and my time became fully occupied with the week-to-week running of this developing scheme, leaving little opportunity for social activities. Time spent on my own work was crucial so my outside contact tended to be with fellow artists. At weekends I would spend time exploring Porthmeor, making notes for prints that I would eventually complete in London. Sometimes I would meet Patrick Heron, who also had a Porthmeor studio, and we would spend hours in discussion about printing trends in Paris and New York. On occasion I would be invited to stay at the Eagle's Nest, at Zennor, where Patrick and his wife Delia had lived for many years.

The gardens of this house overlooked prehistoric sites and coastlands stretching to the Atlantic and from this vista Patrick derived inspirational colour through the ever-changing light and atmosphere; the translation of this response into lithographic terms characterised much of his work for Robert Erskine. It was to remain a constant theme, as reflected in one of the last images he made for the Curwen Gallery, in 1998, which he drew in the garden of his house as we discussed the possibilities of its colour interpretation.

The Arts Council had renovated some fishermen's lofts for artists' use. These overlooked Porthmeor Bay, and Trevor Bell, who was keen to experiment with printmaking and whom Robert had commissioned, decided to link his ideas with the work he was preparing for

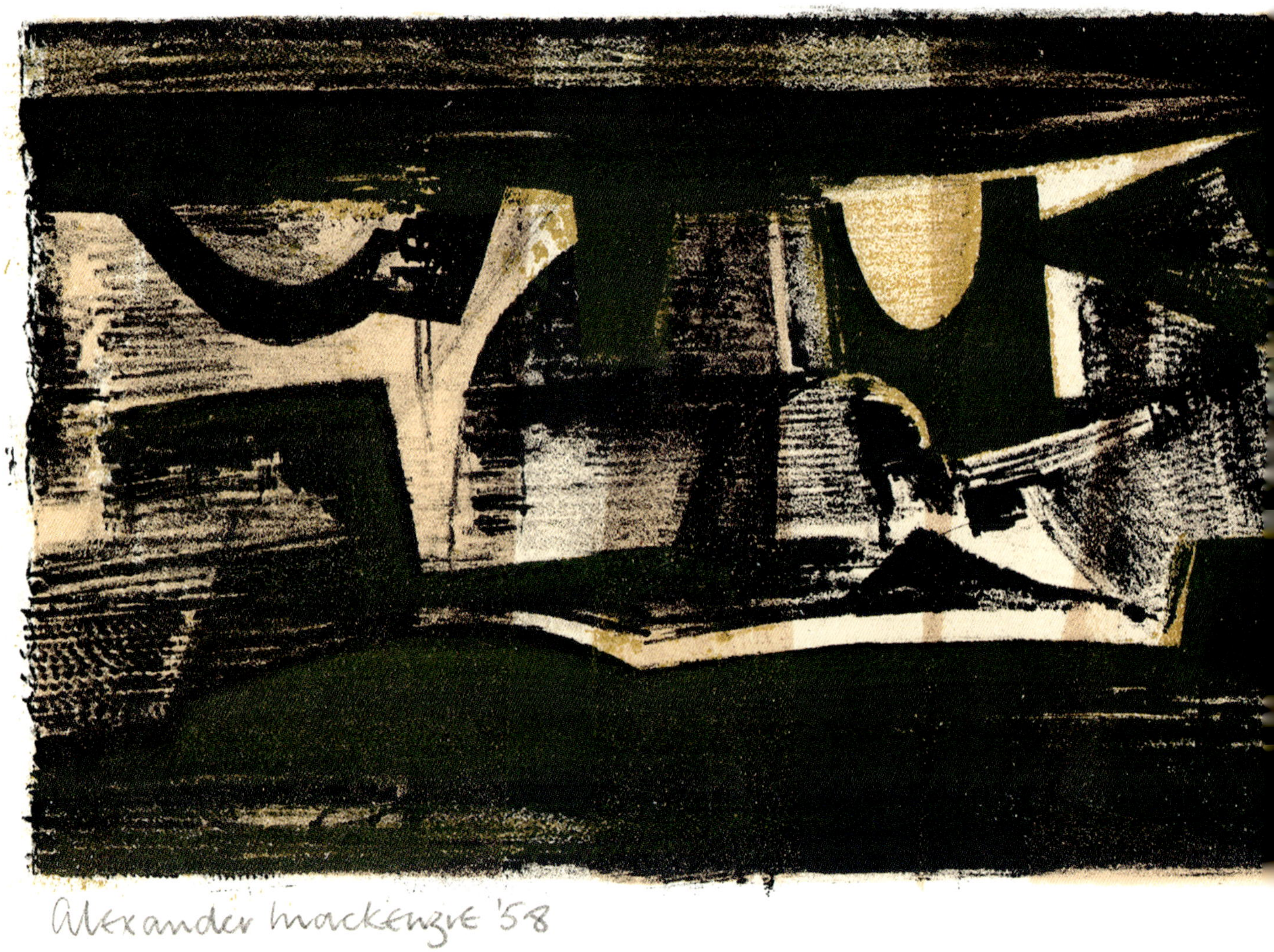

Alexander Mackenzie, *Landscape forms*, proof state, 1958.

a show at the Waddington Galleries in London. This involved often frantic journeys between his Porthmeor studio and the printing workshop to make formal changes to the prints as the ideas progressed.

Life around the studio was taking on a certain pattern centred on the coming and going of artists preparing their work for the St George's Gallery, ready for the summer. Work to be editioned was queuing up and had to be balanced against the time available for artists anxious to make a start. Meanwhile, I had a very encouraging letter from Timothy Simon indicating that progress was being made at the Curwen Press with the building of the studio and that he was already beginning to make the new venture known to his friends in the London art world. Robert Erskine came down for a weekend visit to see what progress had been made and was well satisfied with the results – particularly that the artists he wished to publish were quite happy to carry on their cooperation with his scheme. The studio had become a printmaking nucleus, with many of the artists trying out their ideas in this area for the first time. Karl Weschke would spend much time scraping away at the surface of a stone, fascinated by the curious textures he achieved by using liquid gum arabic and nitric acid. John Wells saw these proofs hanging up to dry and was prompted to try his own variations on this theme, with

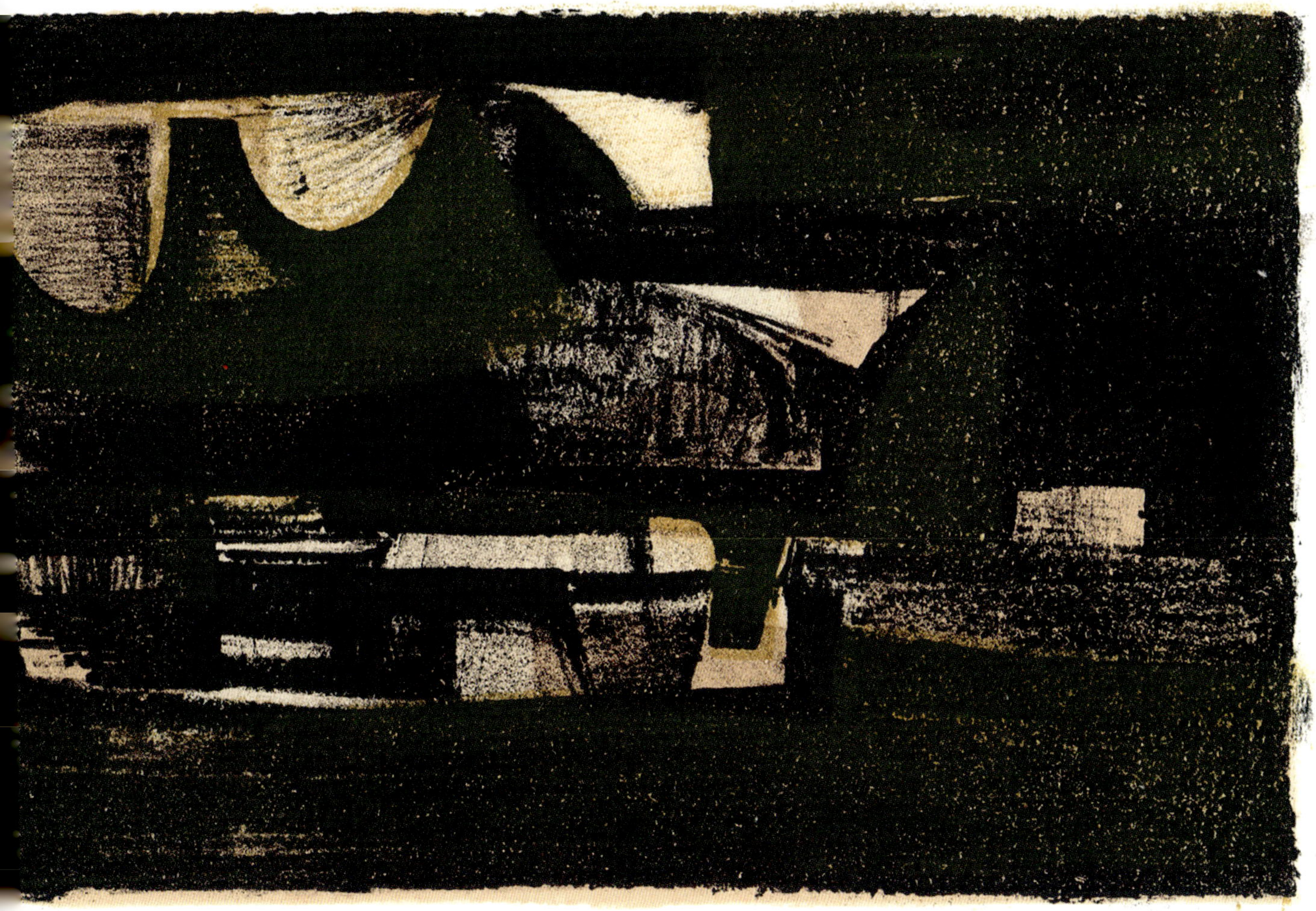

surprising success. Karl, for his part, was quite pleased to have had this temporary influence on John.

The studio's intention was to make sure that from the start the work should achieve a high level of concept and presentation. It meant considerable patience and determination on everyone's part, and often much reproofing, to attain this. For these artists, working mostly in isolation, this collaborative practice brought new elements to their current ideas, but the translation of these into a new medium often presented difficulties. The oncoming summer months were to be devoted to preparing work and to the sending of proofs to the St George's Gallery for approval and their subsequent editioning. Bruce and Monica helped as much as possible, whilst Jenny and her mother provided a domestic background which kept everyone sane when necessary. I still managed to pursue my own work and sent in two large gouache paintings for the Penwith summer exhibition which were accepted and subsequently bought by my first patron, Bruce Connor from New Zealand.

Amidst all this activity I received news from home that my father had died suddenly of a heart attack. Stunned, I made arrangements to go home immediately and attend his funeral. During the few days I spent with the family I took some walks in the locality and became very conscious of the ongoing decline and

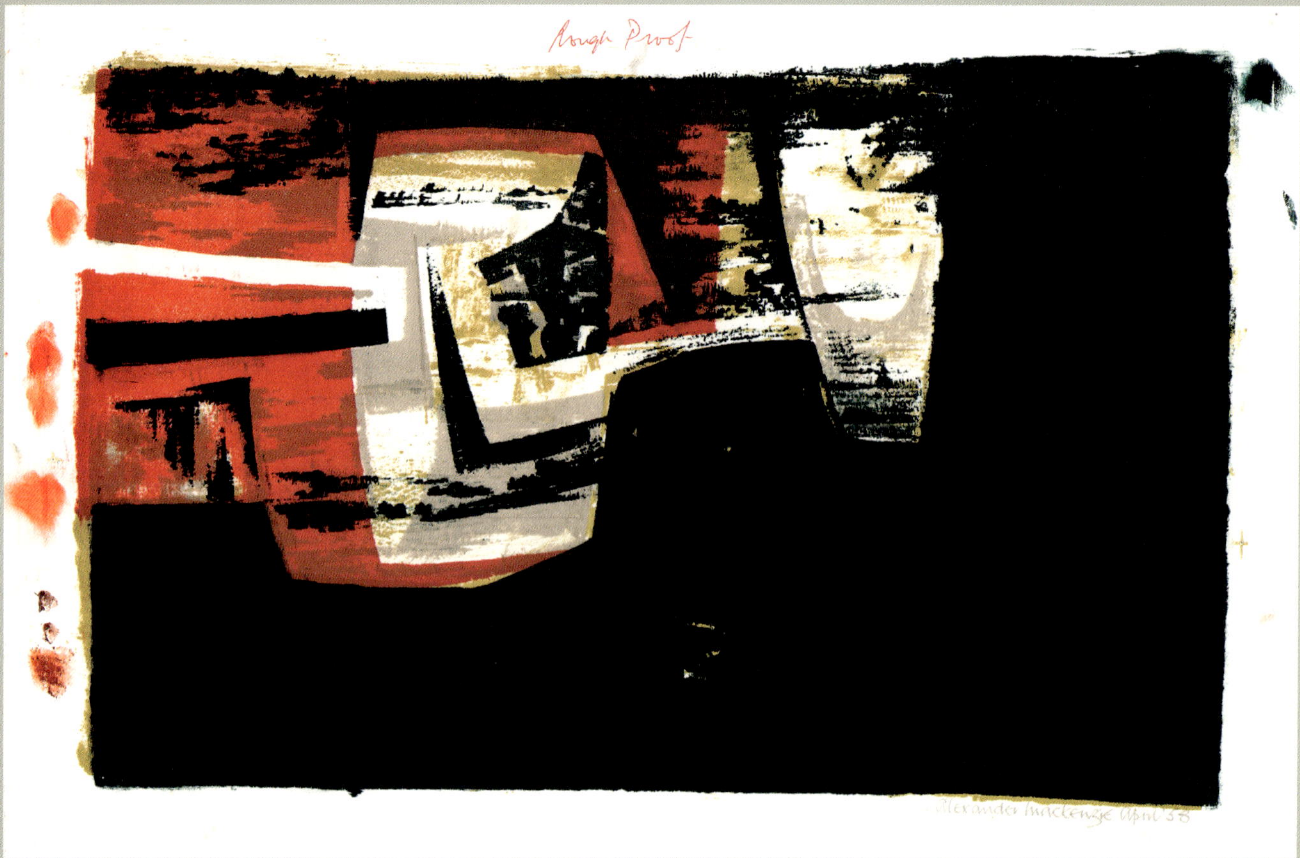

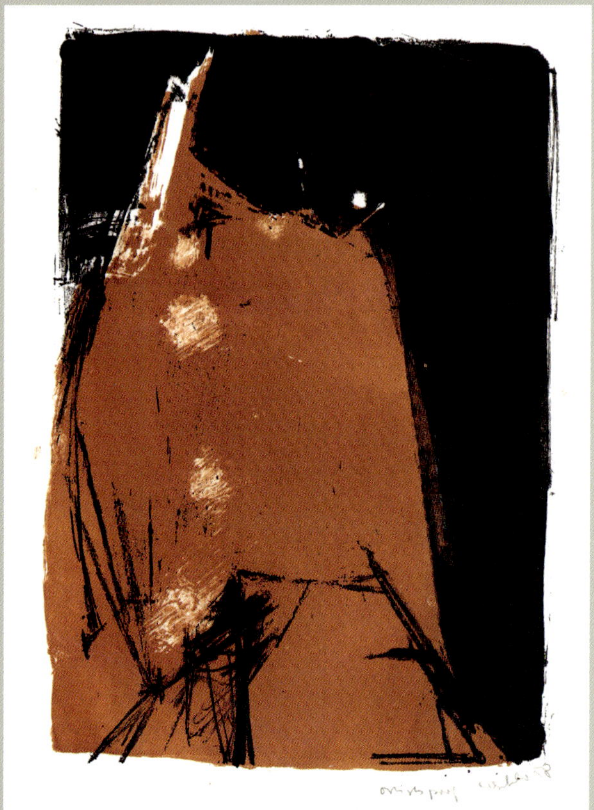

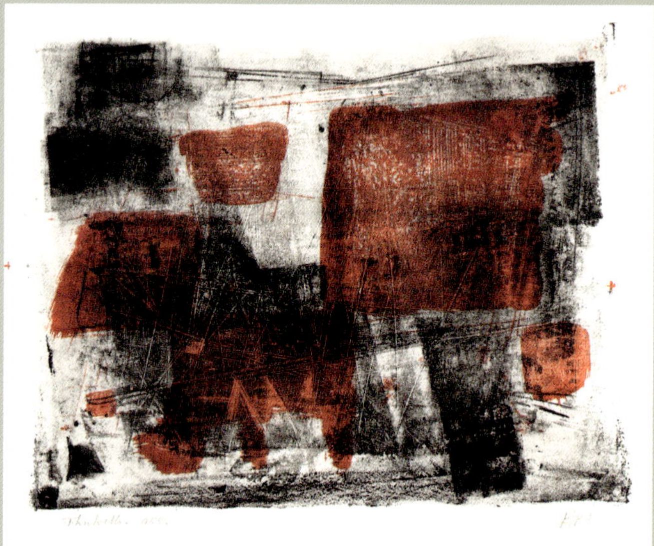

Top: Alexander MacKenzie, *Harbour*, lithographic proof, 1958.

Left: Karl Weschke, *Fissure*, lithograph, 1958. Experimental proof.

Above: John Wells, *Composition*, lithograph, 1958

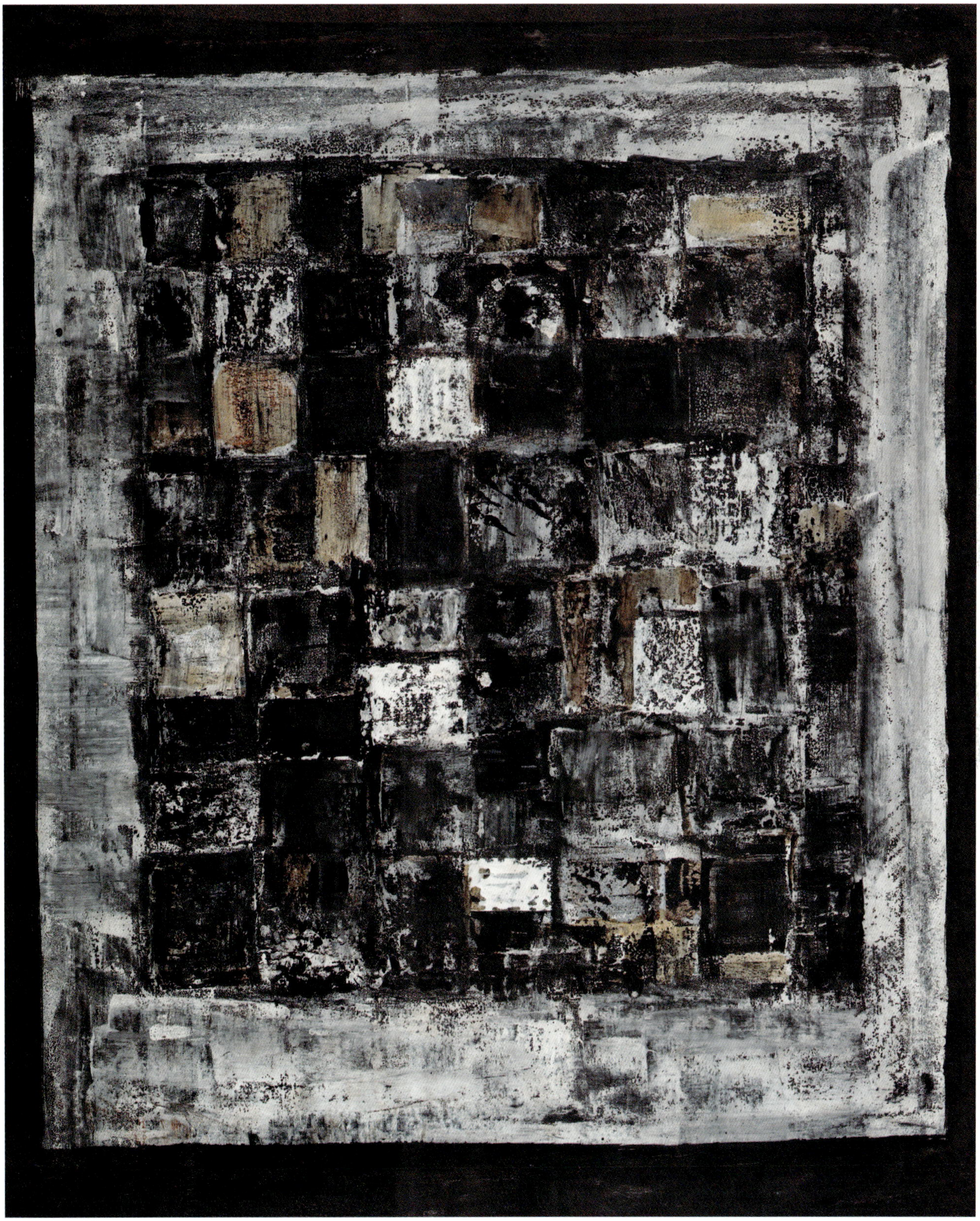

Stanley Jones, *Vista*, *St Ives*, gouache, 1959

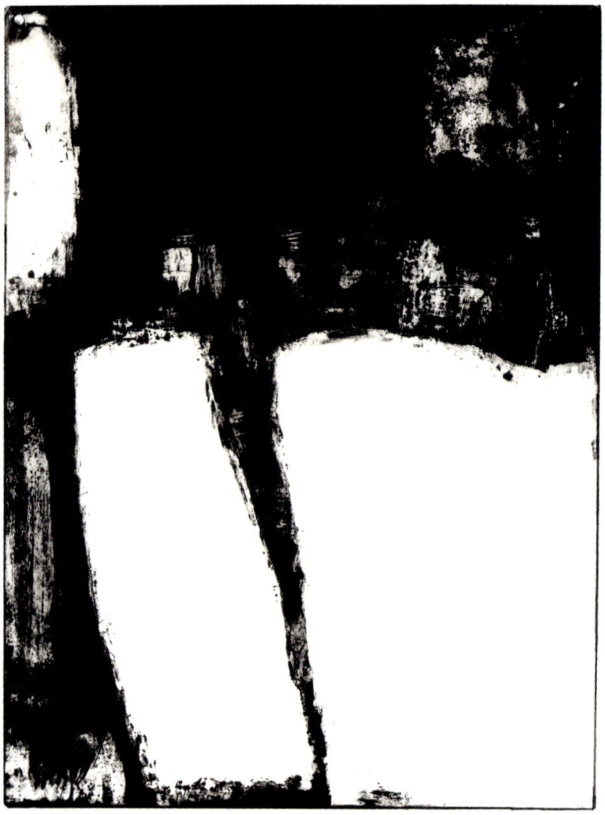

Sandra Blow, *Abstract landscape*, lithograph, 1958. Trial proof.

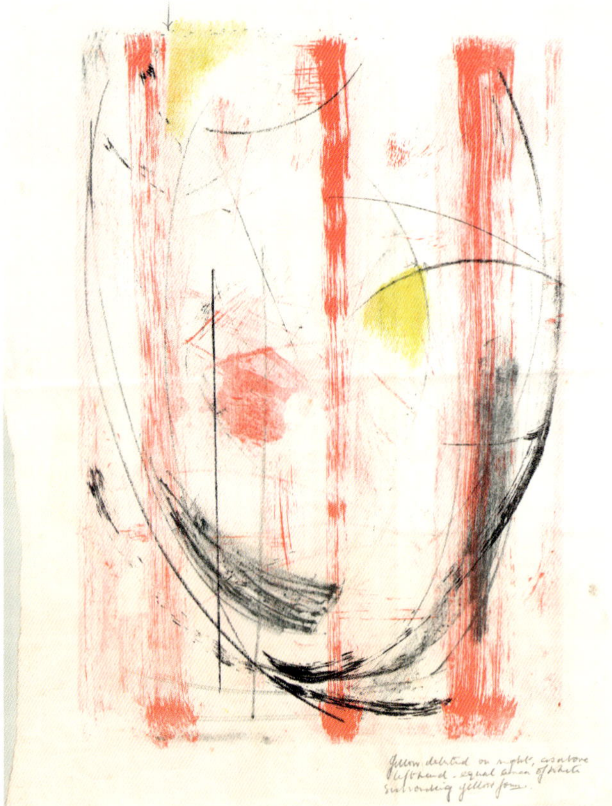

Barbara Hepworth, *Lithographic proof (I)*, 1958. Her first attempt.

closure of the pits and mills. My father's death seemed curiously parallel to this disappearing era; industrial Wigan could never be the same again. My mother would be supported for the rest of her life by family and friends, remaining as she did in such a close-knit community.

I returned to the very different world of St Ives, bemused by this event, which had left such a void in my life. But there were still activities in the studio to be managed and throughout the middle months of the year I continued to work with Robert Erskine, this necessary focus helping me somewhat through the initial stages of grief. More importantly, my thoughts began to look towards London and the demands of the new workshop in the East End. At this point I received an unexpected phone call from Ian Jenkin at the Slade, asking me if I would consider teaching one day a week when I moved to London; a letter would follow explaining everything. Timothy Simon felt it to be a good idea, helping to link the new studio with the world of fine art, imagining that such an obligation would only be for a short time. So began, in October, my weekly overnight journey by rail to London, then back to St Ives in the evening, to resume work the following Friday morning.

Alex Mackenzie, Sandra Blow and Willie Barns Graham were anxious to make a start before the studio was due to move, so we had to be careful about a final date for at least proofing work that could then be editioned in London. I received a letter from Timothy Simon saying that the company expected the studio to start 'operations' on 1st November. It left me little time, considering what would be involved in finishing current work, dismantling the equipment and rebuilding it in the new premises. There was also the work at the Slade, where printmaking was a rapidly growing activity; the classes were very well attended, with many enthusiasts naturally anxious to discover the potential of the medium. Despite the inevitability of the move, there

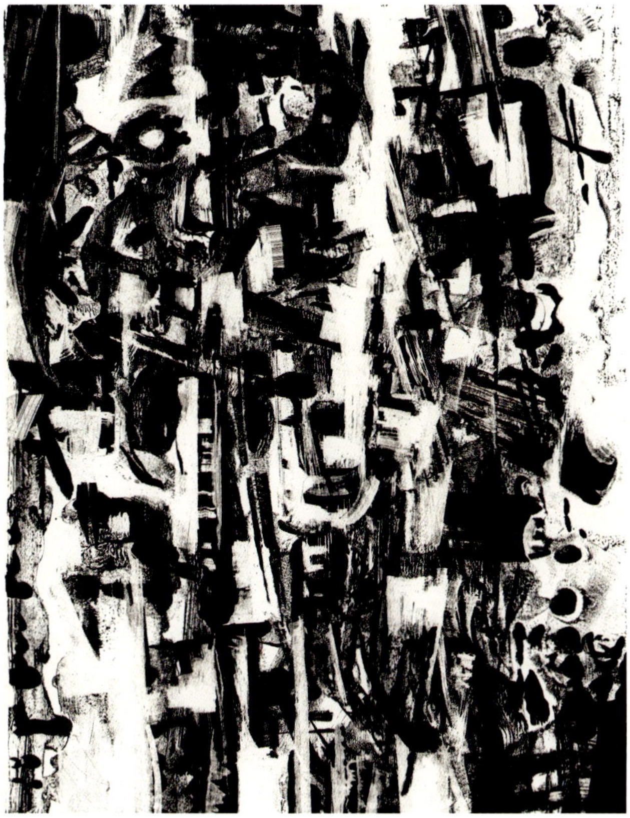

Bryan Wynter, Untitled Proof, lithograph 1958.

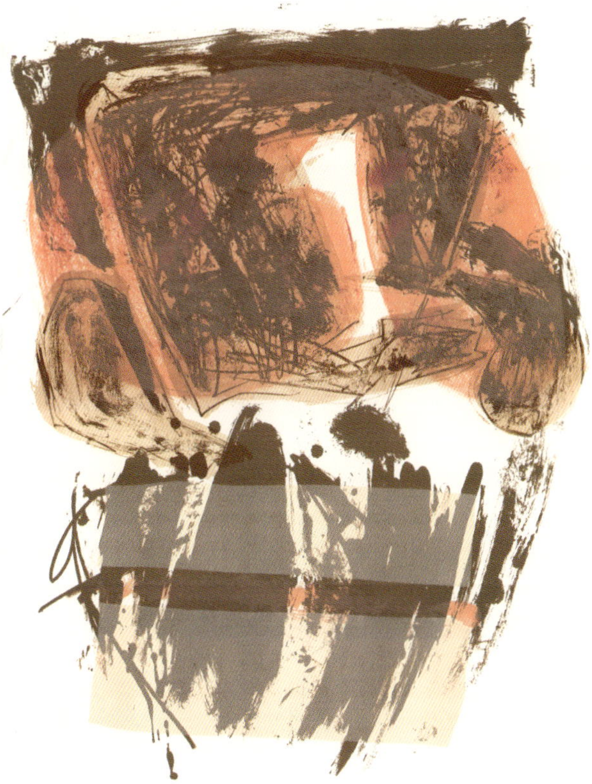

Trevor Bell, *Five Stages*, lithograph, 1961.
Publisher: Robert Erskine.

were those in St Ives who wanted the studio in Fore Street to continue. We had all understood the initially temporary nature of Erskine's scheme and its intended re-establishment in London but the opportunity was there; the ground laid for a future printmaking centre. However, for Bruce, his wife Jenny and Monica, my assistant, life was to progress in very different ways. The domestic arrangements which centred around Bruce and Jenny Taylor precluded the studio's further development – Bruce had his own teaching obligations and life as a sculptor; Monica, my assistant, had started married life with the artist Bryan Wynter in St Buryan, and no on else was available to take over the running of the activity. Thus it ceased when I left for London.

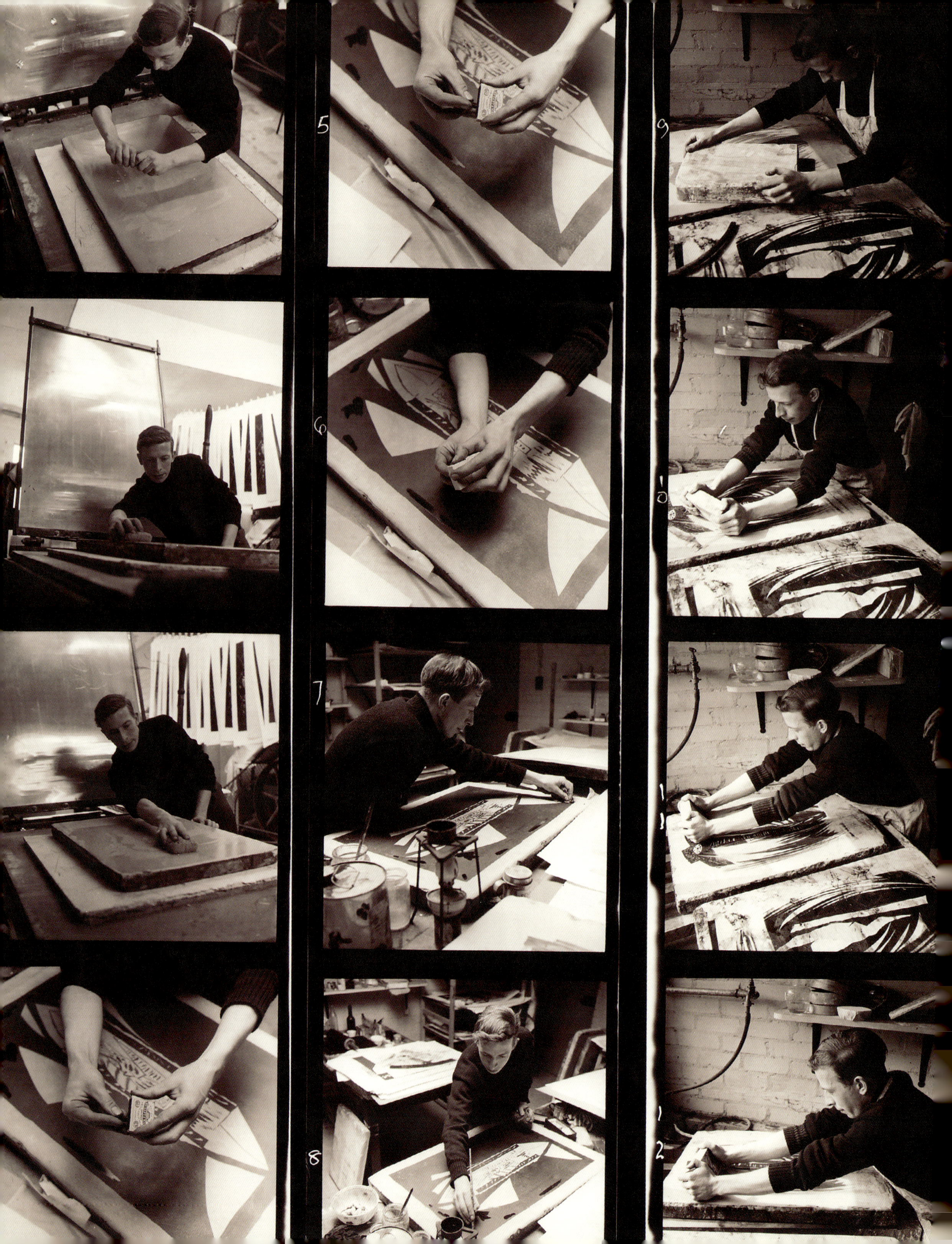
5
6
7
8
9
10
11
12

"We aimed to involvve the artist as much as possible, at every necessary stage, so that the work would reflect its creator's originality."

THE CURWEN PRESS

Beginnings

Reading between the lines with the value of hindsight, the Curwen Press board must have been sceptical about the gamble their two young directors were embarking upon. The commercially ageing printing techniques which had sustained the press between the two wars were becoming difficult to justify now in comparison with the rapidly developing photolithographic processes. In the light of this the studio was an idea that was given a limited amount of time and money. There was no obvious market in the United Kingdom for the limited-edition print and the feeling of other directors was that such a market would take some time to develop. The Redfern Gallery did occasionally show original prints but apart from the pioneering St George's Gallery there were no other practitioners. The onus for the success of the project would fall on Timothy in particular, as sales director, with Robert Simon as the link with the Curwen Press and myself. What none of us could foresee was the development of the print publishing market that began in the early 1960s.

There was also the problem of trade union response to this venture. Because of the trade unions' approach to union regulation, it was felt by the Press to be a wise precaution to keep this 'local' project physically separate from the main factory, thus avoiding possible objections from the factory floor. Resentment was expressed by some individuals about company money being used for such an experimental project. Timothy managed to persuade those concerned that it would actually benefit the printers by providing extra work for them where possible and rekindling, in a new form, the association with artists which the firm was losing. I was eventually granted a dispensation by George Ward, the NGA (National Graphical Association) representative, which permitted me to handle materials on the firm's premises and to advise the printers, who may not have been familiar with the artists and the processes used.

My first view of the new studio occurred at the end of October, with Robert Simon, Timothy and I sitting on storage drums, the space littered with builder's material and smelling of new paint. It was a strange conversion, still retaining the huge heavy stable doors, which led into a darkened cobbled entrance hall. A flight of steps led to an upper room which would be used for drawing, storage and office work. Back at ground level, in complete contrast to the Piranesian gloom of the entrance space, a door led into a press room, where most of the printmaking would take place; this was light and airy – a good working space. Many of the basic necessities were still missing but I was assured by Robert that these were on their way. As we sat and discussed aspects of the workshop it was decided, because we were to be a subsidiary, to retain the name of Curwen, and for the

Stanley Jones inside the new Curwen Studio: preparation work on lithographic stone for Ceri Richards, 1959.

present to add the word 'Studio' until another name was found. And so it remained.

A brief history of Curwen

What had caused this particular company to attach itself to the development of English art and design since the beginning of the 20th century? Since the mid-19th century, when Revd John Curwen had converted his chapel into a printing establishment for the promotion of educational material for impoverished people, it had always occupied a corner site at the junction of North Street and St Mary's Road (in an area of London known as Plaistow). The Revd Curwen was inspired by Sarah Glover and her tonic sol-fa system of musical notation, a technique using moving syllables for teaching sight singing. Curwen made amendments and additions of his own, including the introduction of hand signals to indicate tone and in 1853 he established the Tonic Sol-fa Association. He wanted to spread the use of this system and to this end he started publishing tonic sol-fa sheet music, songbooks and periodicals. This guided the development of the printing business, which grew in size and importance until, by 1896, it formed a sizeable part of the site it would later occupy in North Street. It was Harold Curwen, grandson of John, who developed other ideas for the business. He asserted the importance of employing artists for designing graphic work, to give it spirit and imaginative treatment and introduced adventurous design and fine commercial printing into the firm. By doing so he paved the way for the company's future development and reputation. In the early 1920s, the arrival of Oliver Simon, and later his brother Herbert, led to a flourishing of work with those designers, painters and sculptors who contributed so much to the company's reputation in the world at large.

Settling in

The Second World War had done considerable damage to Plaistow; not only had the printing works itself been bombed but whole streets in the area had been decimated, leaving gaps and bomb-damaged buildings as relics of the raids. By 1958 the area had a distinctly moribund atmosphere, as if quietly anticipating some long-awaited regeneration. When the fogs descended in the autumn – 'pea soupers' were not uncommon – the silence would last for days on end and Plaistow became a lost land. Most artists accepted the drab surroundings outside without question – for it made focusing on the work in hand considerably easier.

That afternoon I was taken on a tour of the works to introduce myself to some of the staff and to become familiar with the geography of these historic premises, some parts of which were unaltered since the time of the Revd Curwen in the 1860s. It reeked of hot metal casting machines, bindery glues, ink, solvents and that overall atmosphere generated by machines that have been running without interruption for generations. A myriad of rooms large and small, passages stacked with huge piles of paper – it all seemed awesome and full of purpose. I remember meeting Alf Defround, the works engineer, whose knowledge and co-operation I would come to rely on for so many years. Then Bert Wootton and George Grout, experienced lithographic printers anxious to know about the studio, and foreman printer Ernie Locke. Mr Locke had for many years been the arbiter of what artists were allowed to print and how such work should be printed. The fact that a 'rival' department had been set up that would not be under his control was not a satisfactory situation for him. At first he thought that the studio was just one of Timothy's 'whims' and he viewed it, and myself, with considerable suspicion.

That afternoon I was also given a set of keys to the studio – I could come and go as I pleased and await the contents of the lorry due from St Ives in a day or so. For various reasons I was still in close communication with people in St Ives and these were contacts I kept over the years that followed. For the next few weeks I got to know many of the Curwen Press staff as, out of curiosity, they came to visit me from their location further down the road.

Plaistow was for me a total change from the picturesque background of St Ives and even more remote from the ambience of Montparnasse. Artists had been used to travelling there since the early 20th century when Harold Curwen had decided to employ numerous designers and typographers of the calibre of Eric Gill and Claude Lovat Fraser. This activity increased in the 1920s and '30s when Oliver Simon and his brother Herbert began their ambitious publishing and printing business with artists, which helped to give the Curwen Press its historic reputation. When Oliver died in 1954, Herbert was left to guide the company's policy and production – not easy in a changing world of print technology where

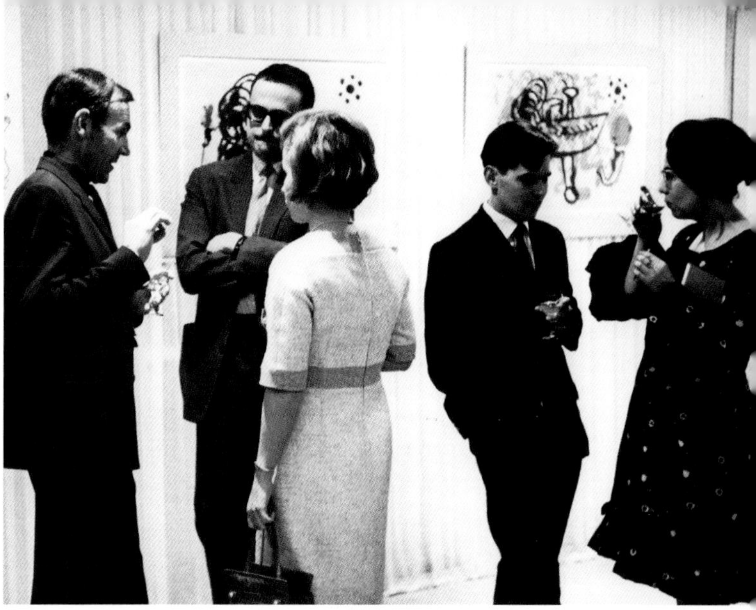

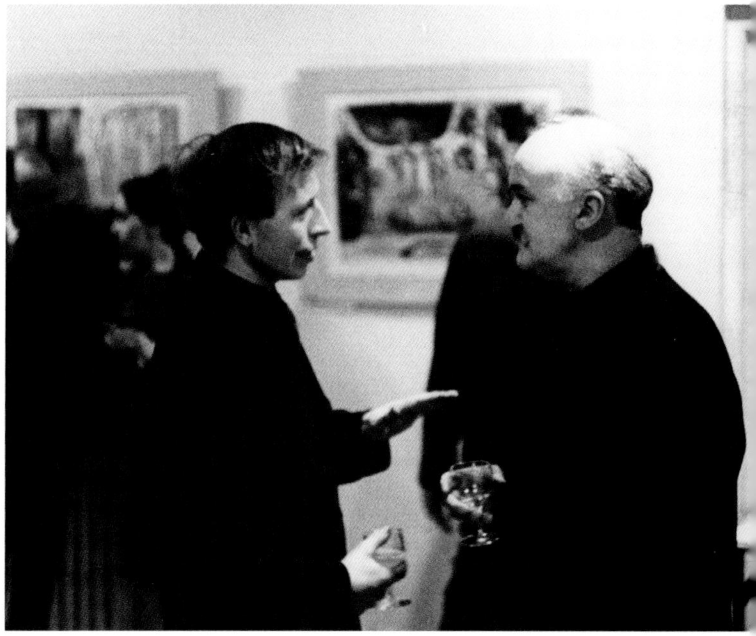

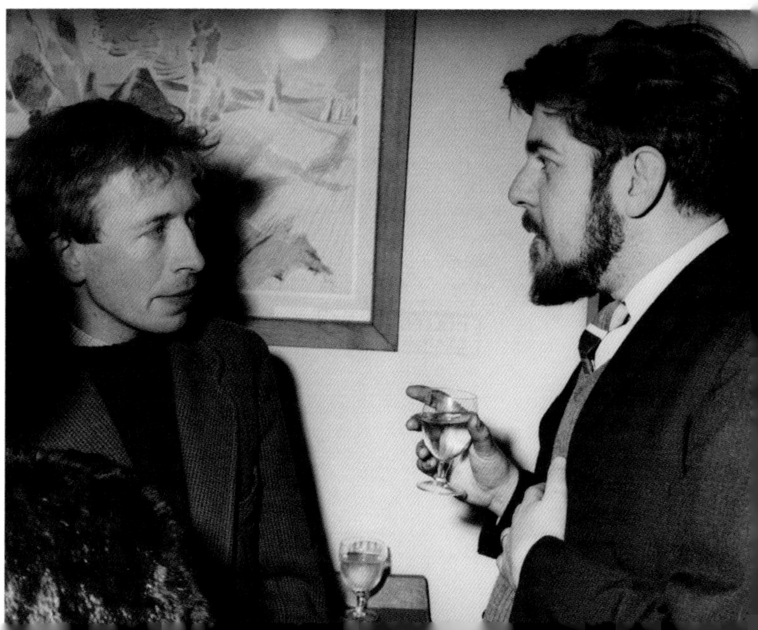

From top to bottom:
Curwen Gallery opening, 1965. Robert Simon (far left), Rosemary Simmons (far right).

Stanley Jones and Robert Adams at Curwen Studio exhibition, 13 Bloomsbury Square, WC1, 1965.

Stanley Jones (left) and Robert Erskine. At the first exhibition of Curwen Studio Prints in the Press's London Office: 13 Bloomsbury Square, WC1, in 1962.

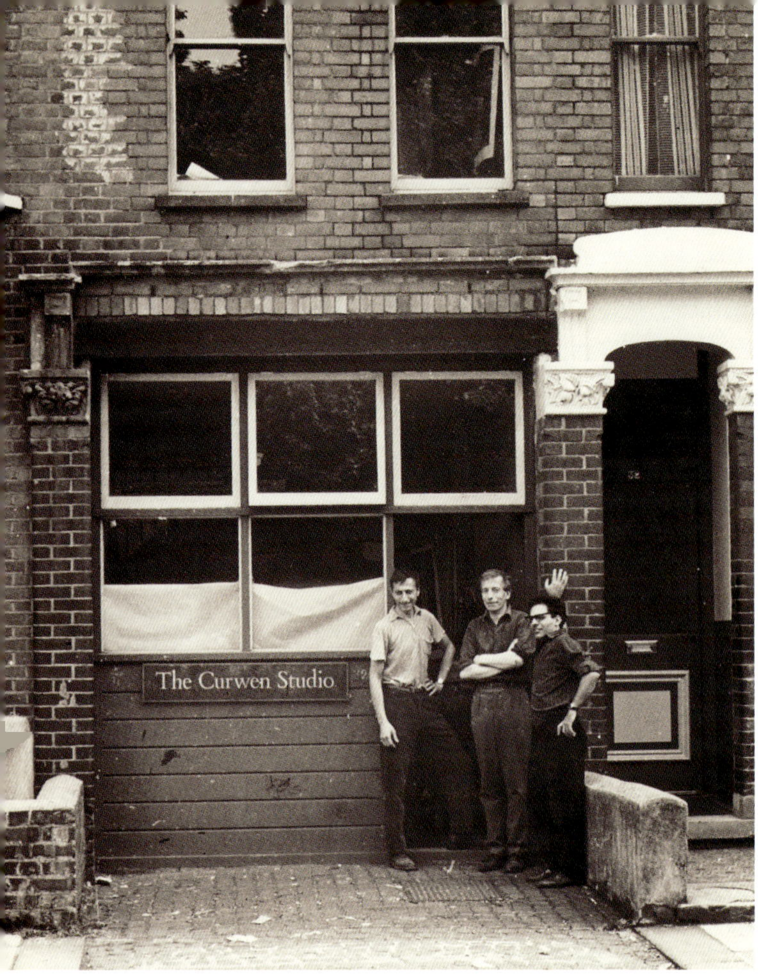

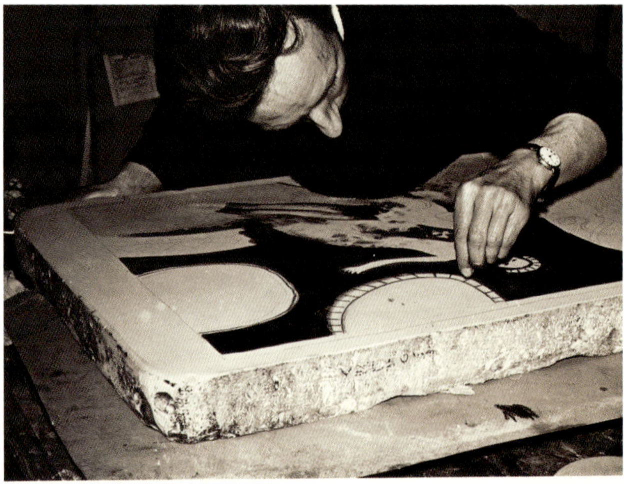

Clockwise from left:

Peter Baer, Stanley Jones and David Zaig outside Curwen Studio main door, Plaistow E13, 1960.

Artist Kenneth Rowell drawing on lithographic stone, 1959.

Henry Moore and printmaker Peter Baer discussing proofs, Curwen Studio, Plaistow E13, 1962.

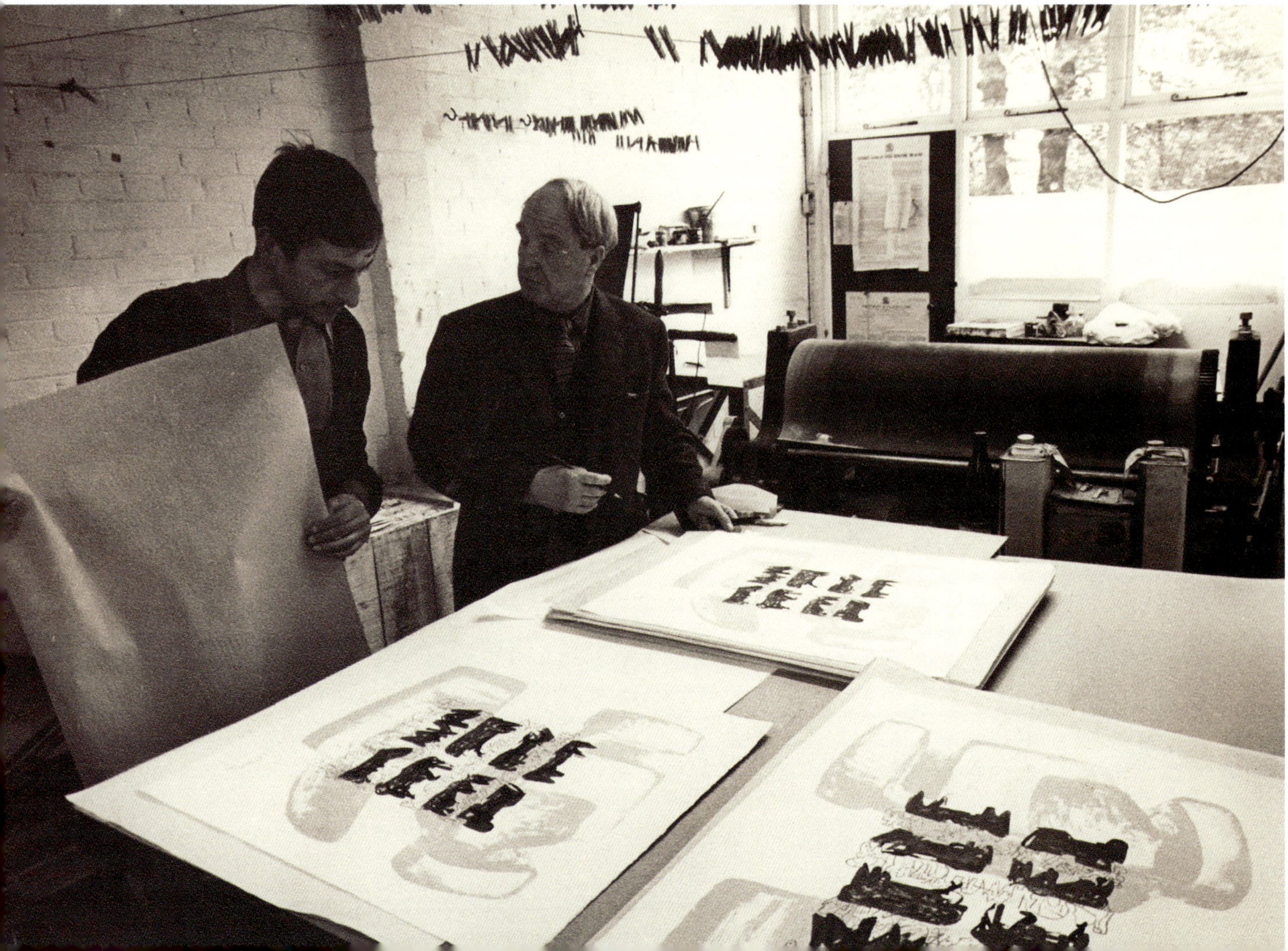

the various unions were determinedly establishing their own members' fixed ways of working. For almost a hundred years, the company had developed on the same site in the vicinity of the long-established East End industries of sugar refining (Tate & Lyle) and flour milling at Canning Town, and the general dock trade of import and export, which had somehow survived the intense bombing of the Second World War. The atmosphere around the works was often tainted by the perfume of disinfectant from the Jeyes Fluid Company opposite, to which the local people seemed totally oblivious.

Timothy Simon had established an office at 13 Bloomsbury Square as a means of communicating with customers – artists, authors and publishers in particular; it was much used in the early days of the studio for meetings of all kinds and the first exhibition of Curwen Studio prints was to be held there in 1962. Robert Simon was in a general managerial position, involved largely with the practicalities of machinery supervision and the day-to-day organisation of the works and its requirements. It was Robert who I had most contact with in those early days, largely because of the basic practicalities of setting up the machinery as well as shelves for the storage of paper, inks and lithographic plates.

It took some time to plan this initial stage, but by the first week in November we were ready to start. The old direct-stone press from the music-transfer room was handed to me for future use; it remains with us to this day, totally usable despite its charred wooden base, the result of an incendiary raid during the Second World War.

Meanwhile, because of the demands of the studio, it became necessary to look for an assistant who would be trained in lithographic printmaking and become a permanent staff member. Such people are not easy to find and much time was sacrificed in finding the most suitable person. Such a role on the one hand demands craft skills and the ability to concentrate for long periods along with a capacity for collaboration not only with various kinds of artists but with other studio printers, too. The time needed to learn the skills is different in every case, with much depending on the individual's determination to pursue their intentions. A major factor is the physical ability to handle presses and lithographic stones as a constant requirement of the daily routines of edition printing.

News of the studio's existence elicited many enquiries from potential assistants, with David Gillison, who had studied lithography at the Slade School, the first to be given the opportunity. However, the search did not stop there. The growing workload in the studio meant I was also able to look for a temporary staff member who might become permanent at a later date. The Curwen Press had an ex-Harley Brothers proofer from Edinburgh, Jock McFarlane, who was quite experienced in this kind of work but was now in ill health and nearing retirement. One morning I received a phone call from my friend Birgit Skiöld, who keenly recommended Peter Baer as a possible colleague. Peter duly outlined both his art-school experience and his keenness to learn lithographic printmaking. Despite the personal difficulties he had to endure from experiences in the war, Peter proved to be a skilled craftsman, sympathetic to the requirements of fellow artists and dedicated to achieving the highest standards of work. He would spend 14 years with us before leaving for a career in teaching.

During these early months I was able, with Timothy, to gauge the background against which we would be operating. Apart from the major art schools such as the Royal College, the Slade School and Chelsea College, there were no other centres practising artists' printmaking. There was, however, Birgit Skiöld, the enterprising Swedish artist who rented a basement in Charlotte

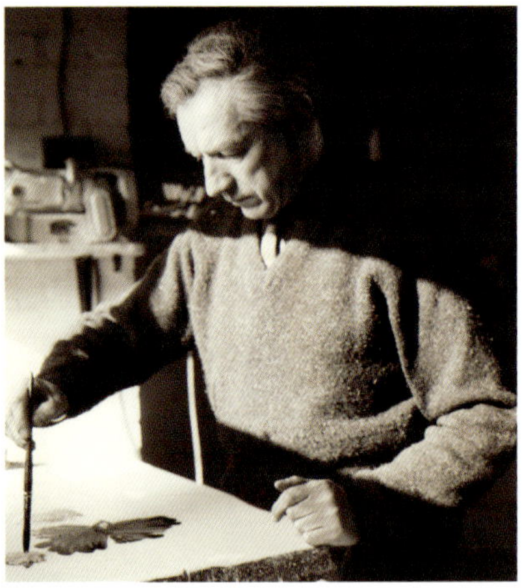

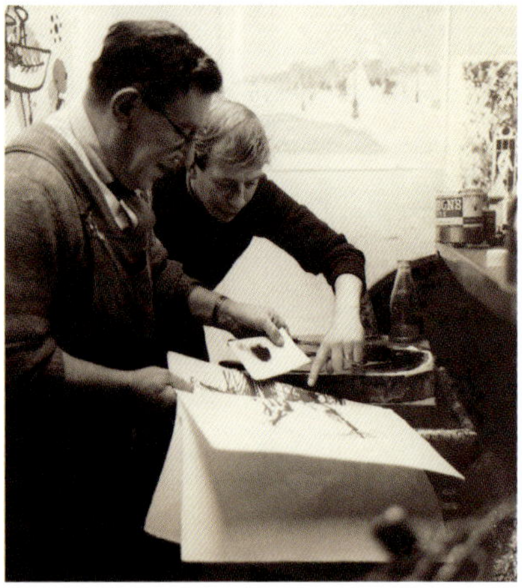

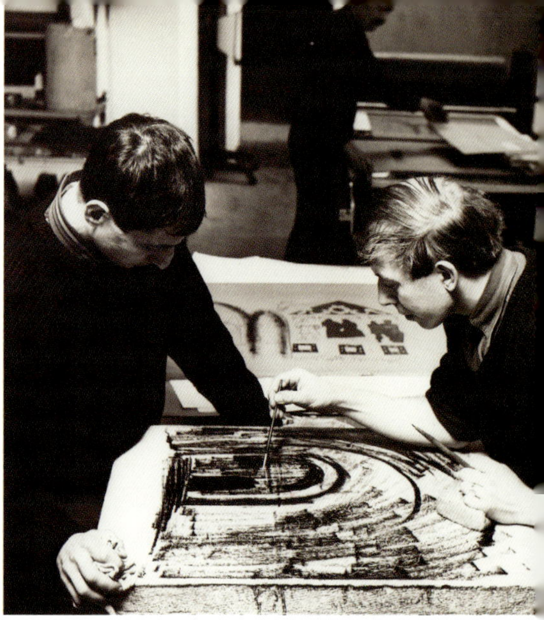

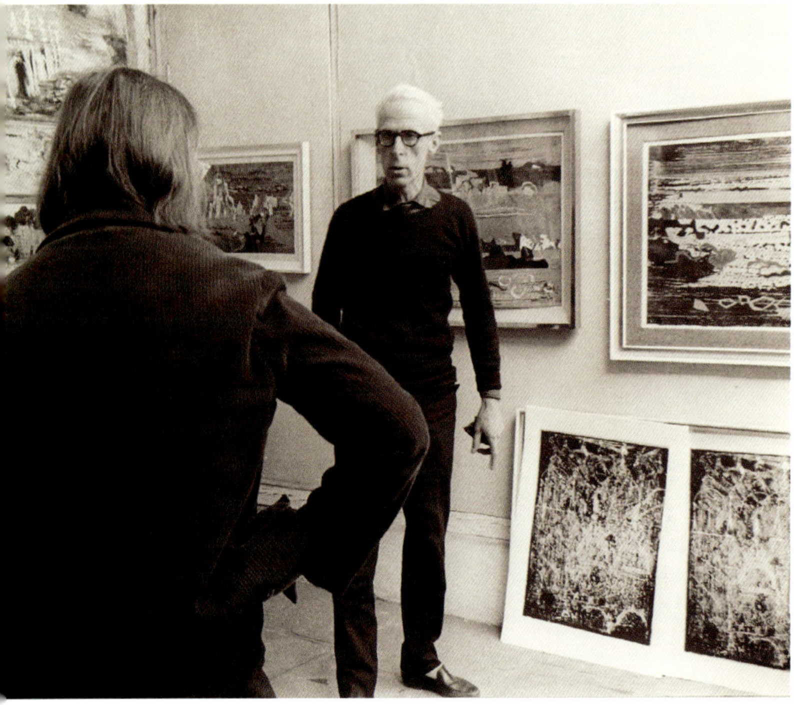

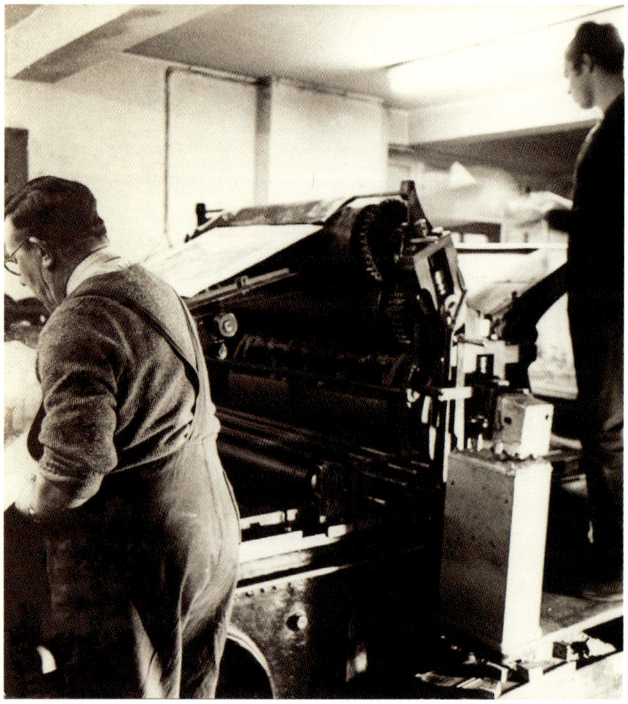

Left to right top row: Ceri Richards drawing on stone image for 'Trafalgar Square' 1962; George Grout (printer) and Stanley Jones altering colour for proof, Curwen Studio, 1967; Peter Baer (left) an Stanley Jones preparing lithographic image for John Piper, 1965, Curwen Studio.

Left to right middle row: John Piper & Myfannwy Piper (left)examining 'St Marco' proof,1961–62; George Grout (printer – left) and David Beadle (right) hand feeding paper through machine, Curwen Studio, 1970.

Right: Stanley Jones, Curwen Studio, 1968.

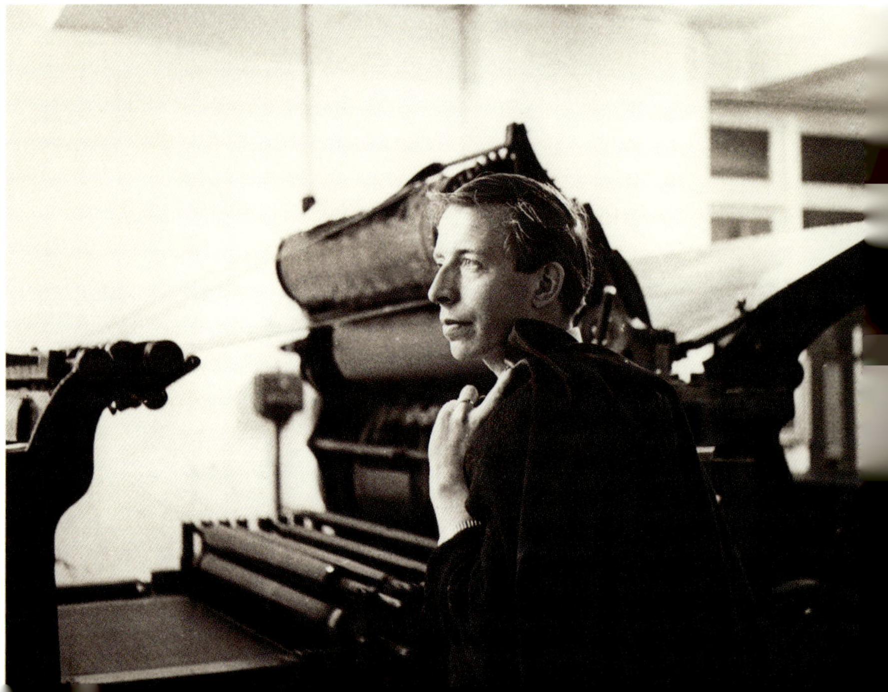

Street from the artist Adrian Heath. Prior to her arrival in London there was no printmaking studio along the lines of a Continental atelier anywhere in London. Only on art courses were students able to gain a practical introduction. It was Birgit who brought to the teaching of printmaking attitudes and standards suitable for post-art school development. She was to remain a constant friend and enthusiast for many years, acting as a catalyst for the emerging print world in London, sitting on committees and generally making her influence and ideas felt with determination and candour. Her studio was a pioneering venture which managed to survive all the complications and politics of the early years to become a bastion of the London printmaking scene. It is not surprising that so many artists took their first steps in etching or lithography in such an experimental atmosphere, where help would come from fellow artists as well as from Birgit herself. Somehow, amidst the obligations of this venture, she managed to pursue her own work throughout, whilst never failing to encourage artists and their publications until illness overcame her life. For us she always remained an ally, particularly in those early years.

At this time, the practice of using the studio for the drawing stage of work that would eventually be produced on the Curwen Press's machines was encouraged. This proved quite successful as it made appropriate use of the facilities of both departments. It also required close co-operation between studio and press, with the result that as time progressed the studio was accepted as a familiar presence in St Mary's Rd. Posters for the London Group (an exhibiting society for printers and sculptors resident in London) drawn by William Scott, and book illustrations produced on stone by Michael Ayrton for an edition of *The Golden Ass* by Apuleius (which were subsequently transferred to plate) are examples of this collaboration. Graham Sutherland designed the book jacket for his biography, published by Lund Humphries, using ideas evolved in the studio – although the design was reproduced photographically, we used grained film, which set me thinking about the possible use of this material instead of the traditional transfer paper. To this end the firm of Vinsent Photolitho, run by Bill Freeman, whose premises were located within the Curwen Press, was duly absorbed into this parent company – a sign of its growing importance as part of the company's future policy.

The activities of Timothy Simon in formulating an overall policy for the studio became his overriding preoccupation. It was evident during 1959 that the studio was attracting publishers and artists and a reputation for the quality of its work was beginning to be established. Robert Erskine was very keen to develop his gallery publishing but needed other people to help in doing this; Timothy wanted to develop their new venture within the Curwen Press so as to keep it within the company's aegis. He decided to turn it into a subsidiary company called Curwen Studio Ltd, with his cousin Robert and himself as directors and myself as studio director. The company secretary, who would deal with its accounts, was to be O.R.G. Williams. It seemed that the Press's confidence in the studio's purpose had been established.

In assembling a body of artists whose work he wanted to publish, Timothy had certain advantages in actually knowing many contemporary artists and dealers. Nevertheless, it would take some time before he had a sizable list to offer from his office in Bloomsbury Square. At this point, around 1960, no one could have forecast the boom in print publishing in London that would soon come to experience. The catalyst for Timothy's enthusiasm for the project was his father Oliver's death some years earlier, after an eminent life in publishing and typographical design. Oliver's brother Herbert possessed a very different temperament, the virtues of which had been to guide the press in the practicalities of its day-to-day running and the maintenance of standards in the crafts of printing. He had an impeccable background of experience and had the respect of his workforce, which he oversaw somewhat in the manner of a benevolent despot. He took an active interest in the domestic background of his workers' lives and would help those who needed practical assistance in solving any personal problems. Knowing them on an everyday basis, he would walk round the shopfloor looking at the work in production and discussing matters with the staff and printers. On the other hand he interpreted the company policies with strict conviction and as a result had the respect of those who worked with him. It is not surprising that, temperamentally, he and Timothy were 'poles apart', disagreeing frequently over policy matters. Even Robert, his own son, who was hoping to make a career in the firm, had yet to establish his own direction within the company. At that moment, however, they were in agreement over the new studio and its future progress.

The relationship between Timothy and Robert Erskine developed apace and plans for artists and their publications were under constant discussion. Robert had been using the Harley Brothers, a firm of printers up in Edinburgh, but for various reasons they had proved unsatisfactory. So John Piper, Elizabeth Blackadder and Michael Ayrton, whose work Robert had hoped to publish with the Scottish firm, were added to our list. In support of this broadening approach, Timothy hoped to make more use of his London office as a focus for publishing activities, an idea that seemed to meet with the company's approval. Numerous articles appeared in the press with the critic Robert Wraight, among others, writing with enthusiasm in the *Tatler* about the new Curwen Studio venture and the rebirth of the artist's print. Only later did critics devote articles in the newspapers to exhibitions of prints such as the annual Graven Image curated by Robert Erskine at the Whitechapel Gallery. (This annual exhibition was initiated by Robert Erskine and the Director of the Whitechapel Gallery, Bryan Robertson, in Cambridge while Robert was studying there. The idea was to present to the public the work of contemporary artists in the UK in whatever printmaking process they specialised – etching, lithography, screenprinting, etc. The work was selected by a committee, while the subsequent exhibition ran for about four weeks. After about three years it was finally transferred to West End galleries, having achieved funding from the business sector.)

In this way, the foundations were gradually established; connections with the parent company and its staff were developing on a weekly basis, with Herbert and Robert Simon bringing visitors such as Rolly Atterbury and Robert Wraight to view this new activity. Perhaps more importantly, Timothy made contact with the publisher and collector of artists' prints, Felix Man, who was keen to commission work on behalf of Wolfgang Ketterer in Munich. Felix Man had the advantage of already having made contact and friendships with many contemporary artists by pursuing the career of a very reputable photojournalist on the staff of the weekly magazine *Picture Post*. This had given him a defined air of authority and a certain hauteur, admirably expressed in *The Print Collector*, David Hockney's portrait of Man. Despite an often difficult relationship with Curwen (due largely to Man's demands for co-operation, generally with Timothy Simon) he was to prove a loyal supporter and was much respected for his historical knowledge of lithography and its unique aesthetic qualities. By contrast, Robert Erskine, as publisher, was keen to expand his activities by commissioning artists and encouraging other potential publishers to join the field.

By late November Ceri Richards was ready to start on his *Hammerklavier* set of prints, an idea that he and Robert Erskine had discussed for a long time. The central images took inspiration from piano music by Debussy, his *Cathédrale engloutie*, whilst others developed ideas already explored in paintings dealing with music and the cycle of nature. The prints served the purpose of affirming and distilling some of Ceri's then current poetic themes, which were to emerge again in later years. For the first time he was able to express himself freely on large slabs of lithographic stone, seeing the vitality of the drawn images emerge as the proofs were pulled. Ceri took to the project with characteristic enthusiasm. Arriving early in the morning he would stand transfixed in front of the stone for hours on end whilst versions of an idea came and went as the lithographic drawing progressed. Anxiously, Robert Erskine would await a proof for approval, only to find the following morning that Ceri had changed his mind overnight and wanted to start again – much to Erskine's frustration. According to Frances, Ceri's wife, this was a normal state of affairs. The new possibilities of the medium also encouraged him in this direction, as he could now try graphically experimental uses of lithography which had previously eluded him. Picasso's ability to do this, which he so admired, was now within his own grasp. In fact, the medium offered him a range of alternatives which he sometimes found bewildering.

Two of the prints were to be done on Japanese paper, supplied by the eccentric Mr Lawrence of Bleeding Heart Yard, because Ceri liked the textural grass surface. As the proofs were printed, colour on colour, it became evident that the shreds of grass would unpredictably detach themselves from the paper surface. There was no other answer but to resecure the strands with archival glue, carefully, each time this occurred. But we persevered and the two editions were duly signed by a very satisfied artist. In those days, artists' editions were limited to a total of 75 copies; above that figure purchase tax was levied. *Hammerklavier* was duly launched at the St George's Gallery and was very well received by critics and the public. It gave Ceri a new world of expression to explore, while for the studio a promising future had begun.

Hammerklavier occupied us throughout the early months of 1959 against a background of building up the studio's equipment. Apart from suitable machinery (we still use the direct litho machine for stone printing) donated by the Curwen Press, there were types of paper suitable for printmaking to be investigated– the market at the time included papers from France (Arches, Rives), Germany (Zerkel) and Italy (Fabriano). There were certain mills in England, such as Barcham Green, specialising in handmade paper, but there was no mould-made paper created especially for printmaking. Reluctantly, Jack Green, the Managing Director of Barcham Green, agreed to supply us with stock but it was his son Remie who took a real interest in providing us with archival paper, realising that there could be a future market here for his company with artists and publishers. After family disagreements, some years later they were able to produce very creditable printmaking paper.

The search for high-quality printing inks was made easier by Curwen's use of such material on a daily basis. The firm of A.R. Gibbon was keen to supply us with lightfast materials, and we also found ink chemists who could advise us on inks suitable for hand rolling. Other necessary materials were easily available within the printing world, and, moreover, the choice was wide.

Much commercial printing was soon to be done on zinc, and many supply companies, such as Hunter Penrose, and F. Horsell and Co. of Leeds, manufactured their own products.

The founding of the studio had fortunately given Robert Erskine a potential solution to the problem of producing lithographic work. It was clear that the Curwen Press wanted to develop the studio as its own business and to cooperate with the St George's Gallery as and when required, leaving Robert to develop his publishing ideas separately. This seemed a good arrangement until other publishers arrived on the scene. After the launch of Ceri Richards's prints, attention was turned to Robert Colquhoun and Robert McBride, two artists who Erskine had tried for some time to persuade to make prints for him, without success. They were living in Suffolk, their work much sought after by dealers. They had an ongoing reputation for drunken behaviour reminiscent of the lifestyle in 1950s Fitzrovia in Central London, but were now living in East Anglia due to lack of funds. Robert Erskine made the mistake of sending an advance to enable them to travel up to London and start work on their printmaking at the studio; they did not arrive. Frantic phone calls produced no result, and in desperation we were asked to search around Soho. Luckily, my assistant at the time, David Gillison, had a car, so we ventured into various watering holes before finally discovering them, very much the worse for wear, in a corner of the Gay Hussar on Greek Street. After some persuasion they appeared in the studio the following morning, still hungover though willing to work – albeit under a 'no alcohol' rule. Surprisingly, during the following days they made efforts to print several editions, working with constant application, and became totally intrigued by the different processes, even vowing to come back again if Erskine would agree. He never did. Other promising Scottish artists that Erskine invited to work with us at this time included Elizabeth Blackadder, whose graphic work was to form an important element in her future life.

As the year progressed, other artists came to work in the studio; Josef Herman came to fulfil a long-declared wish to work for Robert Erskine. The study of two seated miners was his first attempt at stone lithography. He spent much time in trying to etch out the forms of the figures with nitric acid on the limestone until he had achieved the result he desired. Each successive day he would arrive, put on his overalls and workman's boots, and spend the day concentrating intensely on the stone image. He was captivated by the process but when the time arrived to introduce colour he could not decide. So the final editions printed were divided into two: one version in dense black, and the second combining the black with a yellow-ochre background and an umber foreground. The reaction of the people at the press to the work emerging from the studio was mixed to say the least. Due to its workshop methods, the Curwen Press, like many similar companies, had production practices which gave a recognisable hallmark to its work, of which it was justly proud. We aimed to involve the artist as much as possible, at every necessary stage, so that the work would reflect its creator's originality. It was a difficult ideal to follow, for all sorts of reasons, but has been key to the studio's policy since the beginning.

The influx of different artists continued unchecked, with Alan Davie finally arriving as we had arranged during my time in St Ives. His first image, produced partly on stone, involved amongst other colours an emblematic use of red and black occupying the full 'imperial' sheet. The proof caused quite a stir in the London office and was duly titled *Sleep my Angel*.

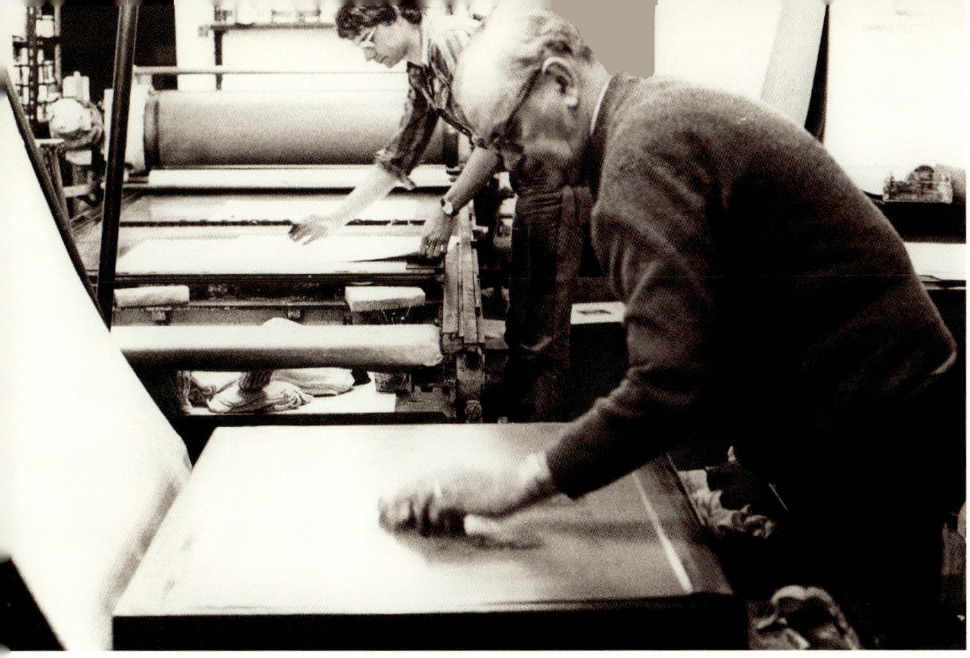

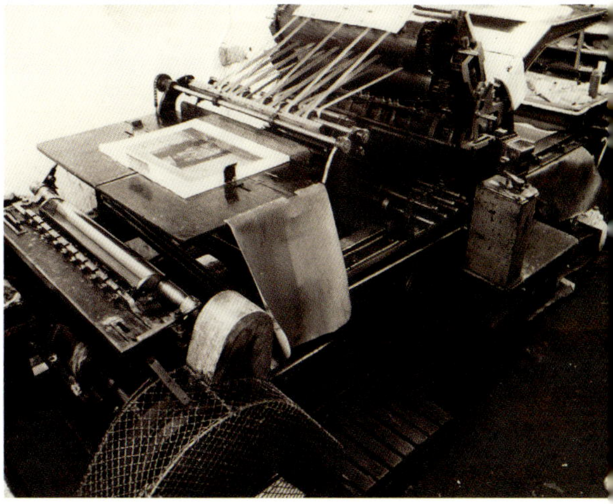

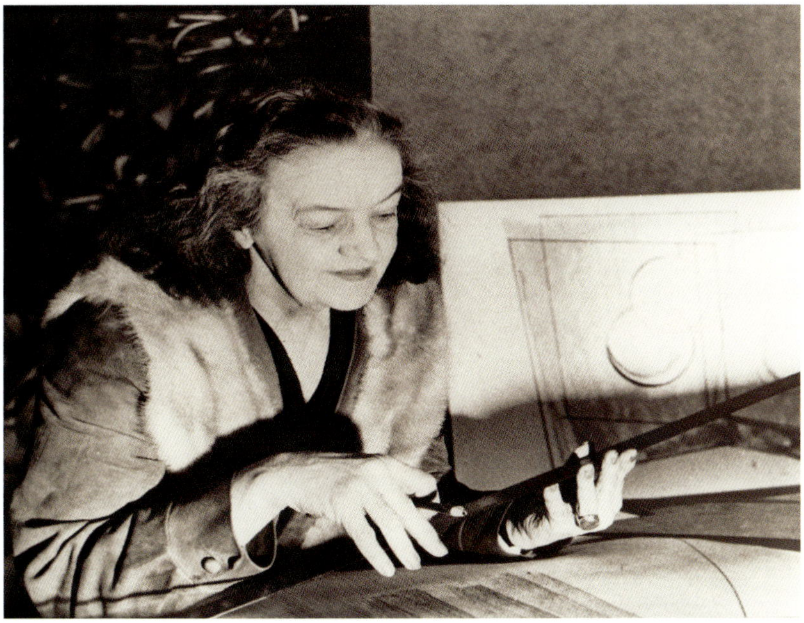

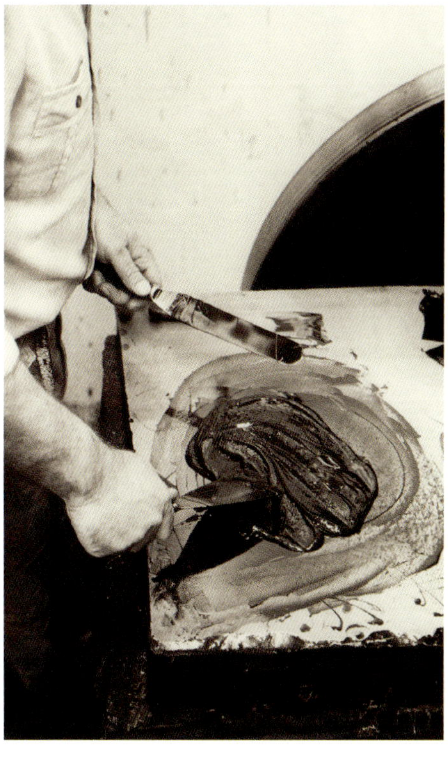

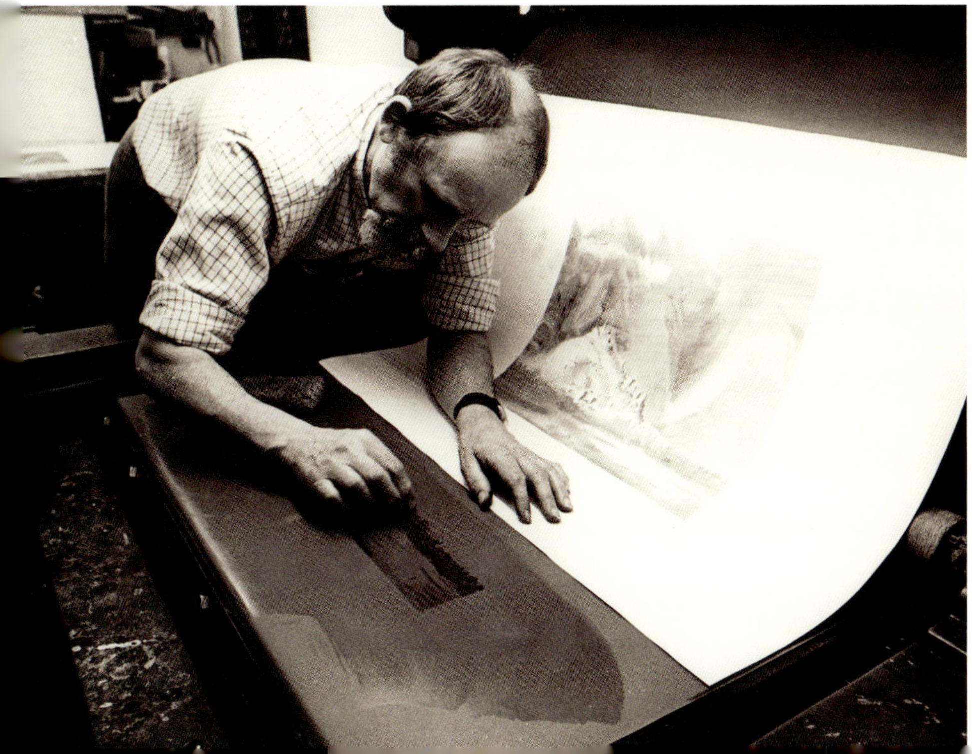

Left to right top row: Bert Wootton (foreground) and John White (background) working on proofing presses, Curwen Studio, 1975; Overview of Ratcliff flatbed printing machine, Curwen Studio, 1967.

Left to right middle row: Barbara Hepworth on lithographic plates in Trewyn Studio, St Ives, 1969; Ink mixing prior to printing edition, Curwen Studio, 1975.

Left: Guy Field (printer) making alterations to artist's printing plate, 1984.

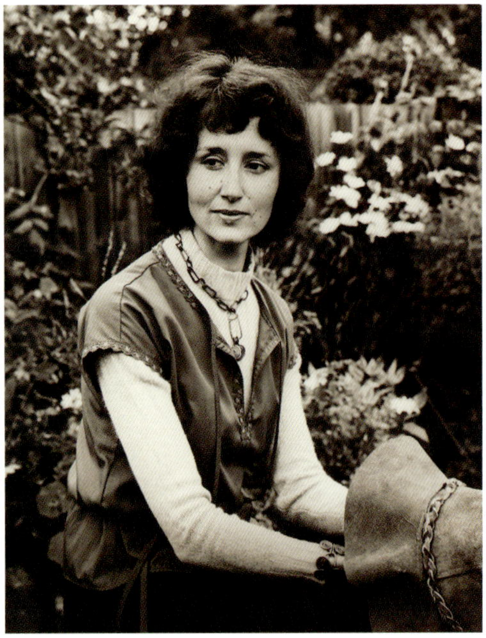

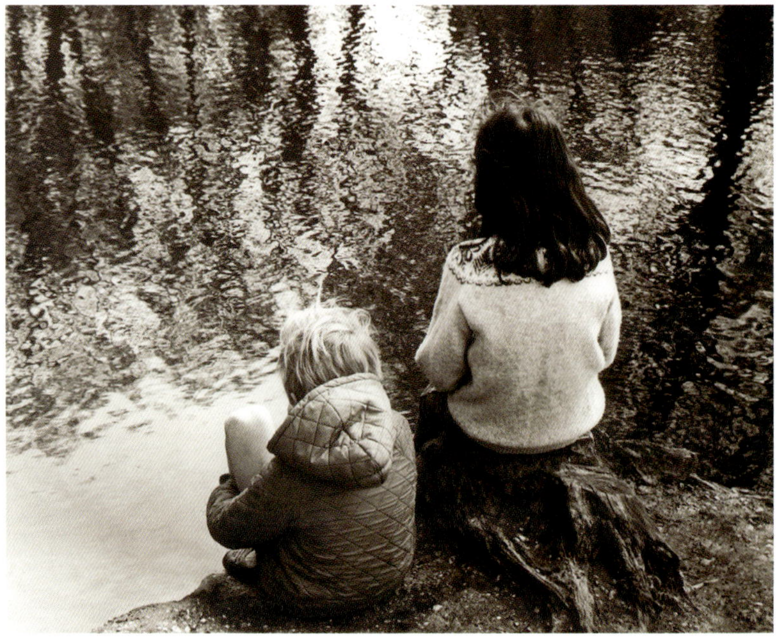

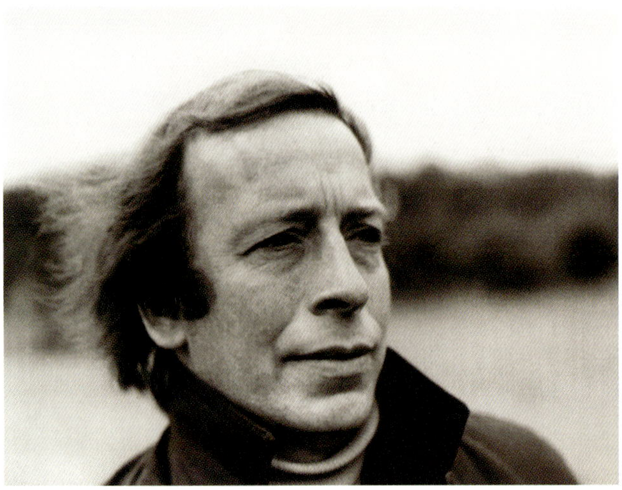

Family group circa 1972 (clockwise from top left): Jenny; Matthew (left) and Liza (right); Stanley Jones.

Then suddenly, to everyone's concern, Timothy was rushed into hospital with heart trouble of a serious nature, surviving only through the skills of a gifted consultant. He was to be away for two or three months, leaving myself and Peter Baer with work to produce for Henry Moore and Prunella Clough. One afternoon when we were fully occupied with this, Laurie Parkin, the head of the bindery, appeared, accompanied by a young lady who he introduced as 'Jenny Stone from the London office – can you show her around the studio?' Such is life. I did not know at the time that I had just met my future wife and my life was about to change irrevocably. Jenny had been recently appointed as Timothy's office secretary in Bloomsbury Square. As a result of my teaching commitments at the Slade, I was living in a flat in Highbury Hill found for me by Mrs Allcock, my landlady from my student days. It was convenient for the Slade on Gower Street, and also for Plaistow, to which I could even cycle in the event of a London Transport strike. I was to remain at the flat until Jenny and I were married in the spring of 1961, at the church of St Charles Borromeo in Bloomsbury, whereupon we moved out of London to our cottage near Ongar in Essex.

Essex

In the spring of 1960 I was looking for a larger place to live. My flat was beginning to fill up with work of various kinds. It was Annabel, Robert Simon's wife, who suggested that I search locally where Jenny lived in the village of Toot Hill in Essex. Her suggestion proved very practical. By cycling around the lanes I discovered by chance an empty semi-detached house, called Lion Cottage, in the hamlet of Clatterford End. I knocked next door, to be confronted by the tall stooping figure of my future neighbour, Mr King. He sent me further down the lane to see the owner, Phillip Millbank, who belonged to a local farming family. I explained my plan to Phillip and his wife, ending with the proposition that I should rent the house from them. After some hesitation they said it might be possible; could I come back tomorrow to discuss the matter further? The following day, to my surprise, they agreed to sell. This meant raising the capital from the local bank but eventually this was achieved.

Fortunately, Jenny's enthusiasm for the house's possibilities equalled my own. Robert and Annabel proved very supportive but the cottage needed a lot of renovation. At least there was a cold-water tap in the kitchen and an earth closet at the end of its wild garden. It promised to be quite an adventure, living in a mixed farming community and working and travelling to London each day, and in all weathers, from Blake Hall Station to the Curwen Studio or the Slade. Making Lion Cottage habitable became for us a weekend project, with Jenny enthusiastically helping whenever possible. For the next two years it was a constant effort, involving my own unexplored building skills, the local council and numerous helpful neighbours in Clatterford End. There were times of near despair, particularly when the building side of matters became especially frustrating or the bitterness of the winter months froze everything solid for weeks. But we were fortunate in many ways in our attempt to establish a home – there was a garden in which Jenny could learn to grow vegetables and I was able work in a spacious garage, albeit only when the weather permitted. There was the Simon family, too – Herbert and his wife Molly, who lived locally at the White House in nearby Ongar, were to become lifelong close friends. It seemed a bizarre solution to live in what was then a very rural part of Essex but for Jenny and me it proved inspirational to the start of our married life, which began in the spring of 1961. Our two children, Liza and Matthew, spent their early years with us in this idyllic farming hamlet, surrounded by farming families whose lives had changed little for generations.

Eventually, in 1969, because of the growing demands of the studio and the need for more space, reluctantly we decided to move further into London when we discovered an Edwardian home in Woodford Green. Inhabited by an elderly lady anxious to sell, and set in a secluded road near Epping Forest, it had been on the market for a long time with no apparent interest from buyers. For us it represented an ideal solution: it had cellars and basements for workshop space and was close enough to Central London. It would be a significant move for the whole family.

Printmaking gains momentum

The lithography room at the Slade was attracting a considerable number of students each week. Moreover, painter Michael Elliot's brother Brian had set up a silk-screen facility near the sculpture school, which under

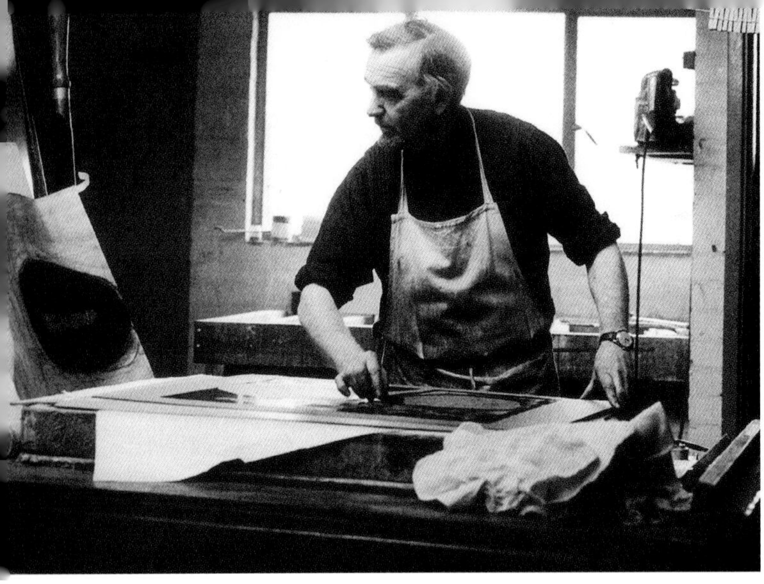

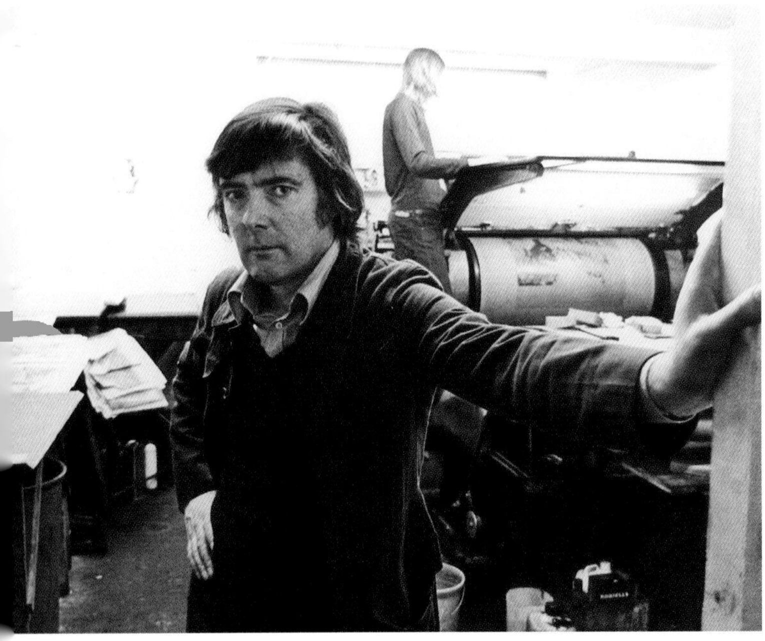

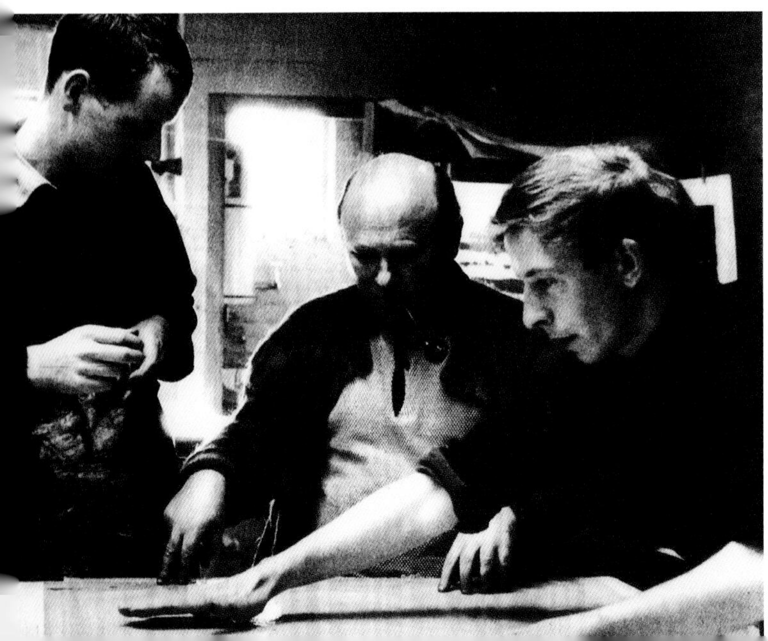

his inspired guidance provided a new creative medium for the students to explore. News went around that dealers such as Marlborough Fine Art were contemplating entering the print-publishing market; at the same time Robert Erskine was also in the process of organising his annual Graven Image exhibition at the Whitechapel Gallery. The link between the Slade and the studio had a good rationale for me in that at the school, for various reasons, I could meet other artists, but it also gave my colleague Peter a chance to take control of matters in the studio and grow in confidence. There was also the additional benefit, when the studio moved to Tottenham Court Road a few years later, that the students could come and see the current images in progress and possibly meet the artists at work. This gave them a glimpse of printmaking as a professional possibility rather than just as an art school subject.

In the early 1960s the signs were beginning to appear both in Europe and America of a developing contemporary market for prints. The New York School of Painting had finally established itself as an international force, whilst in London, Cork Street was leading a new generation of dealers whose artists and their activities now rivalled the Paris scene in their influence. No longer, it appeared, did the École de Paris dominate the art world. There were a number of American artists, many of whom had spent time at Hayter's Atelier 17, who were now growing in importance, having returned to New York to look for printmaking facilities and publishers to launch their work. Tatyana Grossman pioneered the

Top to bottom: William Scott drawing on lithographic plate, Curwen Studio, 1961; David Gentleman awaits his proof, Curwen Studio, 1975; Artist Josef Herman (centre) Stanley Jones (right) and David Gillison (assistant), Curwen Studio, 1960.

artist's print in her lithographic studio in New York, and was later followed by the Tamarind Institute (aided by the Ford Foundation) in Los Angeles.

The founding of Editions Alecto in this country meant the presence of a publisher whose aims were directed at Europe and America as well as London. Having started in Cambridge, Paul Cornwall-Jones soon moved to London with enthusiastic colleagues, bringing a company which would produce as well as publish limited-edition prints by contemporary British artists. Their first commissioned prints were two studies of Westminster School by John Piper, which we printed on stone at a time when John was also producing his view of San Marco and a study of a Brittany beach for Timothy Simon. Unlike ourselves, who specialised in lithography, Alecto was also to embark upon printing etchings and silkscreen editions as part of their output. It would seem that the Curwen Studio had a future competitor on the horizon, well financed and with a comparatively large staff, and soon to include Robert Erskine, who had closed his St George's Gallery to join their board. Administered by Joe Studholme, Erskine and Cornwall-Jones, their intentions were to develop not only in Europe, but also in the rapidly growing American print market.

The board of the Curwen Studio, though much impressed by these developments, kept the studio to a small scale by comparison; it had built its reputation, characteristically, on lithographic skills alone, and thus drew artists and publishers constantly to its doors for

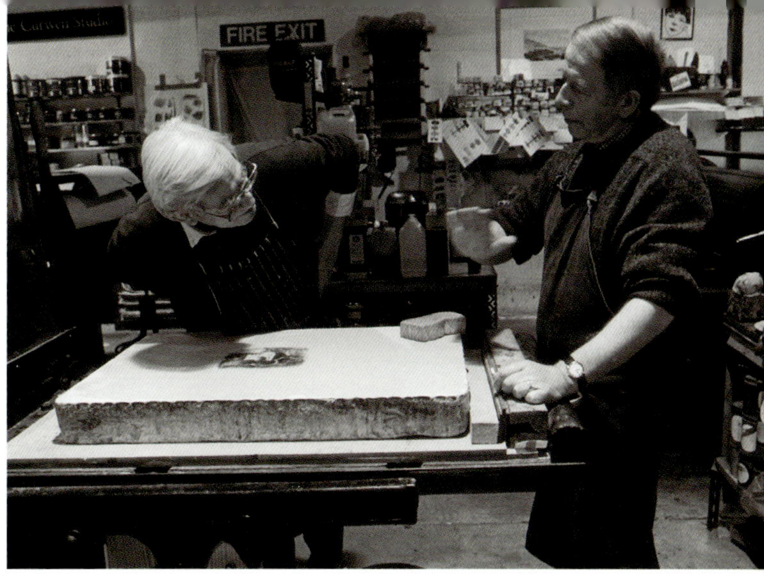

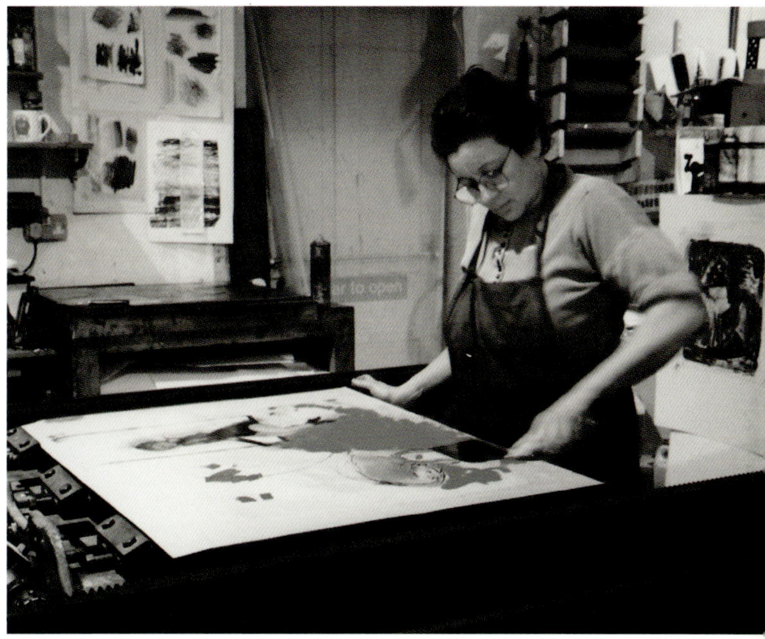

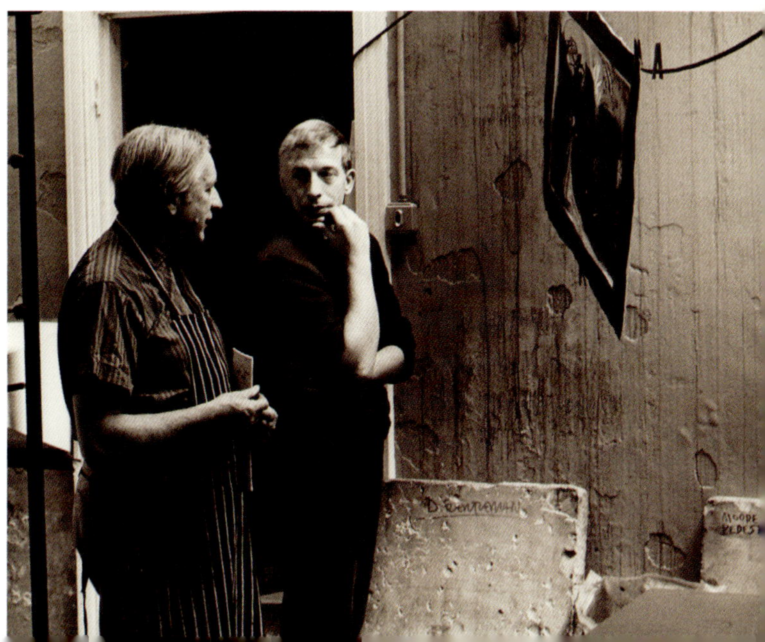

Top to bottom: Bernard Dunstan (left) and Stanley Jones in discussion at new studio in Linton, 1994; Anna Maria Pacheco at work on the proofing press in Curwen Studio, Linton, 1992; Ceri Richards (left) and Stanley Jones discussing a proof, Curwen Studio, Midford Place.

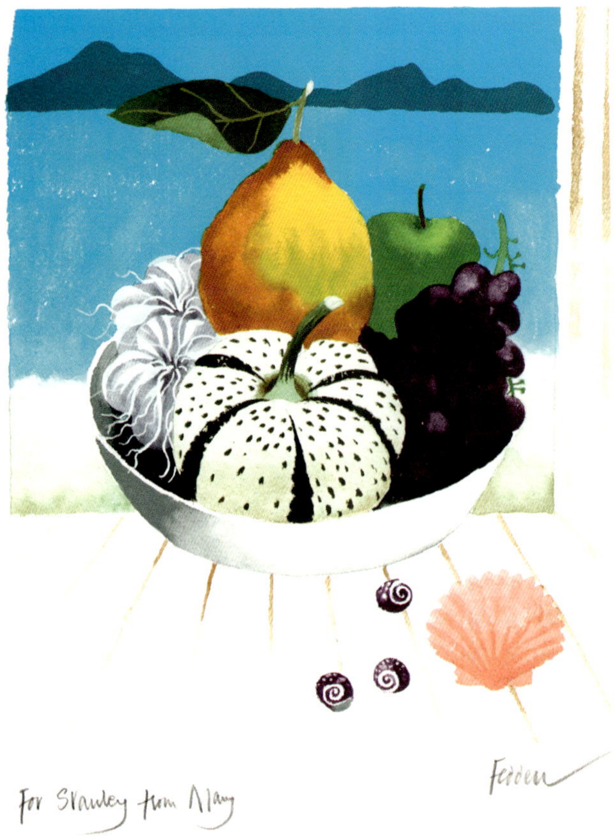

Mary Fedden, *Still Life Fruit and Shells*, lithograph, 2004.

this specialist expertise. However, we also had formidable lithographic competitors in France, Switzerland and Italy, who were only too keen to attract important British artists. The developing silkscreen companies of Kelpra and Advanced Graphics were also rivals in this field. They had evolved their own appeal to potential printmakers with the new photographic processes and the speed of production they brought. However, in the mid-1960s, the fine art world did not look favourably on the use of photography in printmaking – it was regarded as being too linked with the world of commercial printing. However, with the development of new-generation artists such as Robert Rauschenberg, who combined hand-drawn and photographic work in his lithographic prints, the public gradually became familiar with photographic imagery to the point where its acceptance as a *bona fide* medium was inevitable.

Timothy and I were unfazed by these developments. It seemed to us that the two companies, Curwen and Alecto, could exist side by side, since the printmaking world was growing in all respects, allowing space enough for both. Thus much depended on the ability of the various individuals within each organisation to work well with each other and the different strategies each one adopted. You could say in retrospect that it looked like a case of David and Goliath, but this is probably too melodramatic. In any case, in years to come, other unforeseen developments were to influence the separate futures of these two firms.

The arrival of John Piper in our studio indicated the resurgence of what turned out to be a lifelong association. During the pre-war years John had worked as a book illustrator with Oliver Simon at the Curwen Press and had subsequently developed his company Contemporary Lithographs with Robert Wellington until the intervention of the war. He was keen to resume contact with me in the new workshop and to explore new methods and ideas for producing lithographs. The commission from Timothy for a view of San Marco gave him an opportunity to do this, as did the study of a beach in Brittany which followed.

The view of San Marco began as a lithographic brush drawing on transfer paper, over which were splashed copious spots of white gouache. The idea was based on a lithographic study by Picasso of a bird, *Le Gros Pigeon* (c. 1945), also on transfer paper. John's adaptive use of this technique atmospherically transformed the façade of his San Marco – in this case its effect deriving from the then-fashionable Tachist method of painting. Highlights were then touched in with yellow to give the final print an unusual, almost theatrical, vibrancy. This image was then followed by a study of a beach in Brittany, drawn largely on stone and in this instance using collage

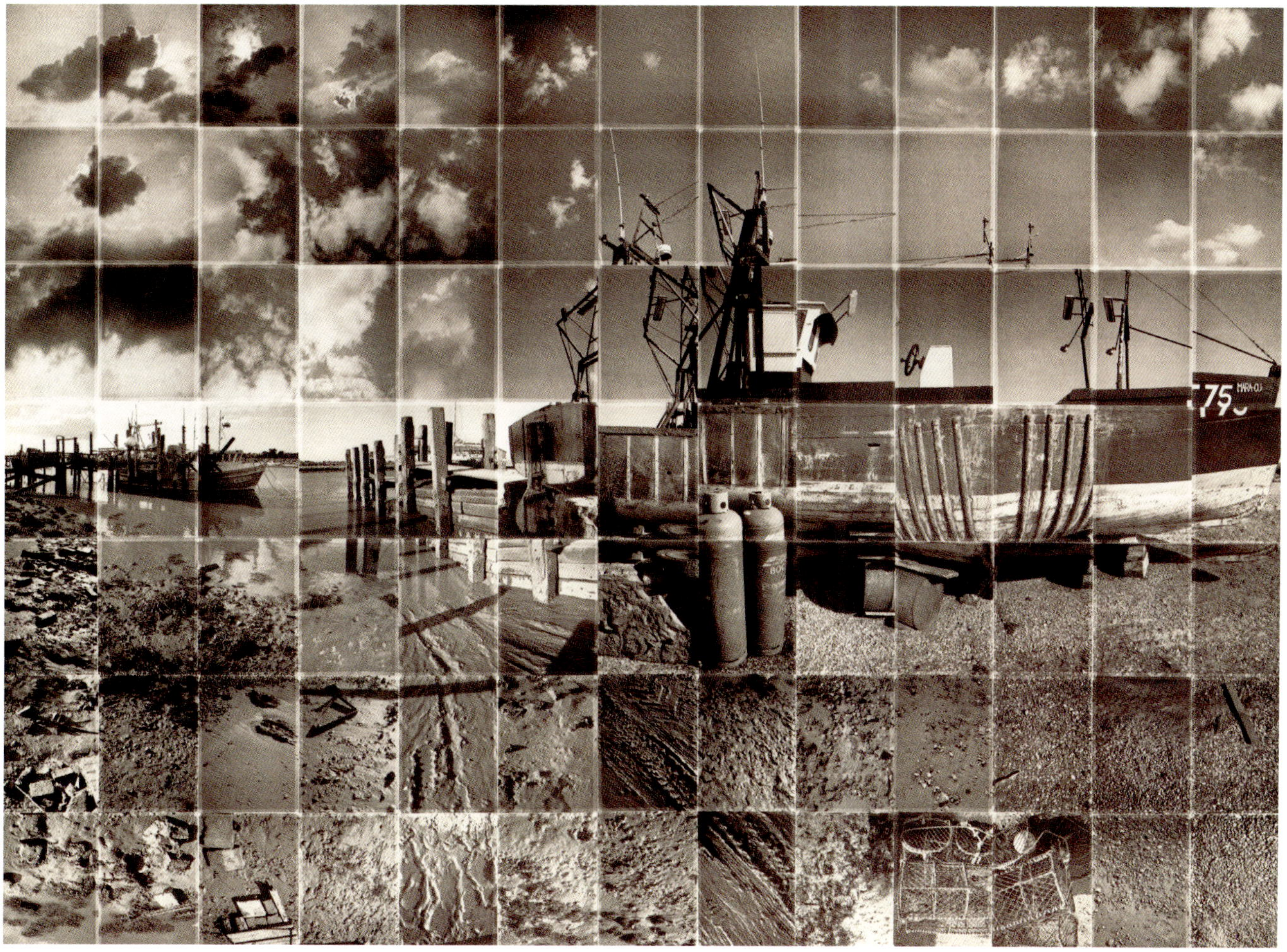

Continuous tone lithograph, photographic origination.

shapes glued to its surface with gum arabic. Over this, Piper floated washes of drawing ink diluted with turpentine and water to complete the graphic details of the landscape. Both images were different in interpretation and each highly innovative in execution. Significantly, more of this activity with Piper was to come at a later date.

Meanwhile, Timothy Simon was devoting himself to commissioning artists with the idea of launching his publishing venture from the firm's Bloomsbury office, which was now beginning to take shape. It was realised by the Curwen Press board that publishing as well as printing was necessary if the venture was to have financial stability into the future; just how much was to be an ongoing subject of debate for many years to come.

Timothy Simon was slowly building a portfolio of prints ready for publication in 1962 and as well as using the Bloomsbury Office for the exhibition launch he also hoped to stimulate international interest by having agents in New York, Stockholm and Oslo. He was encouraged in this direction by Felix Man, a supporter of many avant-garde European printmakers whose publication *Europäische Graphik* was shared with Gallery W. Ketterer in Munich. By this route Reg Butler was inserted into the studio schedules, invited by Man to produce images for his next publication. Over the years Reg became a keen practitioner in the studio, although he was also plagued by the constant desire to invent his own lithographic drawing materials. The problem was he had little practical knowledge of the process, and whilst he preferred to work in his own studio, his methods for producing the work were often obscure and frustrating to all concerned. One

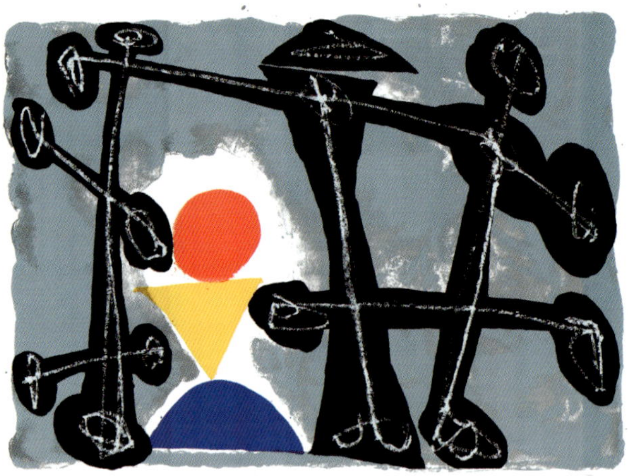

Basil Beattie, *Demonic Stomp*, lithograph with silkscreen, 1988.

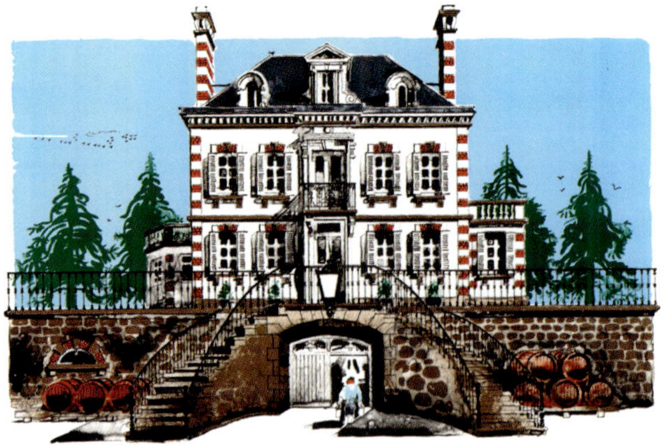

Paul Hogarth, trial proof lithograph, 1985

instance involved a drawing to be done on transfer paper – we sent him three different varieties, none of which, apparently, were suitable for the textures he had in mind. Instead he decided to make his own paper despite my warning of the dangers of using unsuitable paper and coatings. The image subsequently arrived on an unresponsive piece of card together with a list of the various glues he had used. Even Felix was nonplussed. It took five days of coaxing to persuade the drawing to transfer to the stone – largely through the unconventional use of a smoothing iron and steam. Perhaps surprisingly, much to the delight, and relief, of the artist, the publisher and the studio team, the resulting print was very satisfactory.

We now had in the studio a promising group of printmakers able to cope with our growing list of artists and their requirements; formerly, two of these, William Scott and Alan Davie, had made contact with me when I was still in St Ives. William had made lithographs at Corsham School of Art and was keen to satisfy a growing number of dealers, including Timothy Simon, who were keen to publish his prints. It was now opportune for him make a start, which he did during the summer with a work for the German publisher, Ketterer. His methods relied on ideas worked out very broadly in gouache, to be used primarily as a guide for colour, and his preference was for lithographic plate rather than stone. One advantage of the plates was their portability, which allowed him, where necessary, to continue working on them at home. He relied sometimes on accidental mark-making, as in *Barra* (1962), where the circular form so integral to the work began life as a grease stain left by a misplaced coffee cup. He was particularly intrigued by certain occurrences during the proofing of his work which, although based on gouache or watercolour sketches, was an important formative stage in the making of the final image chosen for editioning. Such non-figurative work benefited from an almost serendipitous assembly of the drawn plates, giving Scott an opportunity to select the proof he most preferred. Alterations to colour selection, colour density or to the order of printing could be made, a process that could yield unexpected results and would often alter his ideas completely. These options he carefully evaluated based on their importance to the printed image; sometimes he would take the printing plates home to make final judgements in his own studio. It was a slow, deliberate process, but one which would give him the best results, and very similar to the working methods of Georges Braque, for whom consideration of the print idea took a considerable amount of time. Generally at this point, his prints were characterised by the painterly use of lithographic ink, which allied them quite closely with his works on canvas. There was much proofing and reproofing of the different hand-drawn colour separations until the desired balance of tone and colour was achieved. It was a different way of thinking from that necessary to the act of painting, requiring a capacity to

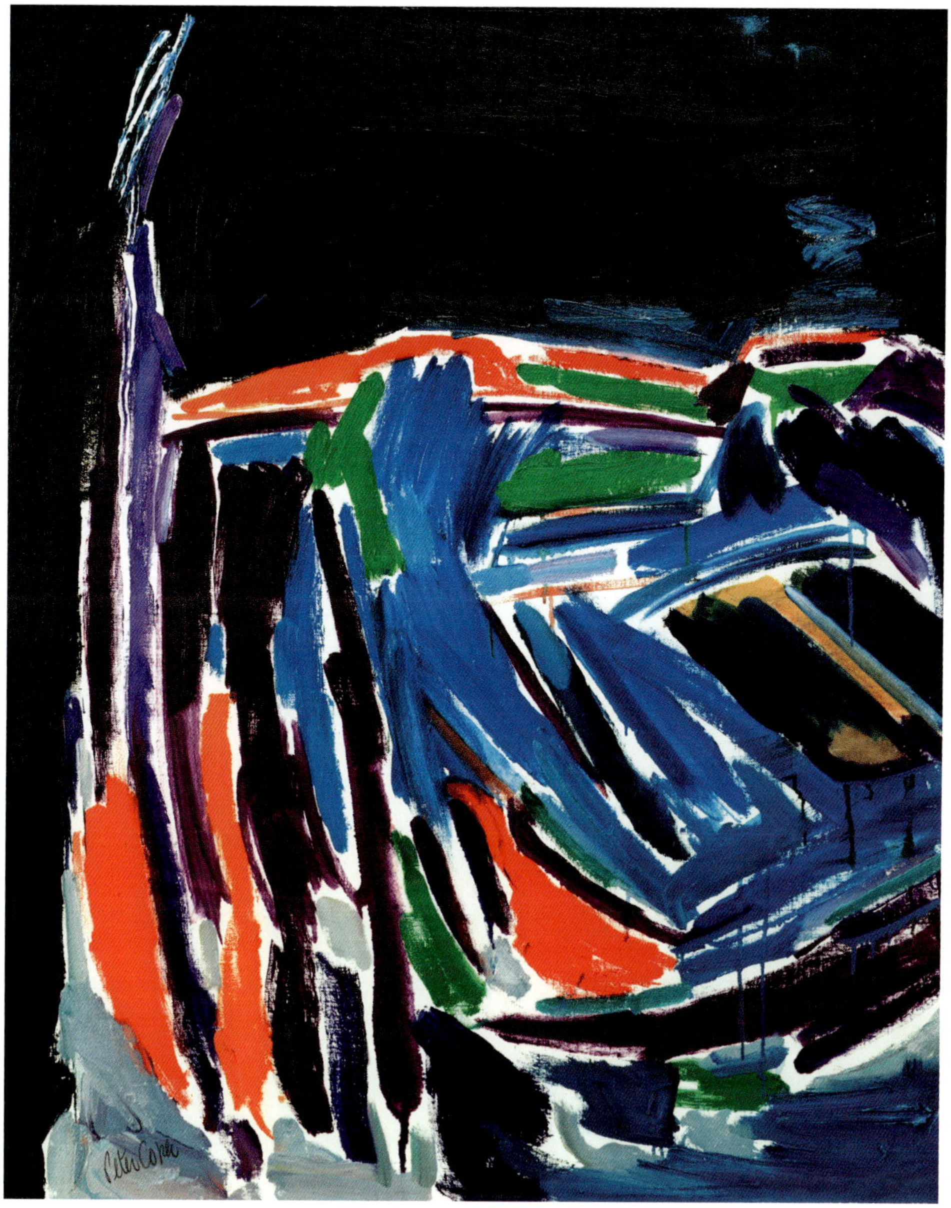

Peter Coker, *Paris Street*, lithograph, 2002.

understand the part played by each colour separation not only in itself but also in relation to the others. Artists vary in their ability to do this. William Scott warmed to the making of prints as an activity that took him into an area different to that of his painting, requiring its own disciplines and practice. He liked the challenge.

By contrast, Alan Davie's approach relied on the many possibilities of colour variations that could be applied to each drawn plate. The proliferation of colour proofs generated in this way suited his serendipitous approach to achieving the most adventurous, if unpredictable, final result. Timothy Simon's commissioning of *Sleep my Angel* in 1962 was the first of many of Davie's prints to be produced in this way.

As well as the more *avant-garde* artists who were visiting the studio at these early stages, those who had already worked at the Curwen Press – mostly book illustrators such as Edward Ardizzone – were frequent

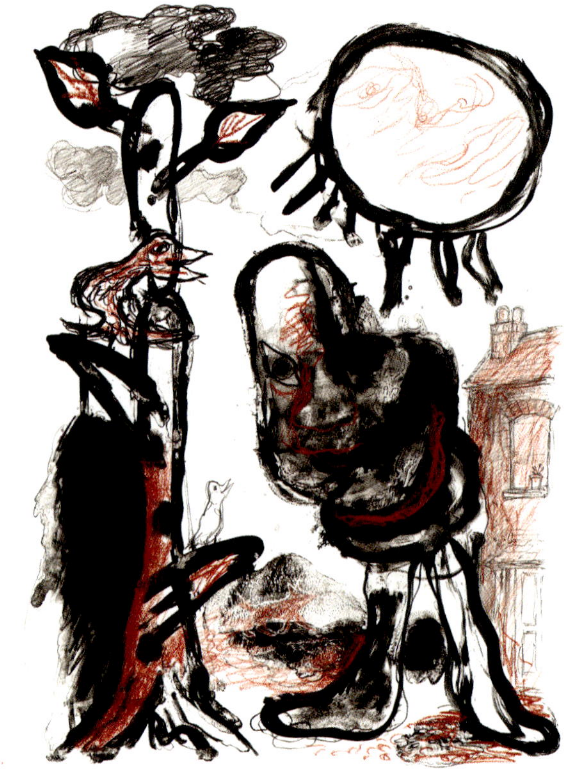

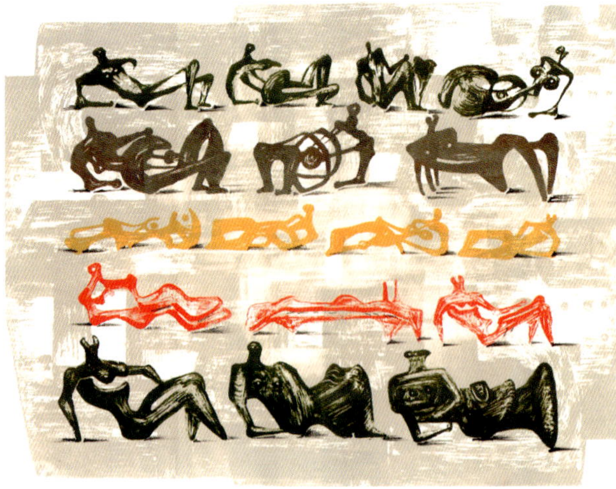

Above: Henry Moore, *Seventeen Reclining Figures*, lithograph, 1959.

Left: Ken Kiff, proof study, lithograph, 2001.

visitors, enjoying the process of working on stone once more. Edward had an ability to befriend the printmakers even as he worked with the utmost concentration, sharing his lunch and his jokes as the day progressed – if you took snuff, there was that also. But his reputation as Diz, the illustrator, draughtsman and author, ensured his status and his appealing eccentricity endeared him to us all in Plaistow. To see the artist's ample figure depart from the studio wedged in his bubble car after a day's proofing was quite beguiling.

In the early 1960s, the possibilities of lithographic printmaking attracted sculptors such as Lynn Chadwick to the studio, at the same time as Kenneth Armitage was making his first two editions for the Marlborough Gallery, which was also beginning to develop an interest in print publishing. Elisabeth Frink, again introduced by Timothy, preferred to work on stones, and for weeks scraped and scoured their surfaces for her *Men in Space* studies. Robert Adams, who was also commissioned by Timothy Simon, experimented with hand-cut rubber shapes in the construction of prints based on his metallic screens. It was evident that artists who saw the progression of these and other works in the studio were influenced by the variety and individuality achievable through the process.

Henry Moore

About this time, Timothy had assembled a list of artists ready for publication which included John Piper, William Scott, Prunella Clough, Josef Herman, Robert Adams, Alan Davie and Ceri Richards. There was also Henry Moore, the making of whose *Seventeen Reclining Figures* was to herald a longstanding relationship with the Curwen Studio.

Henry Moore was the first artist to start work in the studio, due largely to the fact that he had just completed a book for George Rainbird – *Heads, Figures and Ideas* – which was printed at the Curwen Press in the spring of 1959. It was a salutary work demanding time and effort from the artist with the help of Robert Simon, who was

Kim Lim, lithograph, 1992.

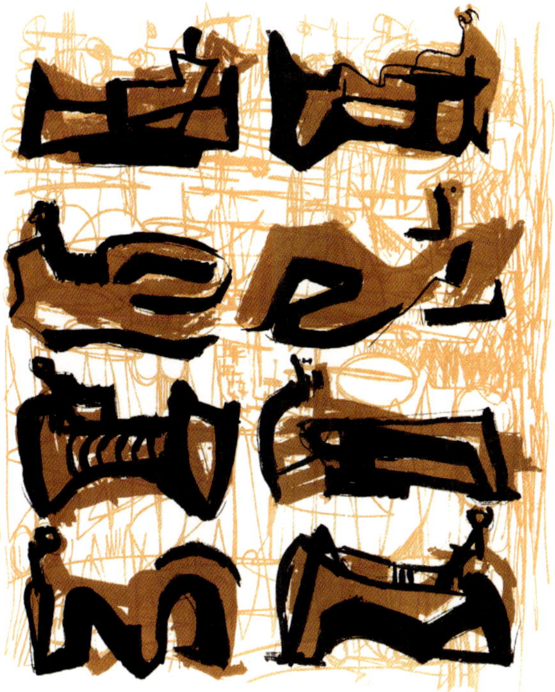

Right: Henry Moore, *Eight Recling Figures*, lithograph, 1958.

in charge of its production. Henry had become aware of the studio's formation and was keen to investigate its possibilities. He was also still teaching part-time at Chelsea College of Art at that point, making it easily possible for him to come to the studio whenever he had the time. Robert Simon brought the artist to see the new studio one afternoon and it was obvious he could see its potential. He happened to have a surplus set of plates that not had in the end been used as intended for the frontispiece of the book. So we decided that we would print them by hand in a limited edition, to be published by Kestner Gesellschaft in Hanover. Though I did not know it at the time, this was to be the start of his lifelong association between Moore and the studio, which would become an important element in both the studio's development and the artist's *oeuvre*. When teaching at Chelsea, Henry would call in to the studio on his way home to watch progress and make any necessary changes during proofing. The possibilities of the medium began to register in his mind.

The first print to be produced, based on plates not used for *Heads, Figures and Ideas*, was the study of *Three Reclining Figures* (1959). It gave him a notion of what could be done in experimenting with the three plates.

To celebrate the launch of Moore's print, a party was held at 13 Bloomsbury Square, where invited artists along with figures from the gallery and publishing world were able to see what the studio was capable of producing at this stage. It was a formative time for British publishers in general as more European publishers were bringing work to London. By now, Marlborough Fine Art had begun its own print publishing venture, which was to have its own West End premises, under the guidance of Bernhard Baer of the Ganymed (sic) Press. The Waddington Gallery followed a similar path by commissioning artists to make prints to exhibit in the gallery. Moreover, the public was becoming aware of the availability of prints, not only through galleries but also by means of mixed exhibitions such as the Graven Image annual show organised by Robert Erskine.

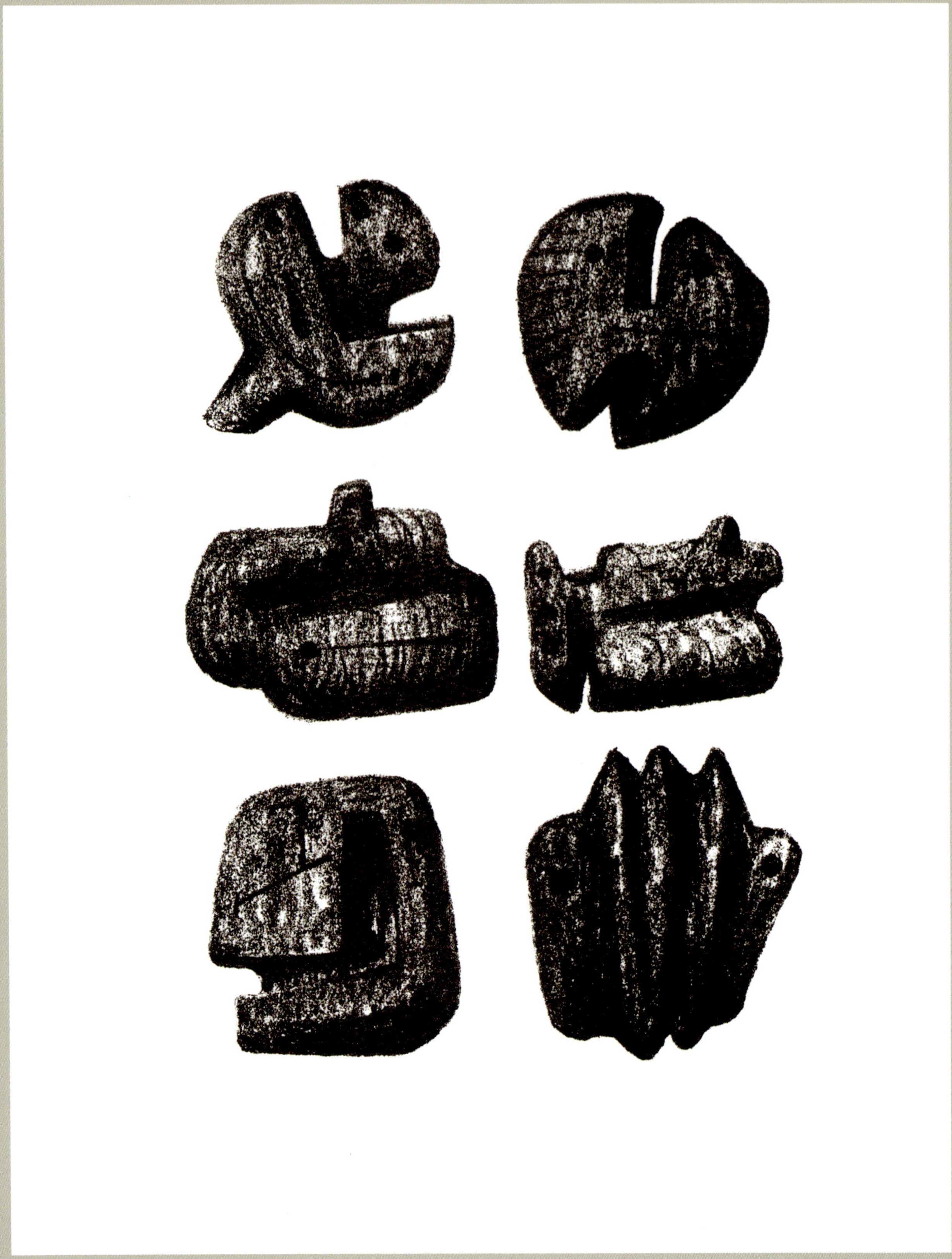

Henry Moore, *Six Stones*, lithograph, 1973, Curwen Studio.

This kind of enterprise was now offering people an opportunity to appreciate and acquire the work of contemporary artists, whilst the practise of making prints to a professional standard was being encouraged and financed not only by professional publishers but also on occasion by private companies like Trust House Forte. The growing attraction of London and New York as important art markets was beginning to boost the activity of print publishing – it gave Timothy Simon's plans for the studio's future an air of plausibility, despite the arrival in London of other competitors such as Editions Alecto and Kelpra, the screen-printers. The Curwen Press's policy of inviting long-acquainted artists such as Piper, Bawden and Ardizonne to use the studio facilities helped to keep a year-on-year balance of new voices alongside already familiar figures.

Amongst this latter group was Graham Sutherland, whose earlier career had been considerably helped by Oliver Simon. Graham was in the process of proofing the cover for his biography, to be published by Lund Humphries. At the same time, Helena Rubenstein had asked him to draw her portrait as a lithographic print from the painting he had made, then in the Tate Gallery. A small stone was selected, drawn and proofed to his satisfaction and shown to Helena Rubenstein. She was delighted and asked for copies to be made. On asking her how she intended to use the image, Graham discovered it was to be a Christmas card, which he felt was inappropriate. Thus he continued with his book jacket, leaving the stone in the studio, forever unprinted.

With an increasing flow of work year in, year out, the subject of possible expansion came under discussion at one of our studio meetings; such a development would involve not only more personnel but also extra space for storage and machinery. It was apparent to us that in its first few years of existence the studio had developed its viability under the aegis of the Curwen Press, and was now considered a subsidiary, going by the name of Curwen Prints.

It continued to attract a variety of artists and publishers, including attention from American dealers, who were already aware of the Curwen name and its reputation. Benton Spruance from Philadelphia was one of the first American artists to work in the studio, arriving in 1961. He was followed by Sam Maitin, Warrington Colescott, James Rosenquist and Man Ray, to name a few.

John Piper

By 1962, the Marlborough Gallery was becoming more adventurous with its print-publishing plans, and had encouraged John Piper to start on a project of lithographs involving 30 images of churches in England and Wales. The resulting series, *A Retrospect of Churches*, was to be his most ambitious use of original printmaking to date. He and I decided to take advantage of this opportunity to explore the medium as fully as possible; thus each subject was chosen partly with this intention. John Betjeman was invited to write an introduction and also suggested some possible subjects. We were all enthused by the project, while at the same time realising the complications of fitting the schedule needed to meet the intended date of publication, in 1964, alongside the demands of other studio work.

The nature of the project meant close discussion among John, myself and other members of the studio staff, to develop the interpretation of each print. In between times, John would disappear, for instance, to design the stage sets for Benjamin Britten's opera *Billy Budd* or to prepare paintings for exhibitions; somehow

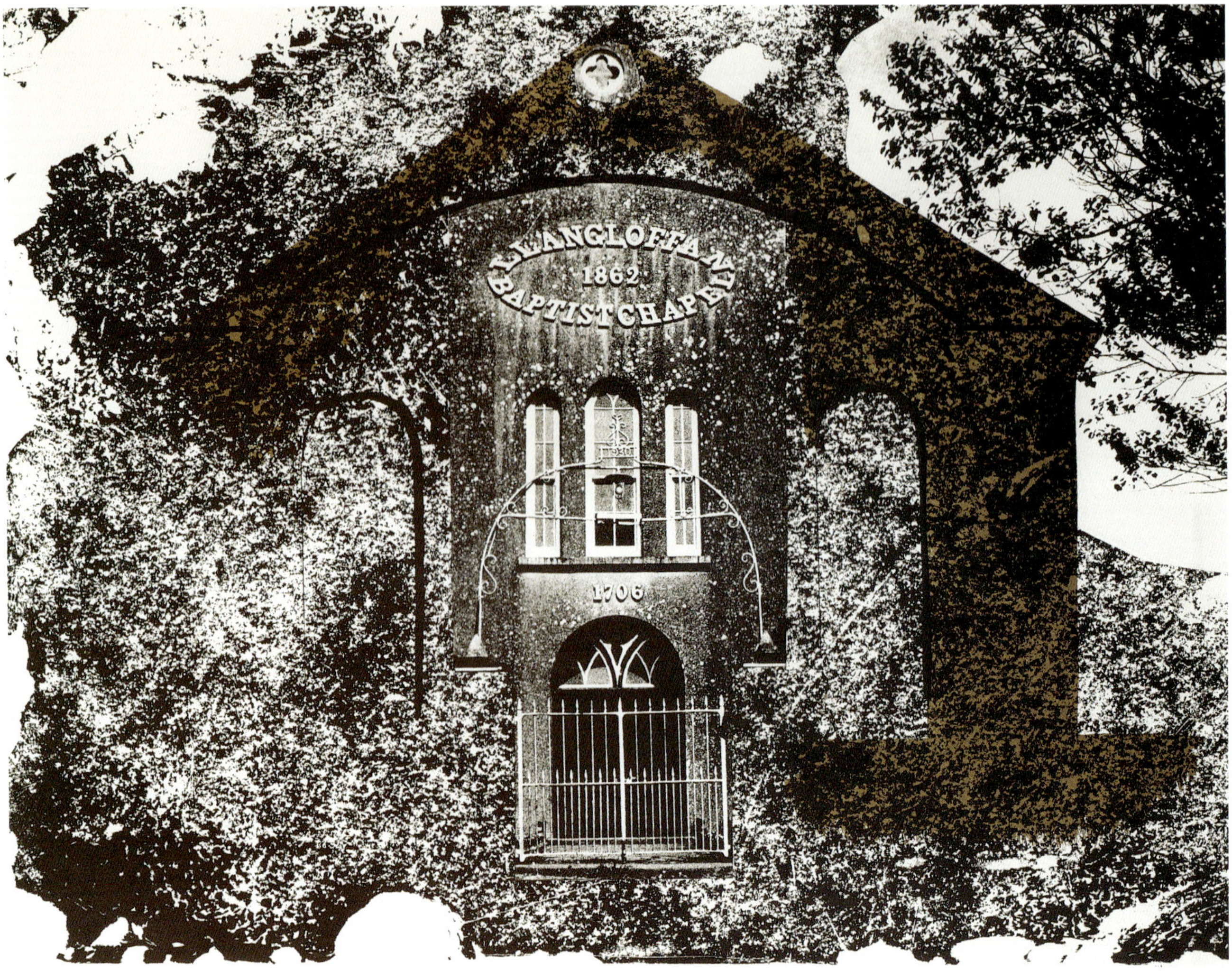

John Piper, *Llangloffan Chapel: Retrospect of Churches*, photolithography and hand drawn lithography combined, 1964.

contact was sustained, often with the crucial help of his wife Myfanwy, herself an art critic who would later become Britten's librettist. A special paper with John's signature as the watermark was handmade by Barcham Green at Tovil in Kent. My hope was that its surface could cope with all the various kinds of lithography expected of it. In the event it performed very satisfactorily on all levels; Remi Green, who took responsibility for making it, had achieved a fine printmaking paper that would subsequently be used by many other artists.

Lithographically, John's chosen images began in a variety of ways. Some were drawn directly onto stone or grained zinc; others began life as works on transfer paper (made in the Curwen Studio); whilst others at a later stage involved grained tracing film – often using collage and frottage work where John thought it appropriate. By choice, the printing was done entirely directly by hand or sometimes by the offset method, if the composition demanded it. We had acquired an offset proving press from the photo-process department of the Curwen Press, known as Vinsent Photo Litho. The offset method of printing was proving popular with many artists, many of whom were now drawing on grained aluminium, partly because of its portability. John divided his time between working at his home at Fawley Bottom Farmhouse and printmaking in the Curwen Studio, where he felt equally at home.

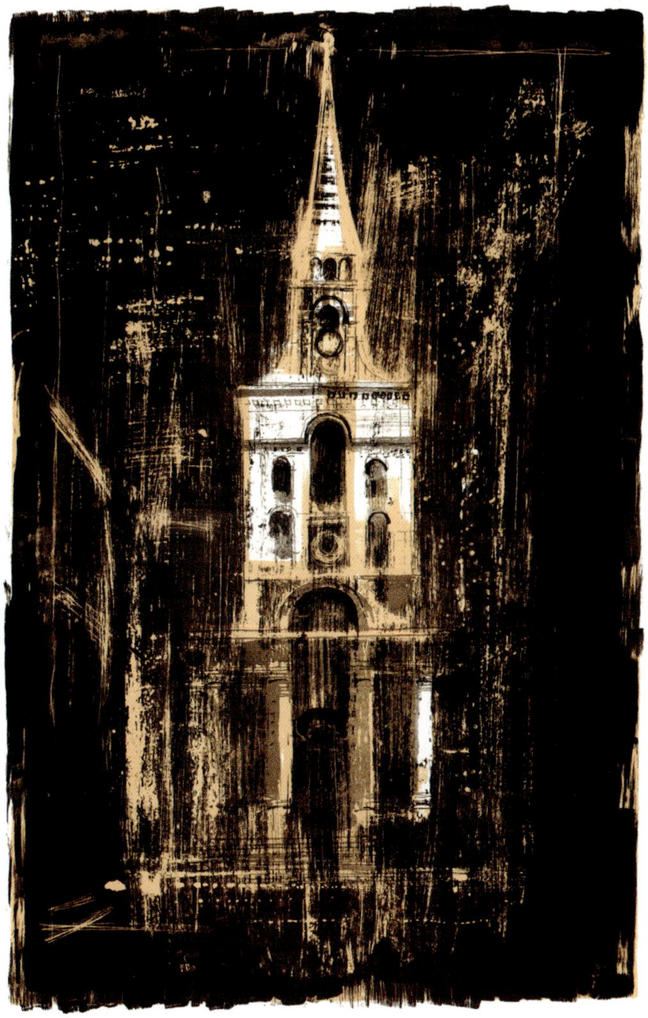

John Piper, *Spitalfields Church: Retrospect of Churches*, 1964.

In printmaking workshops a subtle balance has to be found to make artists feel at ease in their surroundings, retaining the availability of materials such as lighting or drawing tables for individual needs, but, importantly, making sure that help is at hand whenever needed. John liked to have a corner of the studio in which to keep his materials, so that he could work undisturbed on two or three of the prints at the same time – it was a very practical solution. He brought a variety of sketchbooks, watercolours and photographic references to work with; we decided from the outset that the vitality of fresh creative qualities educed from all the different approaches that John planned to use should sustain each of the different images. In short, his interpretation of each subject should be as much as possible through lithographic innovation.

There were many aspects to be considered – for example, the initial suitability of each subject and the lithographic interpretation that John wanted to explore with each one. There were also issues with the number of colours that he felt appropriate for each print, which affected the economics of the project as a whole. The publisher in charge of the project for Malborough Fine Art was very particular about this. It was the largest single project the Curwen Studio had tackled with John Piper – it included 30 separate large images representing different aspects of lithography including one in which we used photography for the very first time. Through all the struggles, I think he enjoyed the challenge.

As John neared the end of the project, his interest in photography developed to the extent that he felt able to experiment with architectural images on a broader scale. He had always been a keen photographer, having travelled the countryside with John Betjeman and making use of a camera in their production of the Shell county guides, published by Faber and Faber. The 1960s opened further possibilities for him to use photography in printmaking, which led to an introduction to screenprinting. This medium was to lead him down different paths to the extent that, with John's approval, the images were often printer- rather than artist-led. Such a change lent different characteristics to the prints, and in his later years, by reducing his involvement in such undertakings, he was able commit more time to painting. However, he would retain his enthusiasm for hand-drawn lithographic printmaking, and the adventures to be had on account of its collaborative nature, until the end of his life.

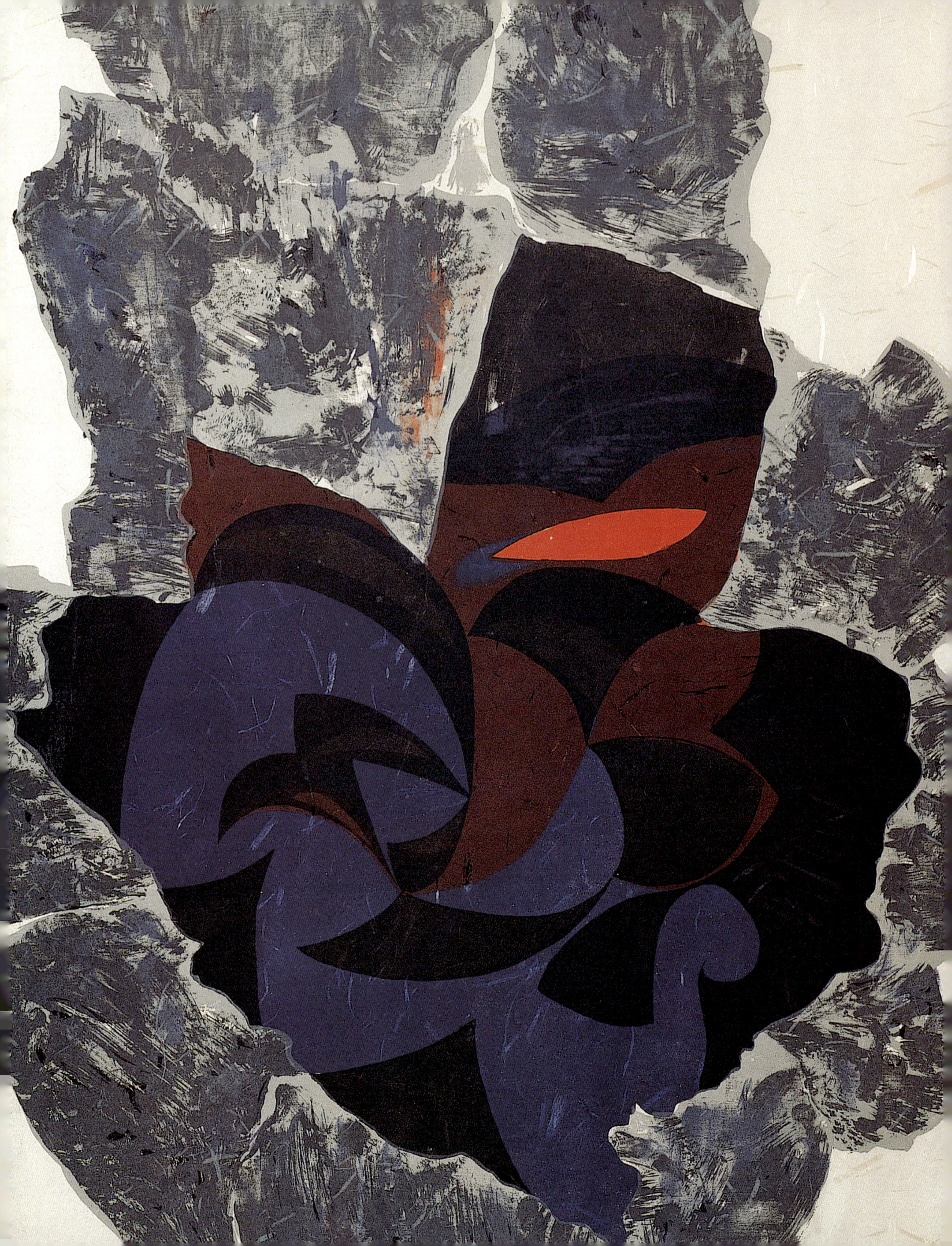

"... the aim was, and still is, always to retain the individuality in each artist's print."

MIDFORD PLACE

In the background, during the course of 1963 and 1964 the Curwen Press had been negotiating a proposed merger with the commercial printing firm of Harleyprint Ltd, with the newly merged company occupying the larger premises of Midford Place, off Tottenham Court in London's West End. Both companies, it was hoped, would benefit from this arrangement at a time when the printing industry was undergoing technical and sociological change. The introduction of photolithographic systems in the commercial world, promising much larger, faster production machines combined with much improved photo-reproduction technologies, had made for much greater competition in the field. To help the two companies in this respect, a merger was thought advisable. This was at a time when the computer-chip technology was set to revolutionise the printing industry, along with every other sphere of life, and the craft of cast-metal printing was becoming an outdated activity. The plan involved the removal to Plaistow of the Harleyprint staff and machinery; whilst the basement part of their premises at Midford Place would be occupied by the new Curwen Studio, which would then have increased space, staff and machine capacity.

Timothy Simon had been exploring the need for the studio's expansion by negotiating with the banks to obtain private funding to find new and larger premises; it would seem that these efforts had been cut short by the proposed Harleyprint merger and the views of the Curwen Press directorate. It was now apparent that they had some faith in the future potential of the studio.

However, there were other aspects to this proposal which needed further consideration. We were being offered a very large offset printing machine which required two experienced printers to operate. It would transform the editioning capacity of the studio but would mean, on the other hand, the introduction of union practice into our workshop. Robert Simon, who explained the various ramifications of the move to Peter and me, felt it to be the future direction of the studio – an opportunity not to be missed despite the change it would mean for the way we worked. My first responses, like Peter's, were very mixed. It would certainly be better to be located in Central London but I would also have to retrain two Curwen printers – experienced but both advanced in years – to cope with the world of contemporary printmaking. How well would they integrate with the other studio staff? How well would their union regulations fit with the concept of collaborative printmaking as we had developed it in the studio?

My own personal feeling was that despite the longer train journey to Central London, the move to Midford Place would have distinct advantages. It would be a much more convenient location for dealing with artists, galleries and publishers, whilst the increased space,

Left: Ceri Richards, *Poisson D'Or*, lithograph, 1959

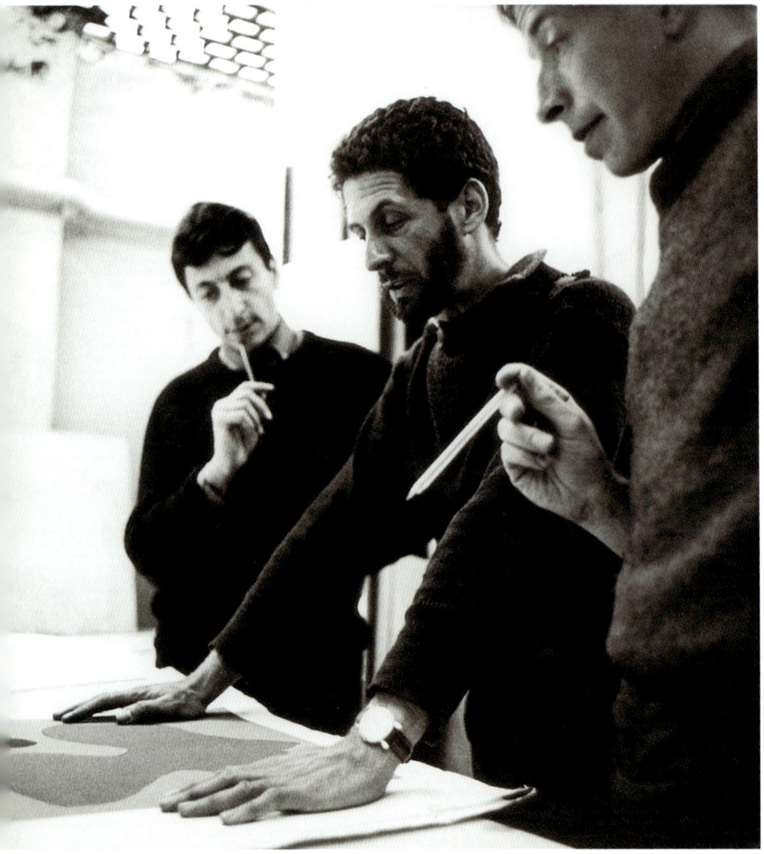

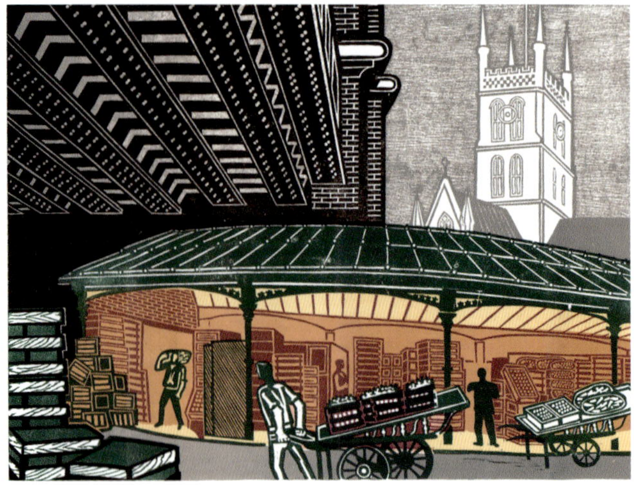

Above: Edward Bawden, *Borough Market*, lithograph, 1967.

Left: Peter Baer (far left), Philip Sutton (center), Stanley Jones, Curwen Press, 1966.

machinery and staff would provide improved and much-needed facilities. I could help my students at the Slade in Gower Street by showing them the studio at work and by offering the possibility of meeting the artists who used it. These matters remained under discussion at the Curwen Press in 1963–4 but for us in the studio what remained most important was the work we were doing for John Piper and Henry Moore.

In the evenings and at weekends I continued to develop my own work for galleries and publishers and became a prize winner in the annual Graven Image show – which helped Jenny and myself to finally build a studio next to the cottage. Then, suddenly, Timothy Simon was taken into hospital for a heart operation and consequently had to retire from his involvement with Curwen, including the studio. He subsequently joined the publishing firm of Duckworth, but throughout his remaining years, until his death in 1970, he was a constantly interested friend and supporter of our work.

Our senior management was now in the hands of Herbert and Robert Simon, who decided of necessity to move the studio to Midford Place. We were about two thirds of the way through John Piper's *Retrospect* when the move began in earnest; it involved various complexities of planning and rehabilitation, as well as dealings with engineers, electricians and plumbers, etc., and constant site meetings. Somehow we managed to keep the upheaval to a minimum but nevertheless it took at least three months' organisation for us and the equipment to arrive at Midford Place.

How best to describe the subterranean corner of a building which faced Tottenham Court Road and had its entrance in Midford Place is not a simple matter. In the 19th century the site had been occupied by large town houses whose coal storage tunnels still ran under the pavement; the only daylight came from panels of pavement lights, making the two principal rooms dependent on constant artificial light. Entry to the studio was from Midford Place via a sturdy, green-painted door followed by a steep, curved staircase. Apart from a fire exit trapdoor in the pavement and an ancient goods hoist, this was the only means of access. The pavement resonated

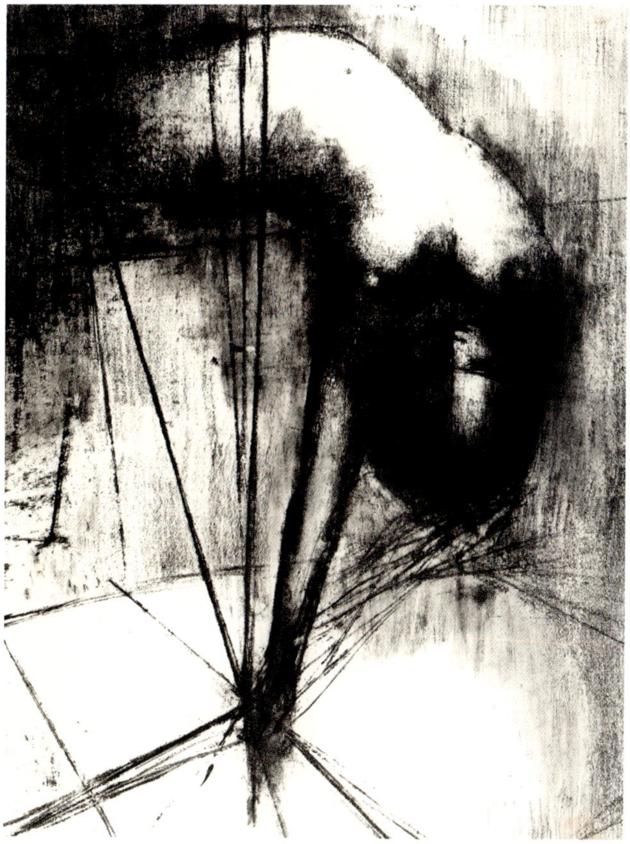

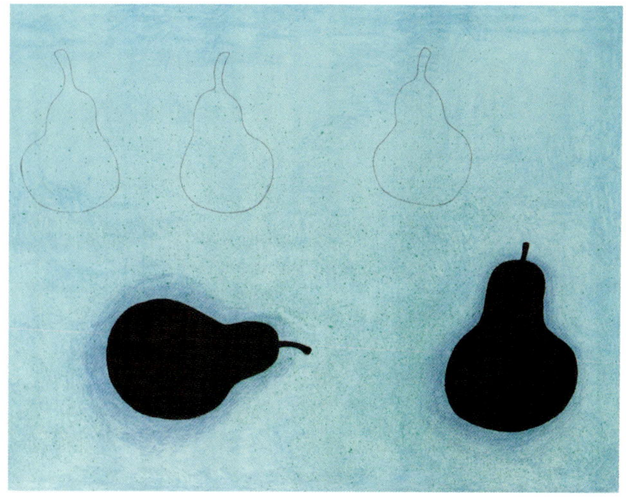

Above: William Scott, *Pears*, lithograph, 1980.

Left: Reg Butler, *Figure in Space*, lithograph, Curwen Studio, 1962–65.

ceaselessly with the constant footfalls of people passing to and fro.

It was decided to place the formidable Ratcliff offset printing machine, whose presence would dominate the studio activity for the next 24 years, in the smaller of the two rooms. It needed considerable coaxing and mechanical modification to cope with the printing required in the studio, having been kept in constant operation since 1927 on a varied diet of book illustration and poster work. Inevitably, Alf Defround, the press's engineer, had to lavish much time and effort on the task of giving it a new lease of life. However, this machine became the crux of the studio's printing activities and was key to producing those fine examples of lithography for which the studio has become known. To manage its intricate operation, the aforementioned lithographic printers from the Curwen Press, Bert Wootton and George Grout, became permanent members of the studio staff , whilst Peter Baer and myself were granted permission to operate in the workshop with them by their union, NATSOPA (the National Society of Operative Printers and Assistants), who would also provide the hand feeders for the machine. The unusual nature of the studio meant the NGA (the National Graphical Association) and NATSOPA unions were very flexible; this was going to be an interesting experiment in relationships. Bert and George's printing skills were unquestionable but they needed guidance in handling the wide variety of artists that would pass through the studio as well as the new lithographic techniques which were being developed. Considerable patience and diplomacy would be required on all sides for this idea to work. It was decided that Robert Simon should oversee the studio's move to Central London, using the firm's existing resources to set up the new venture.

One of the major developments of the new studio was a larger and more diversified staff. This meant more planning and understanding of the developing relationships with artists and publishers and also its parent company, the Curwen Press. Staff from the Press were commercially trained whereas studio staff were already trained and experienced in dealing with artists.

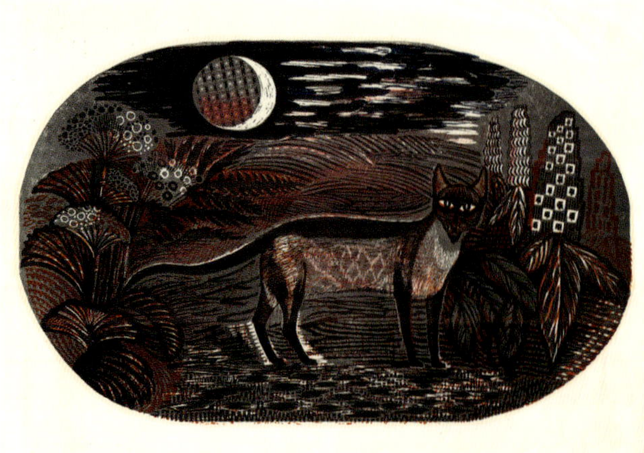
Enid Marx, *Tyger, Tyger*, lithograph, 1975, Curwen Studio.

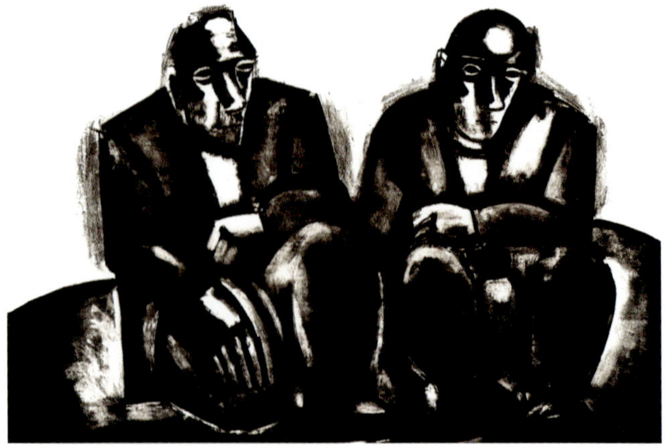
Josef Herman, *Two Miners*, lithograph, 1962, St George's Gallery.

Aside from the two very experienced printers from the Curwen Press, who knew the large Ratcliff machine well, there was also a machine assistant, David Beadle, who had worked for Harleyprint. Peter Baer and I would deal initially with the artists and the creation of their work to proof stage.

Robert Simon was responsible for the company's general running. while Rosemary Simmons, who had been Robert's assistant, now joined the staff. Along with Robert she was inspirational in setting up our other new venture, the Curwen Gallery, in nearby Colville Place in 1965. Originally meant as a display adjunct to the studio's activities, under Rosemary's guidance the gallery soon established its own purpose and identity, while remaining with the studio until 1989, when company ownerships were changed. Rosemary's dedication and practical ability would be central to the structural development of Curwen Studio and Gallery for the next two decades. Not only did she introduce artists to the gallery for one-man shows, she also dealt with the publishers involved in studio work and organised extra events including poetry readings by such notable figures as Pablo Neruda. Much of the studio's day-to-day office administration, including the outside contacts that were so essential to a project of this kind, came under her control. During those formative years she was an effective key figure in the growth and development of the company, and able to cope with all kinds of difficult people and situations. In this respect she was to earn the esteem of many colleagues, even the obdurate Felix Man and the often recalcitrant American dealer Edmund Newman.

The progress made in the studio's first five years in Tottenham Court Road demonstrated its potential to the parent company in this growing world of the artist's limited-edition print. By establishing a reputation for the quality of the lithography, which it produced for a wide variety of artists and by all manner of means, the aim was, and still is, always to retain the individuality in each artist's print. This means that the work is primarily artist-led and often difficult to organise economically from a production point of view because the artist is involved throughout the production process but worth the final result. It always requires considerable dedication and patience on everyone's part.

Despite the absence of funding from Arts Council sources, we were able gradually to stabilise the studio's finances, and in good years we gave some of the profit to the parent company. Financial considerations have always remained a delicate aspect of the studio's modus operandi, requiring careful monitoring every year. As with any longstanding business, they are part of the reason why its policies have needed reinvention from time to time as circumstances dictate.

By 1968, Robert Simon had decided to pursue his own interests outside the studio and to withdraw

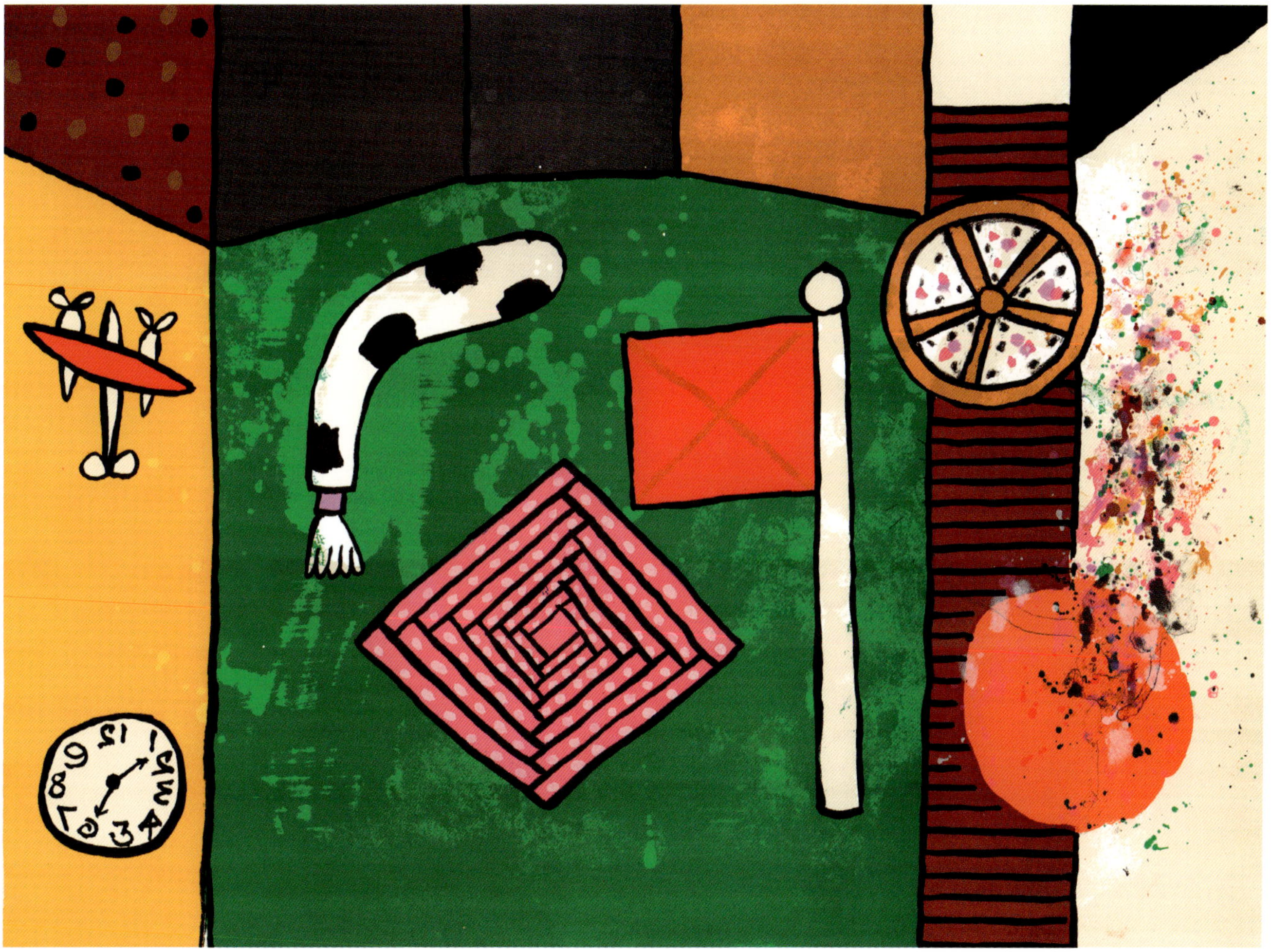

Alan Davie, trial proof, lithograph, 1970. National Gallery, Edinburgh.

from managerial work at the Curwen. He had played a pivotal role in transferring the studio to Midford Place and introducing Ossip Zadkine, Oliffe Richmond and the Hungarian artist Mirea to the studio; his last studio project had been to work with Harold Cohen and myself on a series of prints in which Harold had evolved images of complex photographically originated overlays – causing the printers much pondering and frustration. Robert was still to keep his advisory role with the studio and press but the day-to-day running of the growing studio was now left to Rosemary Simmons and myself, with Herbert Simon in overall control. One of the first steps we took was to reduce the top-heavy size of the board of Curwen Prints, making it more manageable and rational. In the days when my wife and I lived in Clatterford End we had become very friendly with Herbert Simon and his wife Molly, then residing at the White House in Ongar. Our friendship had grown over the years, for he had a genuine enthusiasm for the studio and its aims.

With his brother Oliver he had helped to steer the Curwen Press's fortunes through the thirties and forties, and had achieved a distinguished reputation amongst his fellow printers, having an eye for typographical design and its practical production. Within the works at Plaistow, Herbert was highly respected by the staff, who received praise where it was due but also fierce criticism if the need arose. His arrival in the studio, while meaning a new departure for him, was not entirely unforeseeable, since many of friendships that he had built up in

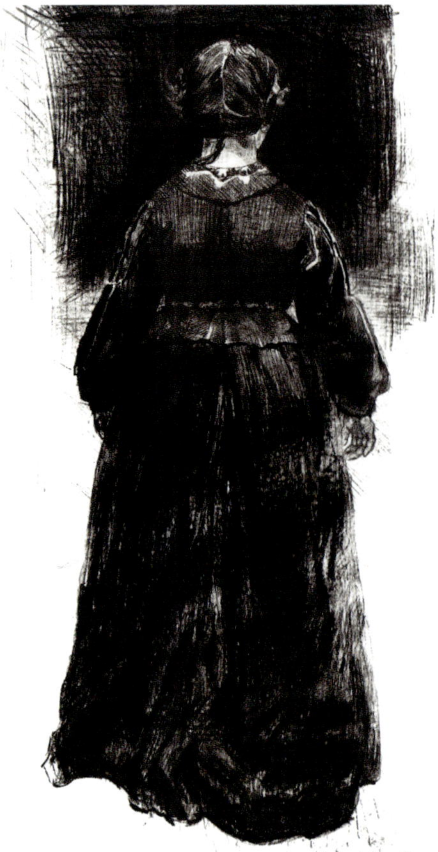

Paula Rego, *Jane Eyre*, lithograph, 2003.

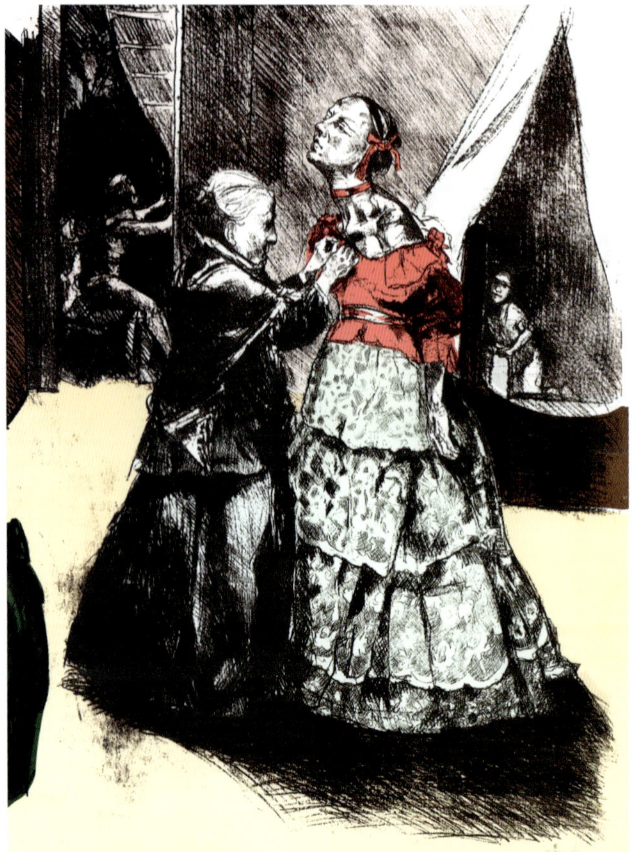

Paula Rego, *Jane Eyre*, lithograph, 2003.

Right: Man Ray, *Untitled (III)*, lithograph and screenprint, 1969.

the art world through the 1930s and '40s – with Marcus Brumwell and Barbara Hepworth, for instance – would become important at a later date. He and I had a rapport which sustained us until his death in 1970. As a family we occasionally stayed in the White House whilst Herbert and Molly took their holiday, usually at Walberswick. It was fascinating for the children to enjoy the rambling house with its green, secluded light and bosky garden, quietly hidden behind the high street in Ongar. His position in the company aided the relationship between the studio and the Curwen Press and its staff, now under the direction of Basil Harley, which manifested in all kinds of mutual practical cooperation on a number of printing projects.

It was Herbert who helped promote the studio's interests among the Curwen Press board, some of whose members were not always sympathetic to our intentions. This situation was to continue until the studio and gallery were acquired by John Hutchings, a director of the Curwen Press, in 1982. At this point I think it would be fair to say that there were different attitudes within the company towards the public image of the Curwen Press, a debate which took into account both its illustrious past and the type of image it ought to convey in the present day and in the future. Crucially, it involved considerations of finance for new machinery and staff, space for production, and the preservation of craft ideals in a rapidly developing and increasingly computerised technological world of modern printing.

In the studio, we already had an established body of publishers who used us for their own purposes. We had developed a reputation in Europe as specialists in lithographic printmaking but our own published output remained modest. Editions Alecto was by contrast a much larger company with a considerable staff of printers, administrators and salespeople. As well as the United

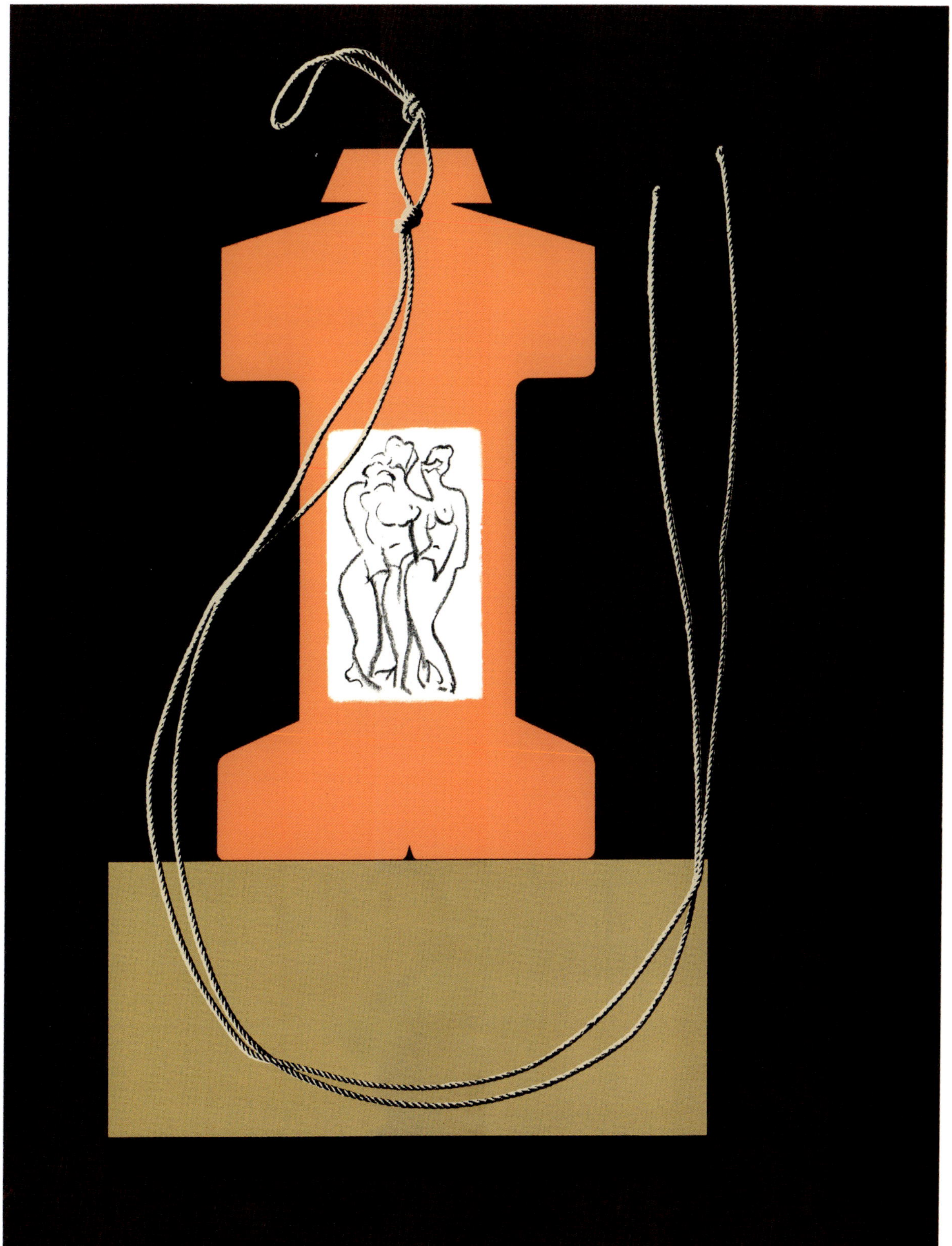

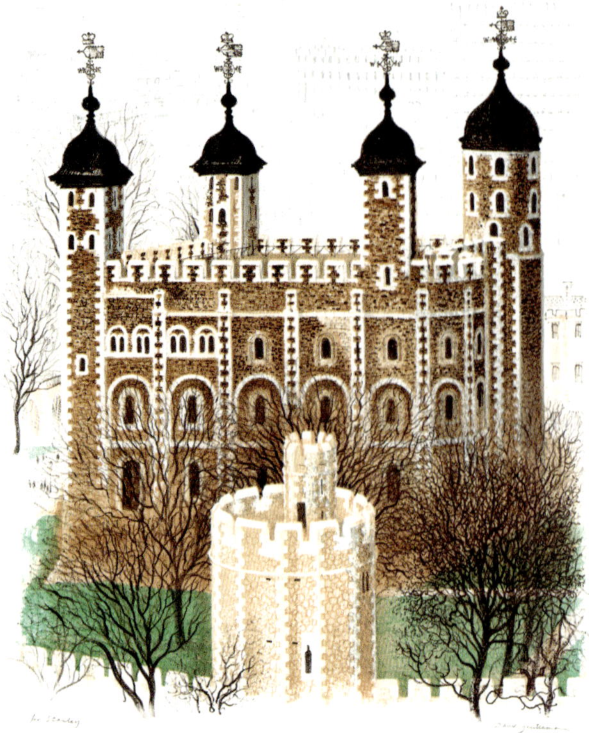

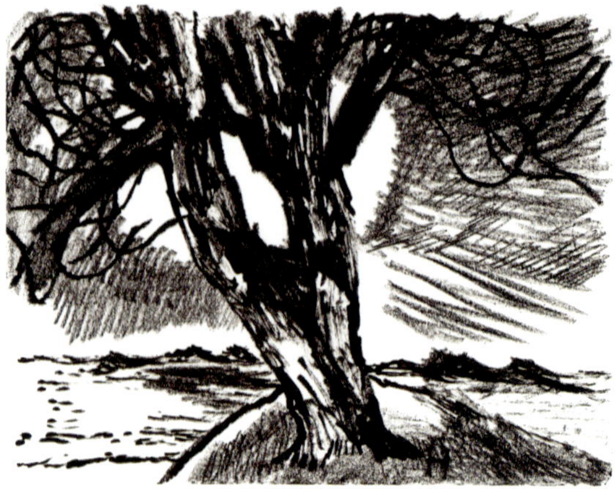

Above: Albert Houthuesen, lithograph

Left: David Gentleman, *Tower of London*, lithograph, 1980.

Below: David Gentleman, *Westminster School*, lithograph, 1992.

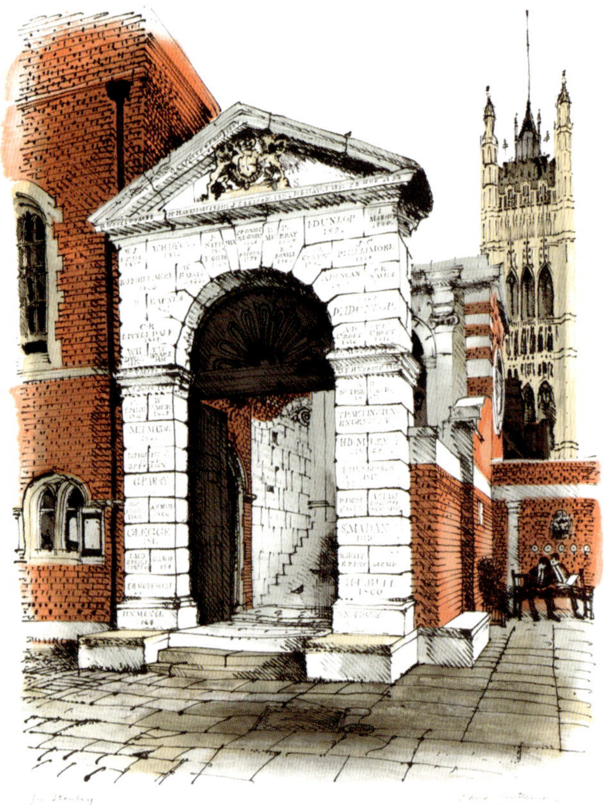

Kingdom, it was active in Europe and America, where its name became well established in the expanding artist's-print world. Eric Ayers and Mark Glazebrook contributed much to that company but it was Joe Studholme who guided its operations until 1981, when it finally closed its doors. Its founder, Paul Cornwall-Jones had left in 1968 to form Petersburg Press as a separate entity. Curwen Studio provided lithographic facilities for both of these companies and it is true to say that many artists worked for both Alecto and Curwen at different times – Alan Davie, Allen Jones and myself, for example.

In the case of Petersburg Press, Henry Moore had asked me to proof some of his images for a book related to Auden's poems. It was an opportunity to use a new method of lithographic printing which I had been developing with Leslie Lawson, a printing chemist from the Algraphy company. Known as 'screenless' or 'continuous tone' lithography, I was keenly aware of its potential for artists using both hand-drawn imagery and photographic source material. John Piper and Henry Moore had both used the method for work of various kinds. However, much care had to be taken over the making of the images on these plates and the UV light control and the press work had to be specially treated.

For these reasons, I asked Paul Cornwall-Jones if we could print the images in our studio, but he and Vera Russell (a co-publisher) had made arrangements for the work to be done in Switzerland and so turned down my request. The proofs and the plates were duly packed off to the printers in Switzerland, and we turned our attention to other work. A few weeks later, I received a frantic telephone call from Paul, in Switzerland, saying that the printers did not know how to handle these plates. Would I mind receiving them back for printing, to help complete the book? I felt that the point had been made, and that, for Henry Moore's sake, no more time should be wasted.

Continuous-tone printing

Perhaps a small explanation of continuous-tone printing is due here. In the mid-1960s the normal commercial method for most work involving photography was the deep-etch process on aluminium plate. The 3M company suggested to me that their research with photopolymers might be of use to artists, as these trials had produced a coated plate which would be receptive to an artist's drawings if these were made with black pigmentation on grained film; the plate would also replicate photo imagery if necessary. The translucent film would be an ideal replacement for transfer paper and in addition the artist could use all kinds of materials – graphite drawing pencils or Indian-ink washes, for instance – that did not contain grease (grease was a prerequisite for traditional lithographic materials). The photopolymer coating also provided great stability for editioning and although particular viscosities of ink were required it was an ideal system for our offset printing machines.

The only drawbacks for me were the chemicals involved, which seemed to produce fumes from the amyl acetate they contained. Everyone in the studio rightly complained about these, so, beginning in 1968, I began to experiment at weekends in one of the cellars that went under Tottenham Court Road, which served as a darkroom for this purpose. The results were quite encouraging even though the only UV light source (required to develop the coating on the plates) was an antiquated carbon arc-light system. However, one advantage of our new location proved to be the old storage cellars where much of this equipment could be installed. It was all very primitive and pioneering and the printers were bemused by it all – that is, until Les Lawson appeared, with ideas similar to mine, and we got down to the long business of refinement. The results without the dot-screen interference were quite remarkable; the accuracy and sensitivity of the technique was extraordinary. Of course, all this work had to be done against a studio background of week-to-week activity but I still managed to involve some of my own prints as part of this experimental stage.

From the beginning of the 1970s onwards, continuous-tone lithography became part of the studio's range of expertise at the artists' disposal. Leslie provided better chemistry and photopolymer plates over the course of these early years, while eventually the arc light was dispensed with and a vacuum frame was fitted into the tiny cellar which enabled better results through a tighter contact of film and plate. Temperatures and light units became important for accurate plate making. But for artists the prospect of greater freedom of expression at the drawing stage and the greater stability of images during editioning was very enticing.

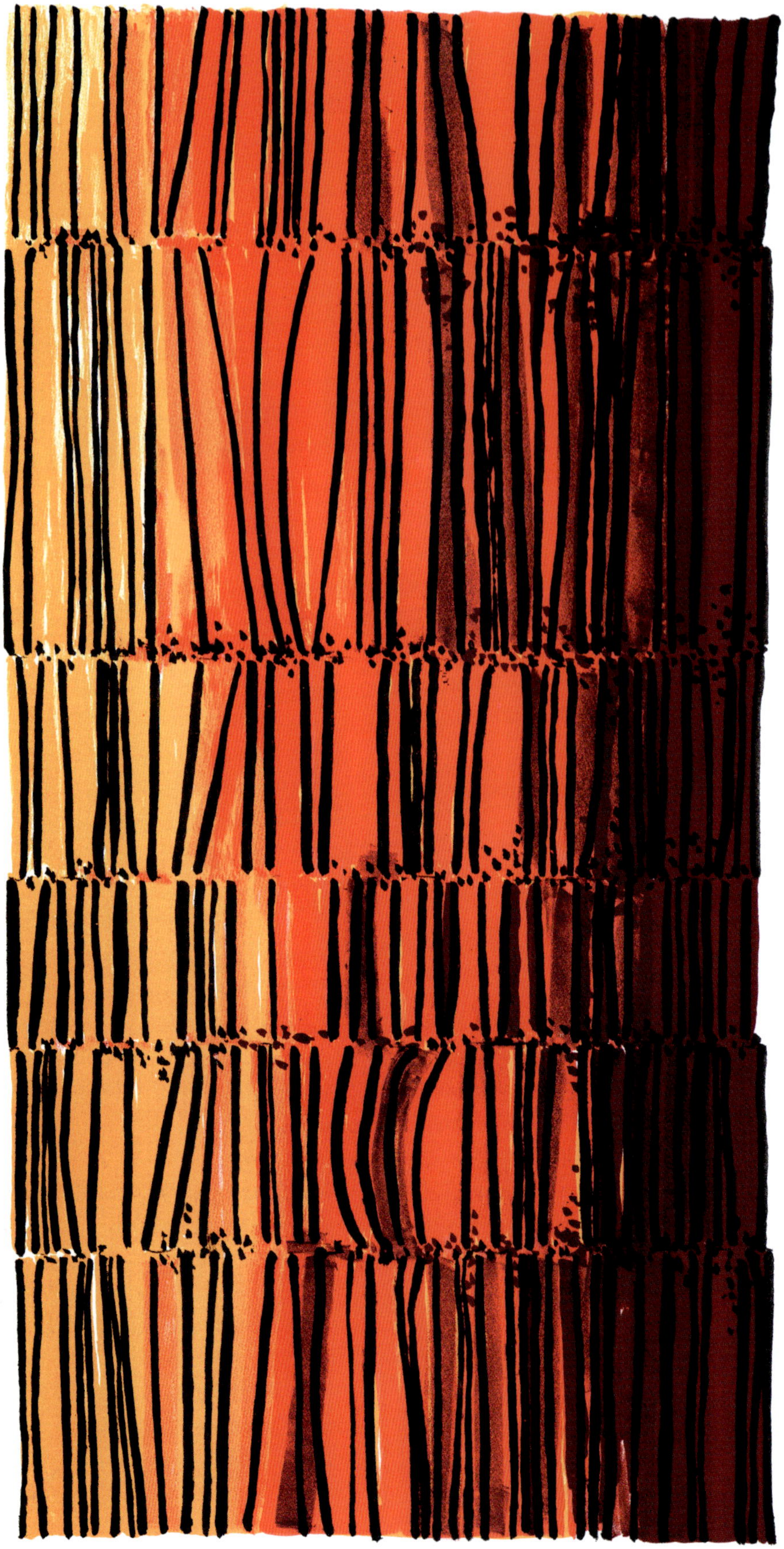

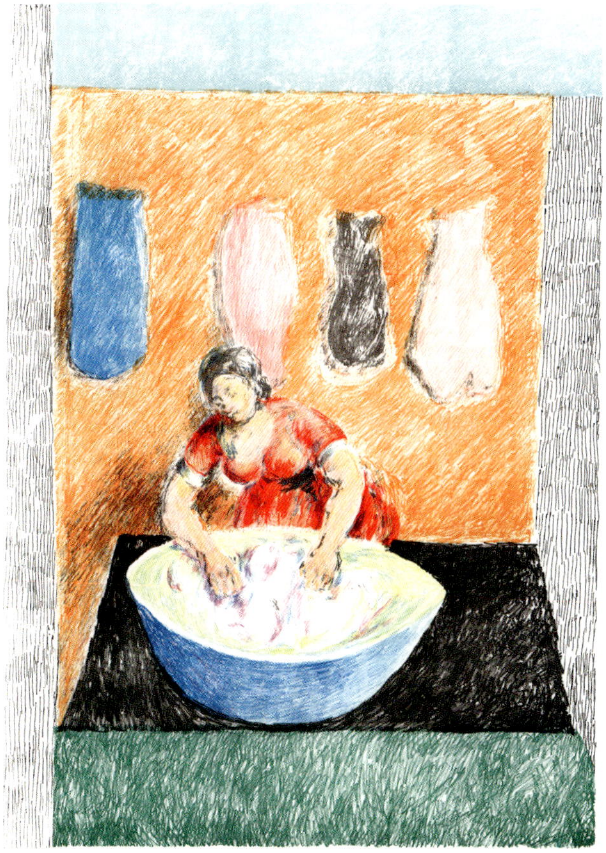

Duncan Grant, *Washer Woman*, lithograph, 1973–4. Observer Art Publication.

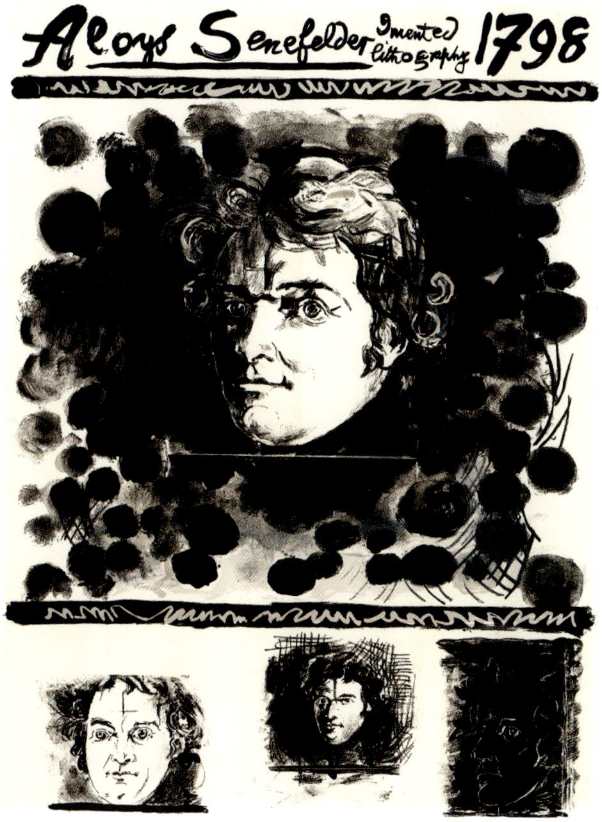

Graham Sutherland, *Portrait of Aloys Senefelder*, lithograph, 1971. Man & Ketterer Publishers.

However, on taking the process to the fine art market in America, Leslie Lawson had a mixed reception, finding much prejudice in any case against the offset printing of artist's original works, but also that, for many printers, to use his special plates would be 'too commercial'. It took a number of years before such methods became acceptable in the US, even though in the UK John Piper and particularly Henry Moore were already warming to this new methodology, with its promise of making new drawing materials available to produce remarkable results.

Left: Robert Adams, *Screen Form*, lithograph, 1973. Penwith Galleries.

Barbara Hepworth

Herbert Simon was keen that we should initiate some of our own publishing as well as providing prints for other for companies. With the help of a mutual friend, Marcus Brumwell, an influential figure in the St Ives art world, contact was made with Barbara Hepworth and a proposal put to her for a group of prints. Initially, Rosemary Simmons was put in charge of the venture, and dates were arranged for the spring of 1968; I was invited to come with my family to spend time working on the project with Barbara at Trewyn Studio. She and I decided to do the work in her studio, which she had made ready for a very concentrated effort, aiming to

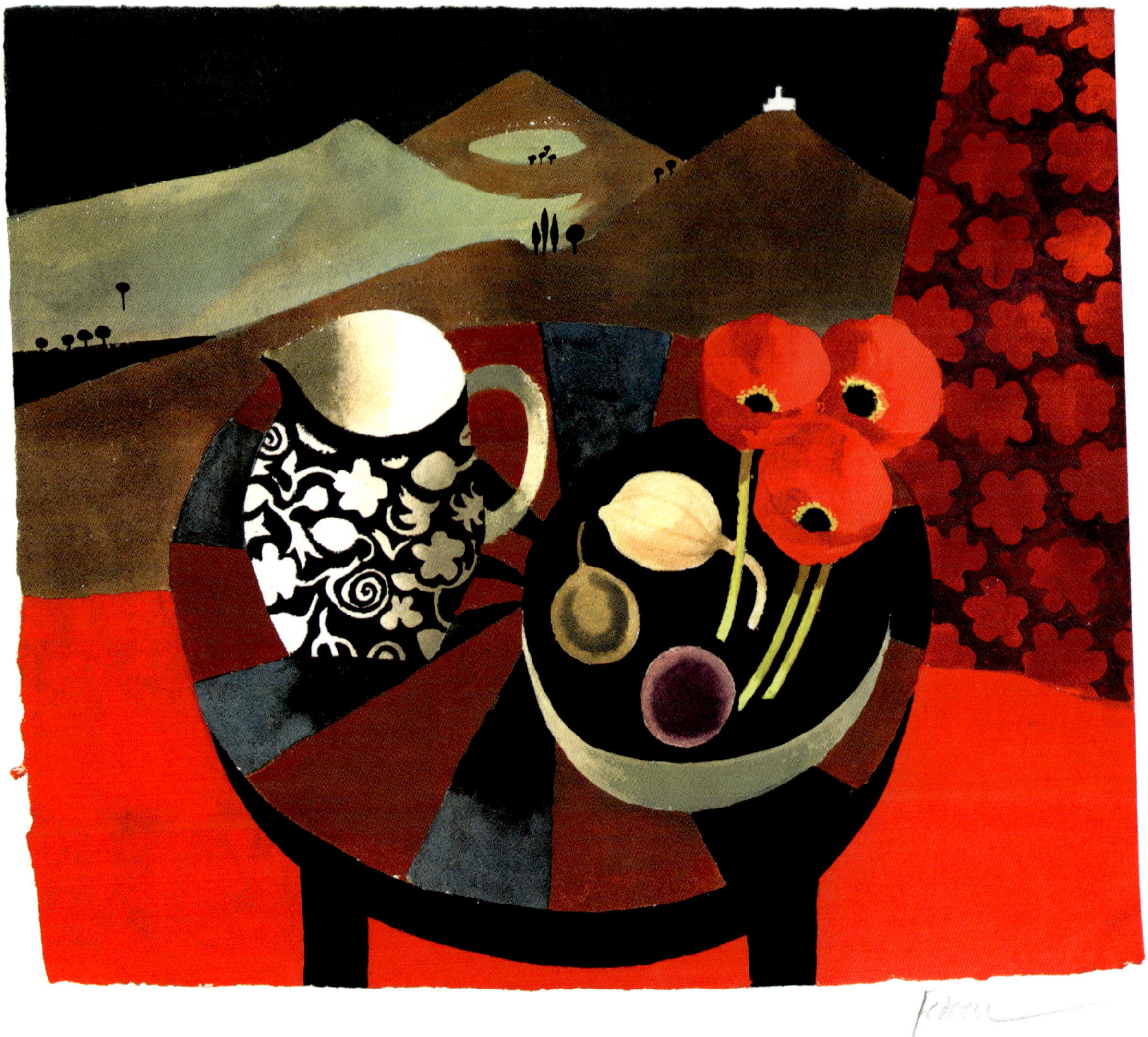

Mary Fedden, *Poppies*, lithograph, 2003.

produce about ten separate works for exhibition at the Curwen Gallery in the autumn. Jenny and the children enjoyed their own adventures and explorations during the day, with the help of Miss Moir, Barbara's secretary.

Each day we discussed and experimented with the different ideas using drafting film and grained zinc plate. At the drawing stage, much excitement came from creating complex working textures, which formed various backgrounds to Barbara's rigid formal structures. These possibilities intrigued her a great deal and she began to discover an unexplored world of space and texture. She became completely absorbed by the intricacies of colour separation; the daily carving was left to assistants – Denis Mitchell, for instance – and everyone was aware of her resentment at any interruption.

Whilst struggling with these poetically based ideas she would rise very early in the morning – around 2 or 3am – and derive inspiration from the atmosphere and organic forms in her garden – *Cool Moon* and *Sun and Marble* are examples of such formed images. The new opportunities offered by the medium drove her enthusiasm and the ideas rapidly began to emerge. At one stage,

I drove across to Falmouth College of Art to spend a day colour-proofing some plates she was anxious to see. This helped a lot, giving her a closer idea of what the final versions would look like. Gradually, the studio became submerged with works in progress, as we struggled to complete the twelve ideas in time for the journey back to London. On the final evening there was a fierce gale blowing, strong enough to scatter papers and films about the room; fortunately, none were damaged, or so I thought. We left Barbara full of anticipation and excitement about the prospect of these twelve lithographs.

Back in London, proofing the work using the plates and films had to begin immediately, with forms to be made for the embossed images. These prints were something of a metaphysical jigsaw to assemble correctly, despite the copious notes. However, Barbara was well pleased with the results and the new form of expression that she had discovered. One mystery, however, remained – the blue background of the print *Porthmeor*. Everything had been very carefully prepared, but this drawing had added textures not drawn by the artist. I decided to phone Barbara and explain what had emerged. There was no doubt that the finished print included unpremeditated qualities – but what would Barbara say? I sent her the proof for comment. In the meantime, thinking back, I realised what had caused the problem: it must have been sea spray blown in by the gale through the open studio window. Salt has an extraordinary effect on lithographic zinc plate, and is normally invisible until printed up. There could be no other explanation. A few days later she phoned to express her surprise and pleasure at the result – particularly the blue background of *Porthmeor*, which she confided in me had been achieved by using 'an ivory-handled spatula'. Of course, what else!

With Barbara's cooperation Rosemary Simmons successfully organised the publication of the editions from the gallery; they stimulated her enthusiasm to the degree that she was very keen to do another group as soon as time permitted. However, to complicate matters, other dealers were eager for her to produce work for them. She had recently moved from Gimpel Fils to Marlborough Fine Art,which was keen to promote their New London Gallery for prints. Unfazed by pressure from Harry Fischer at Marlborough, Barbara stuck to her agreements with Curwen and in 1971 we produced a second series, which gave her further satisfaction in advancing her ideas in lithography.

Henry Moore

As Herbert Simon continued to build and strengthen the activities of the studio in what was a very competitive publishing environment, Henry Moore was again invited to produce work with the studio. The work he had produced for Timothy Simon and Felix Man was a pioneering experience for the sculptor, who had become very conscious of the potential of printmaking. However, it transpired that through an arrangement with his gallery concerning his sculpture, he had consented to have his printed images made in Switzerland as part of a 'gentleman's agreement'. However, in 1968, due to quarrels amongst the principals involved this whole structure fell apart and Henry decided to become his own publisher, thus freeing him from the obligation to travel abroad, and allowing him to follow his own inclinations unhindered.

David Mitchinson, an ever-present figure in the day-to-day activities of the Moore studios, has related, in his own account of Moore's printmaking development, the rivalries and intrigues that occurred amongst the dealers and publishers. It would be true to say that Henry himself, though conscious of it as a background state of affairs, never allowed such matters to interfere with the gradual development of ideas and their realisation in print form. Perhaps the Curwen Studio was fortunate in that we enjoyed a lasting collaboration with Moore for some 28 years, as he developed his ideas in lithographic form.

Speaking first to Mrs Tinsley, Henry Moore's secretary and David Mitchinson (Moore's personal assistant) in the office, Rosemary Simmons and I made a number of monthly journeys to Much Hadham with proofs and variations. He was always excited to undo the parcels we brought and view the results for the first time. At a later stage, when the Gildmore studio was converted purely to accommodate his interest in printmaking, it became habitual to spread the new proofs on the walls and floor so as to discuss possibilities for editioning until decisions had been made. A break was taken at midday, when we would adjourn with David to the Hoops Inn. Here we would often meet other people – dealers' assistants, publishers, critics, etc. – involved with Henry's life at the time. Sometimes visitors were allowed briefly into Gildmore to see the work but Henry was not averse to looking rather pointedly at his wristwatch if someone was overstaying their welcome. He did not much care for interruptions where work was at stake. Publishers were perhaps treated rather differently because they were often involved with the work. One particular French lady, Madame Fifi l'Eall, with whom we did considerable amounts of printing, always stayed at the Ritz in London and arrived at Hoglands (Henry's home) laden with bouquets and sumptuous gifts of all kinds. Needless to say she demanded full attention at all times to the projects with which she wished Henry to co-operate; but we enjoyed the Parisian theatricality of her behaviour, Moore included.

The enduring relationship we had with Henry Moore had distinct advantages for both artist and studio. He had to hand all the facilities and skills that the workshop could offer, and latterly its new continuous-tone systems of lithography, which gave artists a new freedom and accuracy of image making, with the hazards of using incorrect drawing materials on transfer paper a thing of the past. More important still were the long discussions possible about all aspects of the work; even the borders between the image and the edge of the paper were of crucial concern to him. There was always good communication. It was understood that we should keep all the printing plates in store as each edition was completed, for possible future adaptation; the sculptor would refer back to previous prints and sometimes reorganise them as new formal ideas.

As Moore became his own publisher we were often involved in projects with Continental printers – notably Mourlot in Paris, Wolfensberger in Zurich and Il Bisonte in Milan. This helped to make our name familiar with other international publishers. The development of Henry Moore's lithographic work can be traced through the pages of the catalogues devised by David Mitchinson and Swiss publisher and gallery owner Gerald Cramer. They describe an interesting formal journey, not only in terms of etching projects but also in the form of lithographic editions and artist's books spanning largely the years between 1958 and 1984.

During our visits to the Gildmore studio, Henry gave full attention to what the Curwen studio was producing for him; these sessions usually lasted the whole day, with the occasional interruption from his sculpture assistants, John Farnham or Michel Muller. Over the years of collaborative printmaking the images

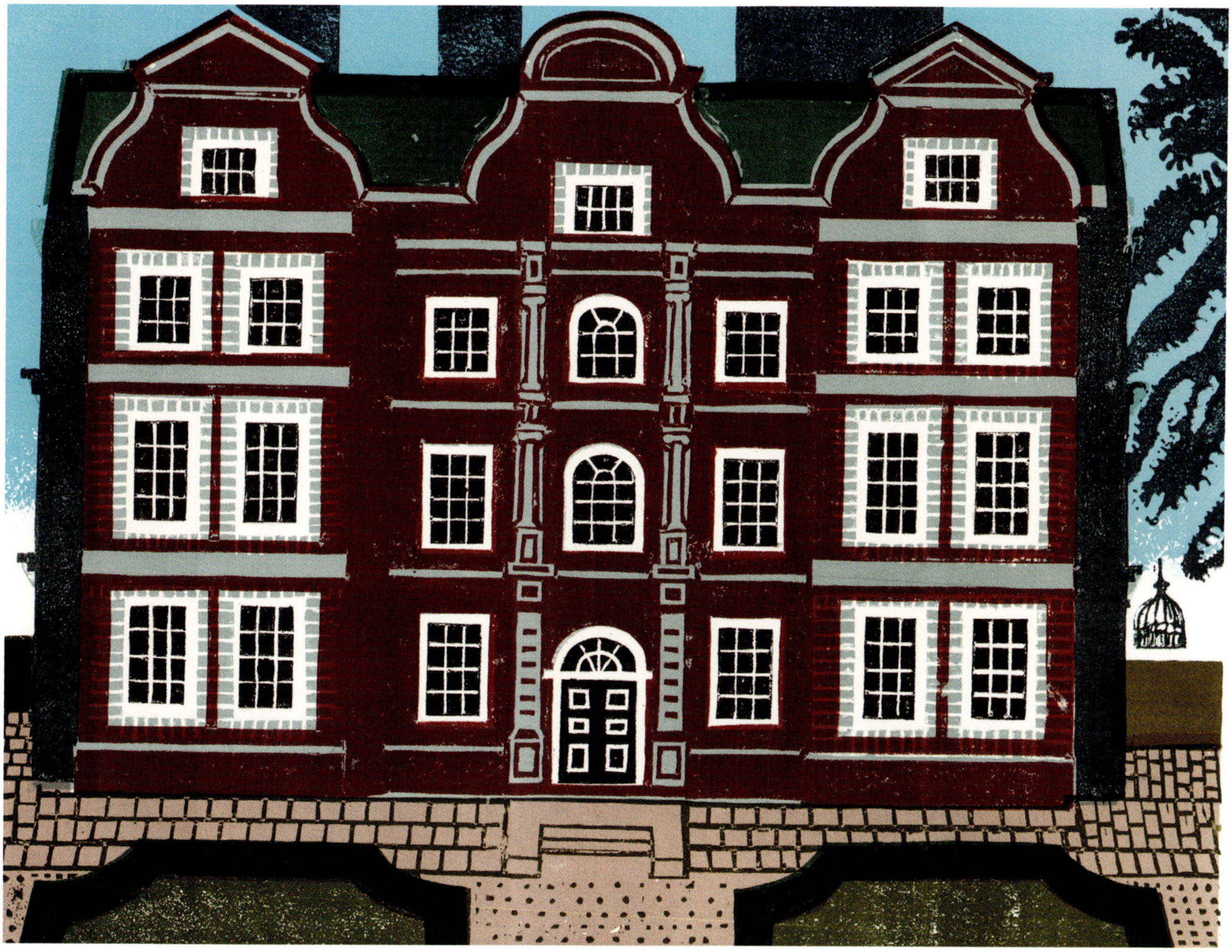

Edward Bawden, *Queen's House Kew*, lithograph, 1988

progressed, as did their method of production – no longer adaptations from preconceived sketchbook material but prints growing out of the proofing process. Moreover, on visits to the Curwen Studio he was not averse to searching under the presses for other artists' images and transforming their failures into his successes. Single lithographic impressions of ideas were often drawn over after many years of being left untouched – there were many such pieces scattered around the Gildmore studio which could be experimented with and transformed into totally different images. Apart from the genuine intrigue of using a medium which gave him new ideas, there was always an element of serendipity in proofing variations from which one copy had to be chosen for the final edition. Sometimes this was a difficult task and a quick decision could not always be made. An infallible solution was to call in Mrs Moore from her gardening occupations, whereupon the problem would usually be solved quite quickly. There were occasions, however, when on a matter of colour preference an edition had to be split and the two different concepts of colour printed in a run of 50 copies each.

It would be true to say that a constant enthusiasm, beginning in 1958, was maintained for this large graphic project; it provided another outlet for expression, separate from his life as a sculptor. It also provided us with a constantly creative activity which made an important contribution to the studio's development. Towards the end, when physical complications made for difficulties, Henry found the prints to be an often useful source of

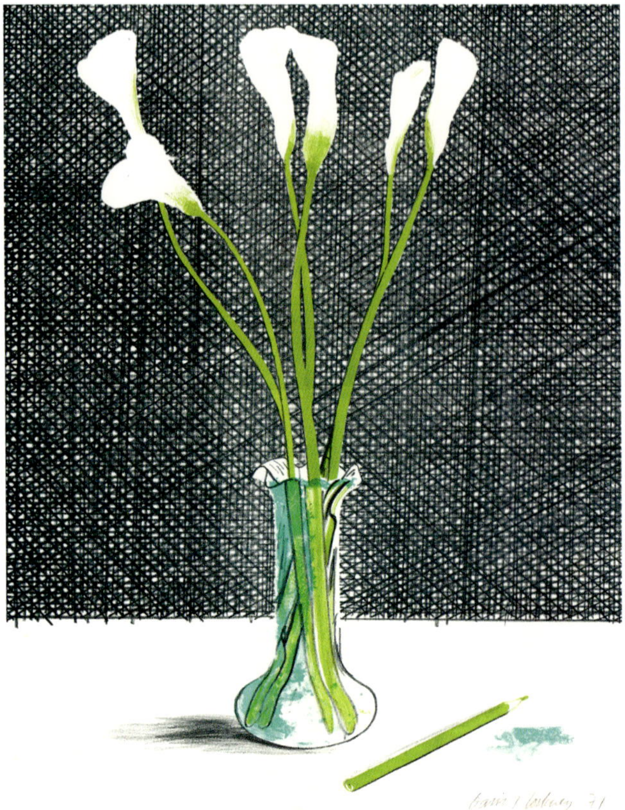

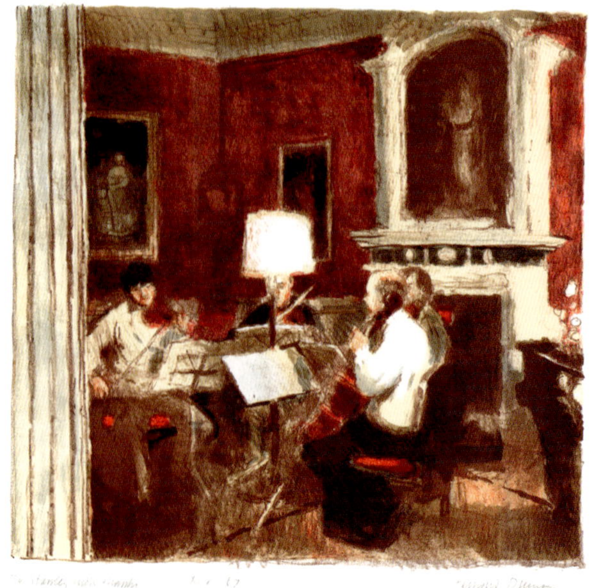

Above: Berard Dunstan, *Gabriali Quartet*, lithograph, 1987. Agnews Publication.

Left: David Hockney, *Lillies*, lithograph, 1971. Man & Ketter Publication.

ideas for sculpture; this was the reverse of how he began on this graphic voyage of discovery. At a later stage, as the amount of work accumulated, it was very important to have administrative help. As well as David, who organised and recorded matters at Much Hadham, Rosemary Simmons meticulously kept the notes and details of the prints and their development year by year. Eventually she was replaced by Jane Hindley, who equally successfully kept tabs on the minutiae of the work with such assurance and interest. Without support of this kind, confusion would have been inevitable for Henry, myself, the printers and everyone else concerned. As it is, the entire prints archive is now available for reference at the Henry Moore Foundation in Much Hadham.

Lithography also captivated other sculptors during these years. Reg Butler first visited the studio in 1962 to produce work for the publisher Ketterer of Munich. Butler had his own press and was constantly obsessed with trying to improve the lithographic process through his own ingenuity, which would often make him difficult to work with. It often meant recourse to unconventional solutions to rescue his ideas and make them printable. *The Figure in Space* (1962–63), commissioned by Wolfgang Ketterer, is a fine example of such work, having been rescued from Butler's homemade transfer paper with the use of a smoothing iron and warm water. Other sculptors, such as Lynn Chadwick and Elisabeth Frink, were more conventional in their printmaking, preferring to use line and wash directly drawn on grained zinc plate. Elisabeth in particular developed a keen interest in portraying animals and figures with a freedom closely allied to her drawings. With delicately drawn washes of lithographic ink she was able to convey character and form in a totally convincing way – subject and medium ideally blending with great economy.

American interest

With the move to Midford Place, the studio had a positive chance to establish itself in the international printmaking world. In addition to the work we did on various projects with European firms such as Mourlot in Paris or Wolfensberger in Zurich, another measure of the studio's development and its growing reputation was that, beginning with Benton Spruance in 1966, barely a year went by without an American printmaker making an appearance to produce work for themselves or a publisher. James Rosenquist was the first artist of the American Pop Art movement to make work in the studio, showing such dedication that he camped on the doorstep from the early hours of the morning to make sure he had time for a full day's work to complete his commission. Because of the growing awareness of the contemporary print in the US and the development of studio facilities there – Gemini G.E.L. in Los Angeles, for instance – in the 1960s and '70s the market for the artist's hand-drawn print significantly expanded. It grew far beyond the high-powered galleries of the major cities but unlike in Europe it did not attempt to involve recognised painters and sculptors.

The Consolidated Fine Art Corporation had as its London representative Edmund Newman, whose main aim was to provide his customers with framed prints of a certain quality. Thus, via mail order, numerous artists from France, Italy and the UK were employed to decorate the walls of American apartments with landscapes and still lifes in a variety of styles and colour combinations. For us and the French printers Mourlot and Desjoubert this service provided a background of work which kept the presses working on a yearly basis, allowing time and manpower to be spent on more complex and important projects. This kind of work also supplied a respite of sorts for the printers, away from the normal rigours of artists and publishers, while also, curiously, honing their skills to cope with future problems.

The printers I inherited from the Curwen Press, Bert Wootton and George Grout, were well versed in working with artists and sensed that the demand for their skills, even in the 1960s, was in danger of disappearing under the looming shadow of photolithography. Their arrival in 1965 along with the large Ratcliff flatbed lithographic printing machine was quite a pioneering step for the studio and brought us onto a level with the French ateliers in Paris. It increased our printing potential but also made it possible for myself and Peter Baer to concentrate on the proofing and image-making side of our work. At a later date, this also applied to the proofing of the work (prior to editioning), when various specialist proofers worked at the studio. The most long-lasting of these was John White who arrived in 1967 and became particularly interested in printing education, and remained working with artists until the studio moved to Chilford Hall in 1989. The printers' membership of the NGA was from the studio's standpoint a mixed blessing, as in theory they were bound to the union's rules and regulations. This meant also that certain wage structures had to be operated, which was similarly the case with the machine assistants, who belonged to NATSOPA. It posed a problem for the studio's finances, which were often difficult to manage, particularly in relation to competition from abroad. However, the innate skills of individual members of staff, plus the guidance they received, helped them to develop their own contributions to the studio's work. As a result, they developed personally in ways which would not have been possible otherwise if they had worked elsewhere. Somehow, against all expectations, the whole improbable equation succeeded in working, with the result that once introduced they tended to remain as studio printers for as long as they could – this was especially true in the case of Bert Wootton, Roy Silvey, John White and Guy Field (all printers and proofers) – applying their skills of lithographic invention and their considerable patience to producing work for artists of the highest possible quality.

In this collaborative atmosphere the reputation of the studio grew by the year. Cooperation at all levels was essential, and we were determined to make it succeed. We did not have many staff problems; occasionally there were temperamental clashes but these were usually solved as a matter of course during the daily running of the studio. The staff came well trained in their craft of printing and took pride and interest in working with artists in this unusual occupation. Today, the same patterns of studio practice are followed at the Curwen Studio at Chilford Hall. One of the important factors over the years has been the relatively small size of the studio in staff numbers – on average between eight and ten at the most throughout most of its life. Good communications are a prerequisite generally but they are particularly important with artists to ensure the progress of their prints through the workshop. Because of the idiosyncratic nature of the work, all kinds of people who supplied us with materials such as paper and inks formed an 'outer ring' of vital personnel; from its early days these sales reps, as they are called, were always keen to visit the studio and see what was being produced. For instance, in the 1970s R.K. Burt and later John Purcell began to supply us with specialist papers. They finally persuaded the St Cuthbert's Mill at Wells in Somerset to produce what began as Curwen Mouldmade, which with the studio's help developed into the internationally known Somerset range of archival papers.

Over the years we have used a variety of the best ink manufacturers from all parts of the world but the firm of A.R. Gibbon has remained for us a constant resource. Since the early days of the studio, when a highly knowledgeable Ben Lyon, Sales Director at A.R. Gibbon, first gave me advice about inks and lightfastness, we have always relied on their ink chemists to solve any technical problems. It has always been important for the studio to keep a check on manufacturers' products of all kinds, particularly chemical products, since without warning changes are often made that could destroy days of work by a given artist. Fortunately, today this is a very rare occurrence.

The early decades of the studio were much concerned with the use of traditional stone and zinc-plate materials; William Scott, Alan Davie and Josef Herman would use both in the same print, while Lynn Chadwick preferred to work on zinc alone. Any photographic image-making had to be provided for us by the Curwen Press and their specialist platemakers, on deep-etch aluminium. The development of continuous-tone lithography, as already described, changed all that.

The 1970s

It took the best part of two decades to establish the studio's position in the thriving world of original print publishing and the economics of running it were often difficult. For instance, we managed to survive periods of recession, even a three-day working week in the early 1970s, which contrasted starkly with years full of progress and activity. In the bleakest times the Curwen Press would have probably benefited from the studio's earning capacity. Apart from the constant work provided by Henry Moore and the publisher Edmund Newman, there were other artists who found lithographic work to be a formative and important part of their activity.

One such was Albert Houthuesen, who around 1972 began to produce work for the Waddington Gallery, a long series of prints that was to give inspiration and encouragement to his final years. He became so involved in the process of lithography that in his final

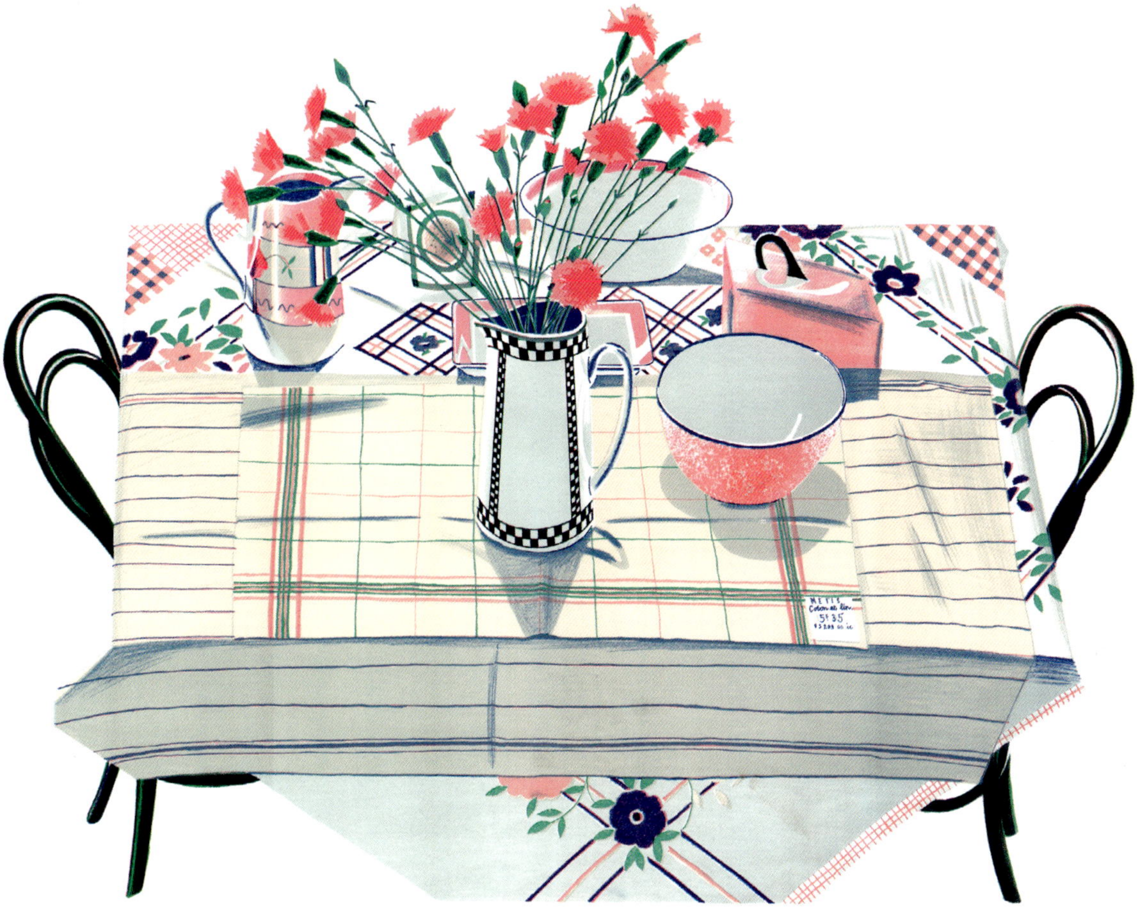

Glynn Boyd Harte, *Still Life*, trial proof, ithograph, 1976.

years it provided him with an essential and constant link through our studio to the outside world. Despite an early life ringed by family tragedy, with support from his wife Katherine, who was totally devoted to Albert and his aspirations, he had succeeded in fulfilling his lifelong intention to be an artist. I went many times to their home on Love Walk in Camberwell to discuss with him his emerging ideas for prints. He became so excited by printmaking possibilities that at the time of his death Richard Nathansen, his dealer, and I still had many more years of work before Albert's editioned output would be complete. The body of images he produced with the studio stands as a remarkable graphic achievement in the portrayal of the human condition.

As the 1970s began to take shape, certain patterns began to emerge in the print publishing world, allowing artists broader means of access to the public. A print biennale supported by the town of Bradford had been initiated and provided a useful indication of what was being published in the UK and abroad. In London, a body of artist-printmakers dissatisfied with lack of public exposure formed the Printmakers' Council – a society whose aim was, through organised exhibitions, to showcase contemporary advances in printmaking of all kinds. We had a basic committee of Michael Rothenstein, Anthony Gross, Bernard Cheese, Birgit Skiöld, Agatha Sorrell and myself – all determined to promote and encourage experimentation in printmaking in what were still pioneering years; revolution had not yet reached the historical Senefelder Club, formed to promote the artist-lithographer in the nineteenth century, or the Royal Society of Etchers and Engravers.

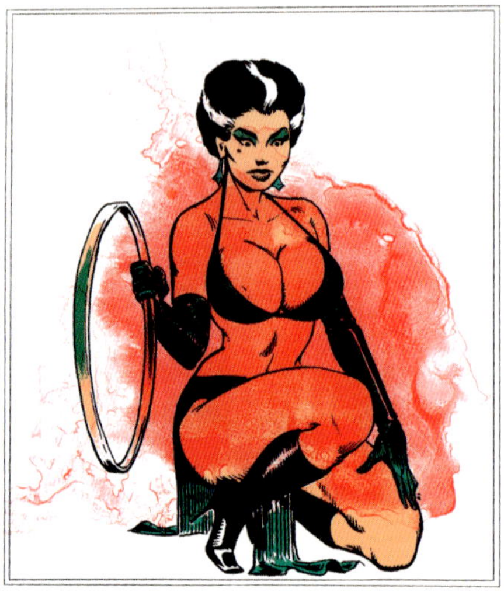

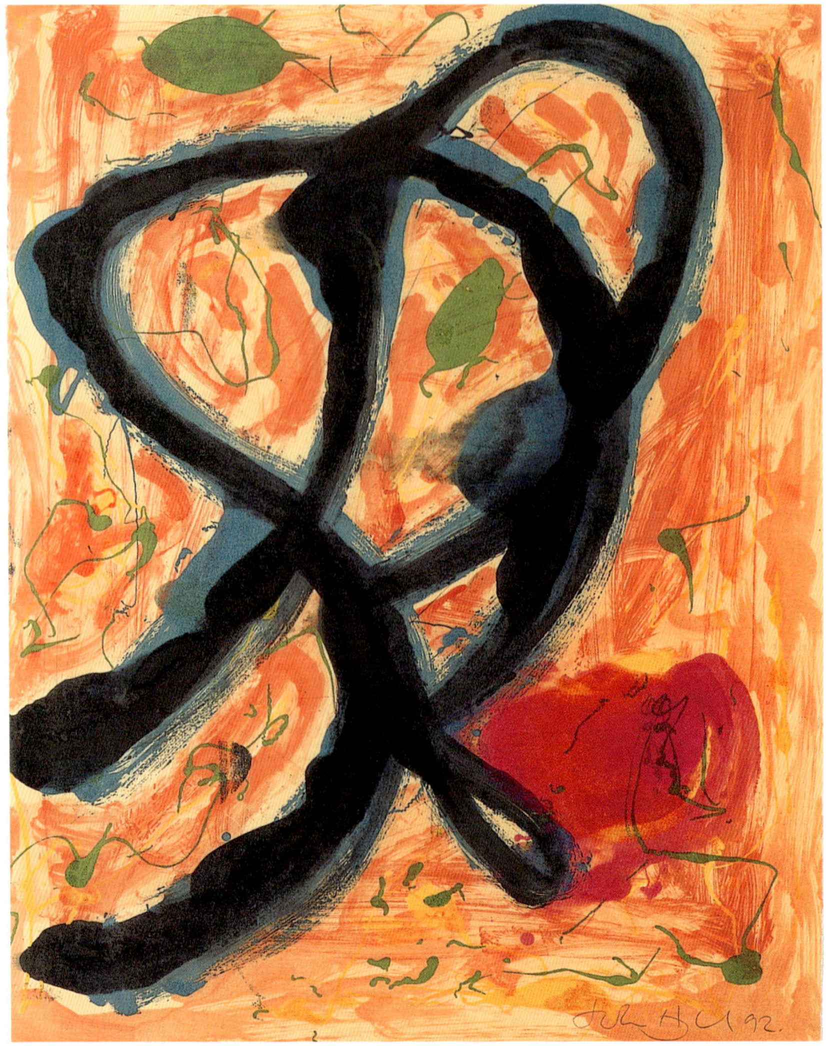

Above: Alan Jones, *Right Lady*, lithograph, 1970. Petersburg Press Publication.

Right: John Hoyland, *Untitled*, monoprint, 1992. CC Editions Publication.

As a studio we were able to produce a wide range of lithographic prints for publishers and artists of many kinds, reflecting the growth of interest from public and private collectors alike. Even the Sunday newspapers indulged their readers in the possibility of acquiring signed original prints in limited edition form, with the added incentive that such works might increase in value. The original print market was rapidly developing its own levels of valuation derived from the example of the New York art market. This widened the entrepreneurial nature of the market in this country. For example, the publishing venture Observer Art, started by the British Sunday newspaper *The Observer*, had discovered that the Bloomsbury painter Duncan Grant was still active in Sussex, and decided to commission him to produce some lithographs for publication. Carol Catley, who was put in charge of this particular project, felt that Duncan had been ignored for too long and was overdue for reassessment by the art world. She felt we should travel to meet the artist at his home, Charleston in Sussex, to discuss matters.

In December 1972, after a bleak journey in an unheated Mini, we arrived at Duncan's house, where he lived alone, surrounded by decorated furniture, paintings and drawings which in the half-light so readily evoked the memory of his Bloomsbury companions. With his gentle manner he made us feel welcome, and over lunch he admitted his total ignorance of printmak-

printmaking while at the same time becoming very interested at the prospect of coming to London to see his drawings set down on plates in the studio. I gathered it was some time since he had visited London and the prospect of seeing Fitzroy Square again added to his enthusiasm. A few weeks later he was brought to the studio by Carol, where he became part of the staff during the making of his three prints. To celebrate the printing of his work we bought him a leather belt for his trousers, which were held up only by a neck tie and had the habit of falling down at unpredictable moments.

One of the most important events of the 1970s was the founding of a contemporary print archive at Tate Britain, then under the directorship of Sir Norman Reid, who was keenly interested in artist's prints. The Curwen Press and the Studio were approached to donate works that would help form the basis of the collection. This donation became known as the 'Curwen Gift' and it was duly exhibited at Tate Britain in April 1977. Pat Gilmour, a writer and authority on British printmaking, produced an admirably researched catalogue - 'Artists at Curwen' - to accompany the exhibition. A similar show from Kelpra Studio, featuring their gift of screenprints, was to follow a year or so later and received similar appreciation. It was now true to say that, at last, artists' printed images had achieved a new status of public appreciation in the UK.

Topographical prints

Apart from what could be described as the experimental printmaking pursued by the *avant-garde* artists, the studio had also encouraged more traditional forms of lithographic work such as topography and the illustration of limited edition books. Bert Wootton and George Grout were already familiar with some of the artists who had built reputations in these areas. John Piper had begun at the studio in Plaistow with two views of Westminster School and then returned to us to make *A Retrospect of Churches* and other later landscape works. His work contributed much to the further development of English topographical painting and printmaking. But there were many other artists who worked with us who, either by choice or at the instigation of their publishers, used topographical subjects as a starting point for their prints.

In 1966 Edward Bawden was commissioned by Herbert Simon to produce a series of *Six London Markets,* which began their lives in the form of linocuts that were first proofed by Edward in his workshop. He and I then transferred the images to lithographic plate ready for editioning, enabling him to make afterthought alterations to colours or textures. He possessed a remarkable sense of craftsmanship and design that was 'fit for purpose', having worked for the Curwen Press since his early days as a student at the Royal College.

Others were to follow. David Gentleman became a practitioner in the studio in the late 1960s, after working for the publisher Edmund Newman. He rapidly became involved with the possibilities of colour lithography, and soon had a steady series of publishers anxious to employ him, not only as a landscape printmaker but also for limited-edition book illustration work. Through constant practice, he has developed his own lithographic drawing characteristics, so that he can choose to operate on either stone or plate, depending on the nature of the subject matter and the intended treatment, aided by his many years' experience in lithographic interpretation. Throughout the following years David was to work for a wide variety of publishers, who commissioned him to interpret into lithography subjects derived from cities such as London and Bath. Other projects involved the atmospheric portrayal of mansions set in the American South or the broad sweep of the East Anglian countryside. Whatever the chosen subject, each print is approached with thorough preparation and consideration of composition, colour and texture; little is left to chance.

Topography also offered a way in to printmaking for Paul Hogarth, who found in the medium an ideal process for developing the watercolour ideas initiated on his worldwide travels. Beginning by drawing on zinc plate in a traditional way, he rapidly adopted the possibilities of transparent grained film, as he found he could draw his colour separations much more accurately by imposing one sheet on another. This was very important to Paul, since he rarely used colour overprinting, relying instead on a unified pen line to hold the composition or the architectural detail together. It proved particularly successful as a means of developing his sketchbook material either for landscape work or book illustration commissions. Working with printmaking, he came to make significant use of the whiteness of the printing paper, both in terms of colour balance and particularly as a key element in pictorial composition.

Other artists were to work in the studio as part of this 'topographical' group. Beginning in the 1970s, Albany Wiseman would go on to produce many editions, commissioned by various publishers, in which the architectural or historic nature of buildings was usually the dominant factor. His skill as a draughtsman had enabled him, with the help of the studio, to mould a particular lithographic style that was well suited to such a clientele. Painters such as Glynn Boyd Harte were only partially involved in the portrayal of architectural subjects, but in his case decorative elements themselves often played a major role. Glynn's enthusiasm for lithographic printmaking captured a joie de vivre which somehow reflected the pattern of his multi-faceted creative life. Subjects for the prints ranged from London to Paris, landscape to still life. It was he who brought Sir John Betjeman to the studio, seeking his approval for the illustrations to *Metro-land* and *Temples of Power.* John liked to come and sit, watching everyone at their various tasks, fascinated by the emerging images, which he called 'artistic alchemy'. When time was pressingly short, the portability of zinc plate lithography enabled Glynn to draw the work at all hours in his own studio close by in Bloomsbury.

Management changes

By the late sixties Herbert Simon had decided to retire as head of the studio and gallery, and its general governance fell temporarily to Basil Harley, then chairman of the Curwen Press. These would be increasingly difficult times for the parent company, with problems of general finance, strong union obduracy and a directorate which could not agree on a policy that would guide it through the technical changes that were occurring in the printing industry. Other printing firms of comparable size and history were wrestling with similar difficulties. Thus, in 1982, it was an inspirational act on the part of John Hutchings, a member of the Press board, to buy the Studio and the Gallery from the Curwen Press. He and his wife Jill would be instrumental in preserving the studio from the complications which would beset the Curwen Press and, in 1984, finally overcome it.

Although connections with the parent company remained, the Studio and the Gallery were free to develop in their own ways. It was thought, when Rosemary

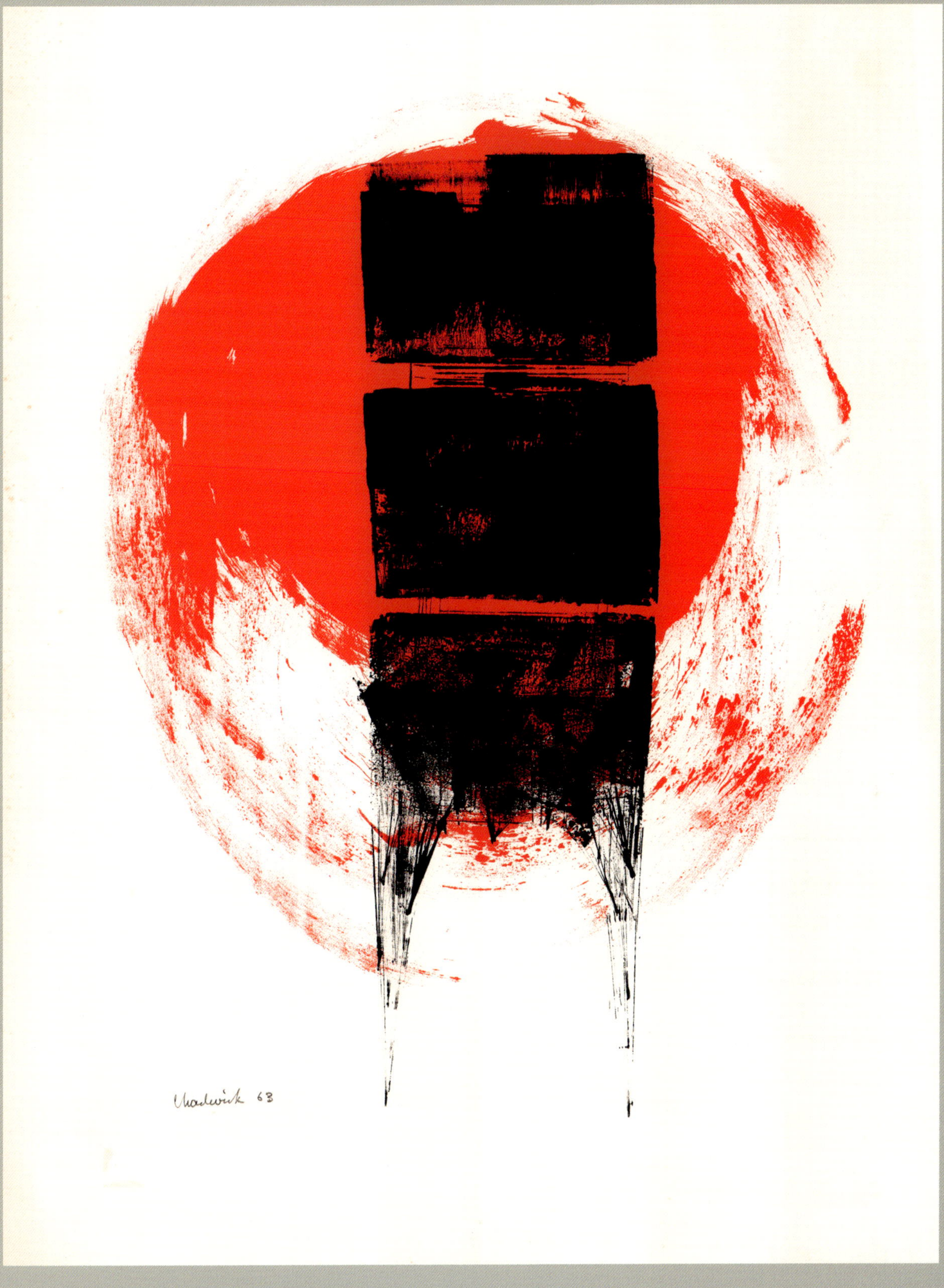

Lynn Chadwick, *Untitled*, lithographic proof, 1962–63.

Simmons left the gallery in 1975, that a new managing director should replace her to carry on with this essential activity of print publishing and administering the gallery. Stephen Reiss, who was finally appointed to fill this role, came from an art history and music administration background, having not long before distinguished himself with Benjamin Britten in establishing the Maltings concert hall at Snape in Suffolk. Together with John Hutchings, and in association with Sir Hugh Casson, the President of the Royal Academy at the time, Stephen formed a company, Business Art Galleries, which enabled him to open a new publishing venture at the RA. For several years he managed to publish prints made by academicians in the Curwen Studio, thus offering these artists a much broader public.

Luckily, by this point the studio had built an international reputation for the quality of its lithographic printmaking and was not reliant on one particular resource for its work – this had never been a wise policy to follow in any case. Therefore, although Stephen contributed much to the general running of the company, it was John Hutchings and I who took it upon ourselves to secure the studio's future with a wide spectrum of publishers and artists. Apart from the growing variety of individual publishers such as Imre von Maltzahn or Gimpel Fils, especially significant for us was the arrival of Christie's Contemporary Art in the mid-1970s, set up by two entrepreneurs, Myles Cooke and David Case. We were able to help this new venture for many years by supplying artists and printing their editions.

Perhaps the most adventurous publishing event for the Studio in 1970 was the commissioning of John Lennon by Edmund Newman of the Consolidated Fine Art Corporation to produce prints for the rapidly growing world of Pop Art collectors. Newman had an assistant, Anthony Fawcett – described by the writer Ray Connolly as 'a self-proclaimed art critic and a likable hustler' – who was given the task of organising this venture. He later transferred his allegiance to John Lennon and became his personal assistant. Central to the project was a series of prints drawn by Lennon concerning his escapades in Amsterdam with Yoko Ono in one of their Bagist events designed to combat prejudice and promote world peace. In England, the publicity generated by this peace 'gesture' guaranteed them more notoriety for a while. However, for two or three weeks the studio weathered all the complications such as the public attention and media interest generated by John and Yoko, and the work was duly completed – only to be banned by the police as obscene when it was put on exhibition in the West End of London. The prints were quickly sent to Canada, where they were signed by John prior to publication; sales of the prints in North America reportedly reached £150,000. The pair were keen to plan more studio work, having enjoyed its collaborative nature, and promised to return. Sadly, however, future events would prevent this happening. It remains probably one of the most bizarre episodes of the studio's time in Tottenham Court Road – the celebrity world invading the quieter world of printmaking.

The international nature of London's art world and the Studio's evolving reputation meant artists were always being invited by publishers to make original graphic work with us. In the spring of 1972, James Rosenquist unexpectedly arrived on the studio doorstep late one Thursday evening – in a frantic hurry to produce a poster for his London exhibition. To their credit the staff rallied round and we worked late into the small hours of the following morning, with the artist, more than satisfied, finally departing in a taxi to the Mayfair Gallery. Such an occurrence demanded special treatment, as did the visit of Man Ray, who had received a commission to produce several prints for the Consolidated Fine Art Co. in New York. He was fascinated by the possibility of experimenting with lithography on zinc plate – again, it was often a question of working well into the night for a concentrated ten days of production in the studio. For future use he took back to Paris folders of proofs, which grew from his many collaborations in the workshop, mostly arising from themes he was exploring for his publisher. His enthusiasm for the work, of course, involved the printers too, who when time permitted were treated to his stories of Parisian life!

By 1969 my family was settled into our house in Woodford, which Jenny and I began converting into accommodation and studio space. The basement made an ideal facility for printmaking, while the loft offered plenty of opportunity for painting. The next few years were partly spent acquiring suitable printing machines so that I could work at home on my own printmaking, as well as at Curwen Studio. By the early 1970s, during term time I had agreed to teach two days a week at the Slade – a convenient arrangement, due to the close proximity of the studio. It also gave Peter Baer and Bert Wootton room to develop their own skills in running the day-to-day business of the studio.

The printmaking department at the Slade under Bartolomeu dos Santos had also evolved its own standing in the educational world of fine art printmaking. It grew strong enough to be able to award a significant MA in printmaking and achieved a worldwide reputation for the quality of its departmental courses. Many generations of Slade artists benefited from what it offered in etching, lithography and silkscreen, as well as computer-based technology. A policy decision in the late 1980s to change the department's orientation to 'mixed media' marked a radical change – fortunate were the students who knew it in its heyday.

The growth of printmaking activity brought into the Curwen Studio not only professional artists and publishers but also an outfield of occasional practitioners from other walks of life – for example, Jonathan Gilli, the TV film-maker who published the work of Glynn Boyd Harte (Warren Editions), and Keith Michell, the well-known actor who began life as an art student in Melbourne before going on the stage. Keith produced many prints in the studio, usually based around Shakespearean subjects. Harold Pinter worked with Harold Cohen on an illustrated version of his play *The Homecoming*, involving many experimental photographic images.

In 1975, Jenny had taken the opportunity to move into further education by studying English language through the Open University, but she was also offered a place at King's College as a mature student, graduating in 1979. Liza and Matthew benefited considerably from their mother's example, going on to local high and grammar schools and eventually to university. These were the years when during the summer holidays we explored the Shropshire landscape. In the 1970s, alongside painting and printmaking, black and white photography began to play an important part in my work, and our sorties into Shropshire gave me some remarkable source material. It was interesting relating my photographic work to the research Leslie Lawson and I were doing into continuous-tone technology.

The research itself involved months of patience and frustration involving time outside normal studio hours and additional costs. Encouragingly, however, it was now normal studio practice for artists to work directly onto various types of grained film. This was due to the availability of photopolymer coated printing plates which opened up opportunities for photographic and hand drawn image making.

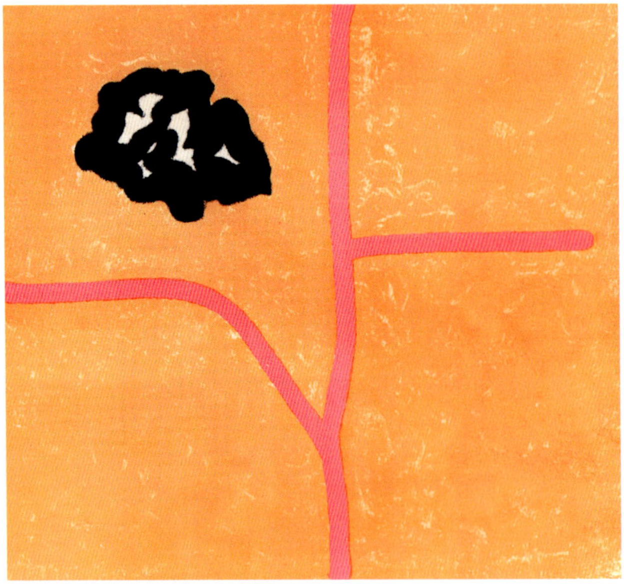

Prunella Clough, trial proof lithograph, 1995.

With the demise of Editions Alecto in 1978, we lost one of our competitors but also a customer with whom we had collaborated on many occasions. After the departure of his fellow director Paul Cornwall-Jones (in 1967), Joe Studholme was left to reorganise the company on a different basis, but he faced competition from Marlborough and Waddington Galleries, plus the new Petersburg Press. Finally, a disastrous fire proved beyond the company's capacity to survive, though it would later to re-emerge in a different form as Editions Alecto (Historical) Ltd. However, the founding of Christie's Contemporary Art to publish and promote English artists' work, would provide the studio with printing work for many years to come. Later, David Case would become an important dealer and publisher in his own right through Marlborough Fine Art, having made a significant contribution to the London's original-print publishing scene.

As we approached the 1980s, the studio's future seemed promising as the world of print dealing gradually expanded. Our annual Christmas party seemed to have become a much-anticipated social event in the West End world of printmaking. We never advertised it but word seemed to spread around every year because it was always well-attended. Of course, the machines had to be wrapped in paper to protect clothing, while decorations were made on the premises, and food and wine was bought from the local shops. The doors were open at six, and from then on a constantly packed flow of artists, dealers, friends and strangers poured down stairs, anxious to join the company and imbibe. At midnight more or less everyone departed convivially in various states of inebriation, while a few kind souls even volunteered to help clear up afterwards so that we could work the following day!

After 1982, with John Hutchings and his wife Jill now running the gallery as well as the studio, the workshop had a more direct management administration than before. Stephen Reiss was running the Business Art Gallery at premises in the Royal Academy, whilst still maintaining his interest and position in the Studio until his retirement in 1982, so there were many Royal Academicians, such as Anthony Green, Leonard Rosoman and Bernard Dunstan, having their prints commissioned. Under this new company structure, the early 1980s were a period of stability for the Studio, whereas our parent company was now experiencing genuine trading difficulties. Matters came to a head in 1984 and the Curwen Press was finally forced to call in the receivers. Many attempts were made to save this illustrious company, by all manner of means, but no purchaser could be found. The demise of an institution that had made such an impression on the progress of printing in the 20th century was tragic. The reasons were complex, involving company policies, management and print union problems. Although it would be easy, especially at this distance, to make recriminations, they are not the focus of this book. In any case, the studio and gallery were now detached from events at the parent company, and would continue to flourish unhindered by this distressing episode.

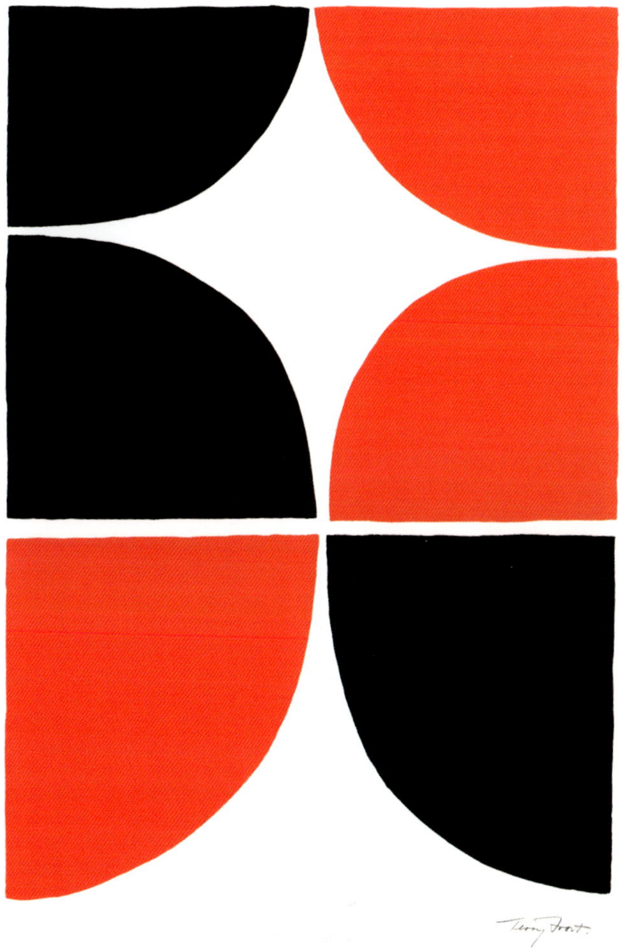

Terry Frost, *Red & Black Solid*, 1967–68, Waddington Gallery.

The union problems which beset the Curwen Press in the 1980s also affected larger printing operations such as those in Fleet Street. Rupert Murdoch's adoption of new electronic technology brought inevitable and radical changes to the commercial printing world, which the unions tried in vain to resist. In the studio, I had been always aware of the possibilities of these new forms of technology, which if used sensibly could benefit both artists and printers. It was essential to be able to offer a choice of process and let artists discover for themselves what creative lithography could offer. The debate in the fine art world about what constitutes an original print still raged from time to time, and even produced a document from the British Standards Association – formulated by a committee of publishers, printers and artists. It did not solve the problem, and to this day the arguments remain unresolved. It seems to me that the answer does not lie in the technology used, whether old or new. A much more logical solution to this problem is to ask to what kind of printed image will the artist willingly put their signature? It is certainly true that the terms 'original' and 'limited edition' have been exploited, their meaning distorted, by a commercial world fond of using a vocabulary normally applied to genuine original prints; this has resulted in much public confusion.

At the Curwen Studio we have always emphasised the presence or at least contact with the artists during the making of their images. It would also be true to say that the printmaker's presence in the studio, together with the printers and other artists working there, can have a beneficial influence on the fruition of an artist's ideas. Henry Moore in later years, for instance, was not averse to borrowing a background from somebody else's print if it fitted his purpose – and he was happy to pay a royalty for the privilege! This of course was quite an exceptional instance but it does illustrate an 'interactive' side to printmaking. Other artists, such as Albert Houthuesen, would spend years making litho-graphic images, appearing themselves only on rare occasions. Albert was to become part of our 'out-reach' staff visiting system and with the help of his wife Katherine, communications with him were constantly maintained. R.B. Kitaj, on the other hand, was very keen to make transfer drawings on plate but refused to leave his studio, preferring to give his instructions on the telephone and use the postal service. Despite this, we had a very constructive relationship with him, producing images for many years, though he never actually came to the studio. His remarkable self-portrait was enhanced by being printed on a stained and singed packet of Auvergne paper which I had rescued from the old Curwen Press. It had survived of the air raids, but, regarded as worthless, had later been put out for salvage in a skip. It admirably suited Kitaj's purpose, and from then on we had to search for other old but good quality remnants of papers (whatever their condition) which would complement his subject matter. It was a daunting task, involving several dedicated paper merchants and collectors; for the artist, however, it was a key element in the presentation of his portrait drawings.

As we approached the last decade of the 20th century a definable pattern of studio activity had established itself. The print publishing world had broadened itself both nationally and internationally, with galleries, biennale exhibitions, journals and magazines now exclusively devoted to the medium. Artists, if they chose, could make a full-time occupation out of printmaking, giving purpose to those art schools offering facilities and tuition in etching, lithography or screenprinting plus the possibility of employment prospects for their students. The Curwen Studio was by now its own recognisable company, and although it was not large in size compared with other foreign companies such as Gemini G.E.L. in the United States, its ability and reputation were widely appreciated. A glance down the studio lists schedules conveys the wide variety of artists using it: constants like Henry Moore, John Hoyland, Ken Kiff, Mary Fedden, Patrick Proctor and Bill Jacklin; topographical specialists like David Gentleman, Paul Hogarth and Albany Wiseman; non-publisher promoted artists such as Sam Maitin and Warrington Colescott from the United States, or Glynn Boyd Harte, or US-born Chester Williams, who had a huge project of prints for the Sultan of Oman. Meanwhile, in corners of the studio, Tracey Emin and Basil Beattie were busy making their first lithographic works.

During these years the nature of the staff changed little. George Grout and Bert Wootton had both retired and been replaced by Roy Silvey and then Guy Field – craftsmen who responded to the artists and their demands with commendable skill and dedication. Space and storage were becoming serious problems and we were fortunate to avoid any member of staff suffering an injury in handling plates or lithographic stones, or in the running of the printing machines. The direct and offset machines always demanded careful guarding, not least from unaware artists. Our Ratcliff flat bed, on which so much depended, was becoming prone to metal fatigue and needed very careful maintenance. For some time John Hutchings and I had been considering the general suitability of the studio premises, which were increasingly in need of renovation, particularly in regard to such matters as air conditioning. Those people who remember the familiar atmosphere of turpentine and printing ink on entering the studio are probably unaware of our constant attempts to improve its ventilation.

Another increasing concern for us was the rising criminal activity in this part of the West End. There were casual petty thieves about during the daytime and weekend burglaries were not uncommon, so vigilance was always necessary. But more sinister was an increase in violent behaviour, often due to drunkenness or street gambling. One morning we were startled by the eruption of a fight in the entrance hall of the building. There was much shouting and screaming, and thinking someone was being mugged I ran up the steps to open the studio door. At that instant the glass in the main door was smashed and a particle of glass cut across the surface of my left eye. Being already blind in my right eye this was potentially a double disaster. I staggered down the stairs, unable to see, and was rushed off to

University College Hospital. I completely lost my sight for several hours. My wife Jenny was frantic but was soon reassured by the consultant, who said the damage would heal after his treatment and the sight would return. Luckily for me, there were no particles of glass deep in the eye. Due to his skill my sight returned and after a few weeks I was able to begin working normally again. Then later a solemn procession of bikers, who had been responsible for the fracas in the first place, came to offer their apologies. Anxious to avoid any police involvement, they promised no more trouble with the office workers upstairs and, having shaken hands in a very English manner, curiously they kept their word.

In 1988 John's negotiations for the renewal of the lease, which were normally a formality, were brought to a sudden head when the owner of the building decided to apply to Camden Borough Council for planning permission to rebuild this corner site of Midford Place. The implications were obvious: suddenly we had to find new premises at a time when the city was booming and space in Central London was at a premium. It was decided to employ a property surveyor who would explore possibilities with me and make recommendations. So began a long hot summer of searching at all hours, finding locations, judging their potential and, of course, considering their overall costs. These attempts proved difficult and the results disappointing. The surveyor was fully aware of the studio's requirements and knew how to negotiate with the various landlords. But to no avail. We had frequent studio staff meetings to inform everyone of the situation and its consequences as the cessation date for the lease grew ever nearer. Incredible as it may seem, the property market could offer nothing satisfactory. Even 'spreading the word' amongst sympathisers, such as our former director Stephen Reiss (now in retirement) and his business associates, produced no positive result.

To help with some of the costs of the inevitable move, a sample of the studio's archive was put up for sale at Bloomsbury Auctions. As an event it actually made the daily newspapers, arousing considerable interest; but even this failed to relieve the atmosphere of apprehension that began to hang over the studio. However, John Hutchings informed me that he had received an offer from an interested entrepreneur by the name of Sam Alper, who had a vacant Dutch barn, situated on his own estate at Linton near Cambridge, which would be ideal as a print workshop. It was conditional on us sharing the space with his own company, the Chilford Press, who were screenprinters – an operation run by Kip Gresham. The thinking was that having the two firms on the same site would offer artists broader opportunities in the making of their prints. I was certainly reticent about many aspects of this idea, so I asked John to wait and see if any other possibilities presented themselves.

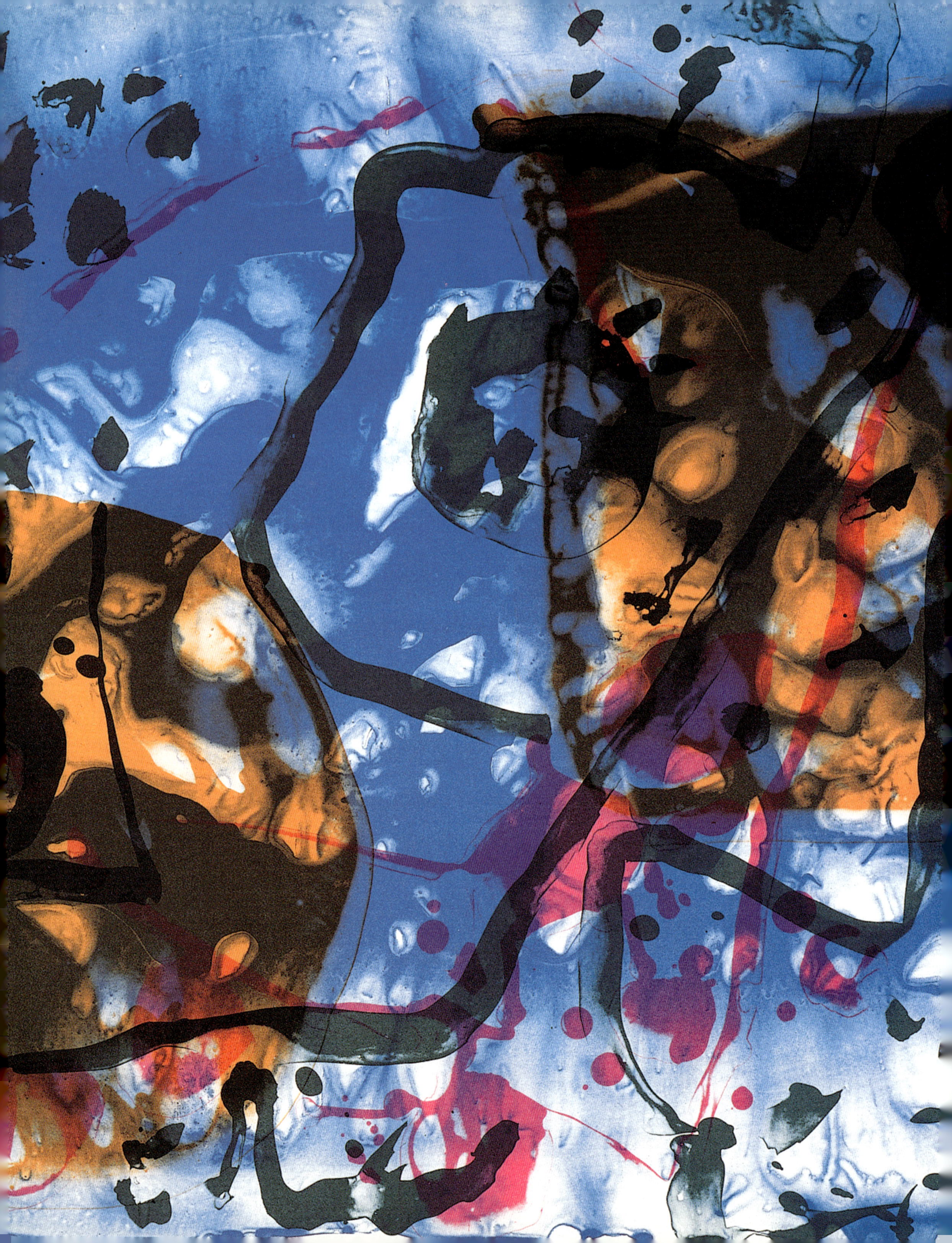

"... it seemed not only inevitable but also the right time to re-invent the Studio once more"...

LINTON

The middle months of 1989 were a time of great change for the studio. I was concerned that the workshop and what it stood for should continue, albeit on a site outside London and with a different staff, but with the same continuing overall philosophy and standards. Jenny and I were willing to explore the possibility of my daily commute to Cambridge along the M11, with all the extra stress that this involved, but we dismissed the idea of moving near to Linton. Jenny was now teaching English literature in local schools as well as privately, while our daughter Liza, now married and with a baby, Lucy, was settled in Sussex with her husband; we did not want to move from our home which was convenient for both the Studio and London. Our son Matthew, now qualified in law, had joined the city firm of Denton Wilde Sapte as a contract lawyer. Moreover, my teaching at the Slade and involvement with galleries made it seem sensible to be reasonably close to Central London. Finally, in any case, who could know at the time whether this project would work out?

However, it seemed not only inevitable, but also the right time to reinvent the Studio once more, and the next step was to tell the outside world of the impending move to Chilford Hall. The news provoked all kinds of response – most of it favourable in that people were relieved to learn that the studio would continue. The current printing staff had decided to go their separate ways, so part of this plan would involve the training of my assistant, Serena Castle; she was keen to further her career in lithographic printmaking and was willing to move with the Studio. After consultation with Sam Alper, John Hutchings formally agreed to divide the company by retaining the two Curwen Galleries and offering Sam the studio with suitable division of shares and capital. So the names and interests remained as before, with the Chilford Hall Press becoming part of the Curwen Studio.

Over the course of the remaining weeks, Leon Rochat and Co. agreed to oversee the moving of the studio machinery and other contents to the new site. For the first time since 1965 production was slowly drawn to a halt as the engineers moved in to dismantle and pack up machines, tables, cupboards and all the paraphernalia accumulated over 24 years. Streams of people – artists, publishers and friends – called in to express both their regrets about the removal of such a well-known facility to a site outside London and their hopes for the future of the new venture. The technicalities were often complex: we could only use the heavy cranes at weekends, by order of Camden Borough Council. It took us three weekends to prepare for this task, and then followed the lengthy business of packing materials such as lithographic stones, plates, prints and paper. As the emptying of the studio proceeded, the rooms began to

Left: Patrick Heron, *Anniversary Print*, lithograph. Published by Curwen Gallery, 1998.

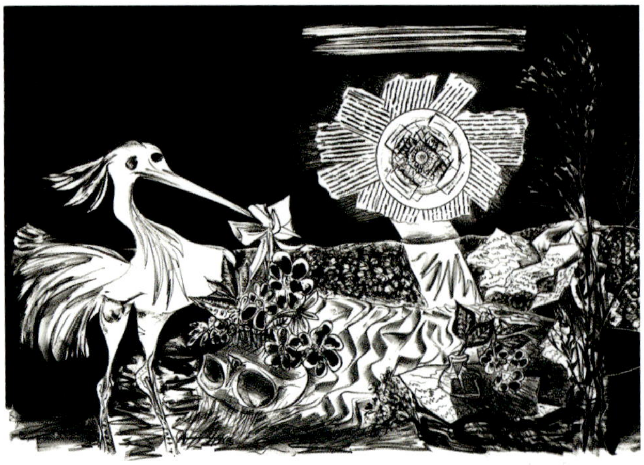

Ceri Richards, *And death shall have no dominion*, Marlborough Fine Art, lithograph, Dylan Thomas Suite, 1965.

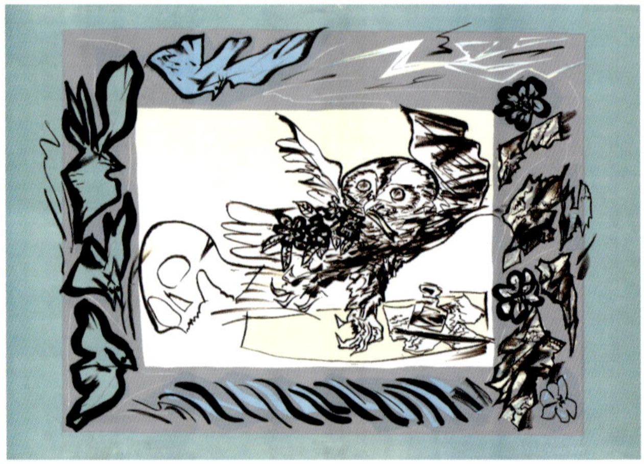

take on a forlorn aspect, revealing the dust and grime of so much activity. Long-lost pens, brushes, rulers, pencils, coins, teaspoons and boxes of crayons – all the detritus of many years' of graphic concentration surfaced again from oblivion. Finally, only pools of old oil marked the spot where the machines had once stood. The Ratcliff, now suffering from metal fatigue, was destined to spend its final days as a gift to the printing museum of John Jarrold at Norwich, where it remains to this day – a working reminder of our time in Tottenham Court Road. Sooner or later we would have to find replacement machinery of a different type – meaning again a different strategy for the new studio. The Ratcliff was the last of its kind and deserved to be preserved. My last action was to remove the studio plate from the front door, ready for it to be taken up to the new site at Chilford Hall; as I turned the key the rooms below lay silent, except for the eternal clatter of feet on the familiar pavement lights in Tottenham Court Road.

My wife Jenny and I now had to reorganise our daily routine because the road to Chilford Hall has meant daily journeys along the M11 – a total of about 50 miles each way. Had we lived nearer to the centre of London, such a drive would have been unsustainable; our home in Woodford Green turned out to be a fortunate piece of geography and was key to the continuation of the Curwen Studio.

Our arrival at Chilford Hall meant a great deal of planning with Sam Alper and Kip Gresham (who was trying to build a silkscreen printmaking studio with Sam's co-operation). Liz (Dame Elisabeth) Frink and Terry Frost had been recent productive visitors. There was the obvious problem of how to combine these two processes under one roof of this limited size. Sam had moved to Chilford Hall to live with his wife and family, and had acquired a reputation as a collector of modern painting and sculpture. Now, in later life, he was active through the Alper Trust, encouraging the appreciation of music, and was well-known locally as an entrepreneur. His association with printing had come through projects he'd been involved in with the stone-letter carver David Kindersley, and he was anxious to preserve the future of Curwen.

Apart from our Dutch barn, the other buildings on site were large conversions used for commercial functions, providing all kinds of employment for local people. A vineyard on the estate had for some years been an added public attraction, and we found discarded bottles to be useful for damping the lithographic stones on a hot summer's day. To begin with there were problems with staff both in the workshop and on the administration side; unlike in London, where there were always possibilities, we had to look carefully for suitable employees, as scarcity often made selection

Above and right: Elisabeth Frink, *Owl*, on zinc plate, 1967. Waddington Galleries

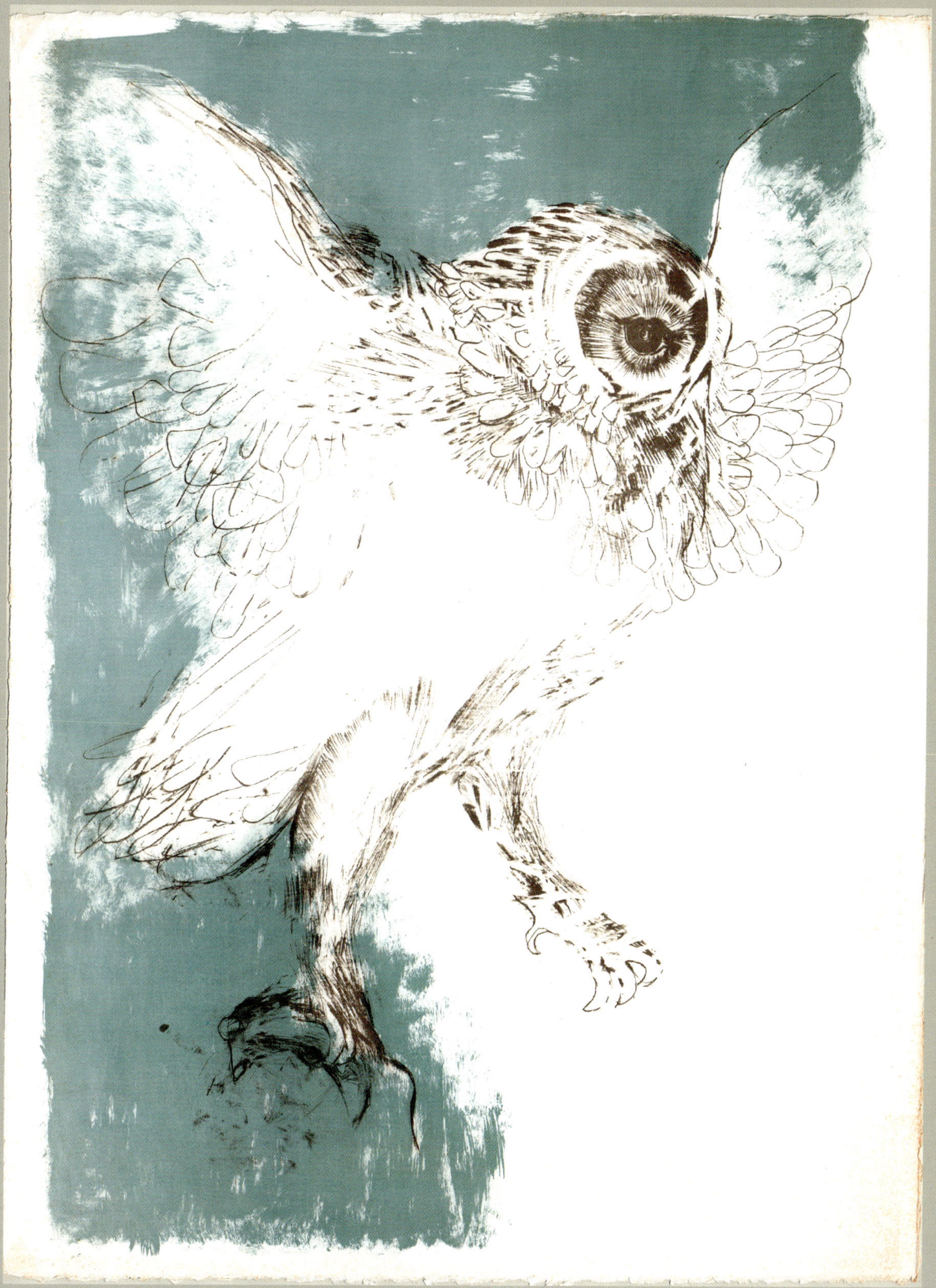

difficult. Serena Castle, however, was making promising progress, and eventually became a skilled member of the studio staff. Sam set about publicising the new venture as much as possible, and indeed this seemed to be one of his major interests. At this stage his office was situated in the administration block of Chilford Hall, where he ran his principal business with his children, Simon and Rebecca Alper. We had our own office within the studio, the materials for building it having been rescued from a derelict local factory. Sam used to greatly enjoy adapting and reusing building materials – his barns had been subjected to this treatment for many years. It does explain some of the more eccentric architectural features to be found on the site.

In many ways the early years at Chilford Hall saw a broadening of the studio's activities in relation to the work – artists could now choose to combine lithography with silkscreen printing – as happened with Prunella Clough, Wilhelmina Barns-Graham and John Hoyland – or remain faithful to a particular medium, as was the case with Ken Kiff, who liked to spend long summer days in his own private world, engrossed in drawing on stone. This element of tranquillity was an occasional characteristic of the new studio, and a change from the usual vibrancy of the Tottenham Court Road. On the other hand, before we had proper heating and insulation, the early Cambridge winters were difficult to cope with, with their unforgiving temperatures and biting winds. Eventually, these problems were considerably eased, but it took a year or so of experiment.

During our final months in London, the studio presses had been involved in printing editions organised by Anna Hunter, a new and enthusiastic dealer who ran the Belgravia Gallery and was keen to publish the work of Ruskin Spear and other Royal Academicians. Anna had also had the idea of persuading the Prince of Wales, whose activities as a watercolourist are well known, to have some of his own images made into lithographs. The results would then be published, and the funds raised could be used to support his charities, particularly the Prince's Trust. This was a bold and unusual proposal for a member of the Royal Family to consider, but she felt it fitted well with his charitable activities. Now in Linton, the project slowly got underway, activated by Anna Hunter and the Prince's aides at Buckingham Palace, who at that stage were also in charge of publicising the event. The images chosen by His Royal Highness had to be delivered to the studio with the Prince's instructions about alterations to size and image. Because of time considerations, the work was a combination of hand-drawn and photographic work, and since the Prince wished to see and comment on the work whenever necessary, I had to take the proof stages to St James's Palace or Highgrove for his personal approval. It needed very detailed co-operation on my part, to ensure that all aspects of the project worked satisfactorily, including the qualification for originality set out by the British Standards Institute. Inevitably, historical events meant there were unforeseeable problems in the making of these prints, but since its launch in the early 1990s the work has continued, guided by the Prince's constant interest, and with the help of Anna Hunter the project is still in active development, and continues to raise funds for the Prince's Trust.

Anna and the Belgravia Gallery brought other artists new to the studio such as Ruskin Spear and Carel Weight, broadening the link with the Royal Academy, while John Sheeran and Bernard Dunstan combined on a project to represent topographical aspects of the RA. The resulting work demonstrated not only the process of lithography, but also Bernard's creative sympathy with the medium. Wilhelmina Barns-Graham came from Cornwall to continue a project that she had begun with me in St Ives, and made full use of the combination of lithography and screenprinting. However, as the early 1990s progressed it was becoming apparent that the policies of the studio did not quite suit Kip Gresham, who began to have disagreements with Sam Alper over its general running. It would seem that apart from clashes of temperament he resented Sam's managerial role and the inevitable restrictions on space for the development of screenprinting. I tried to persuade him to have more patience over the development of the company, but it turned out he had come to the conclusion that he wished to have his own company.

Matters came to a head in the summer of 1995, while Jenny and I were away on holiday, when Kip decided write a confrontational letter to Sam expressing his dissatisfaction with both Sam and the studio's policies. By then his discontent had been apparent for some time. There was no alternative for Sam but to ask him to leave – an altogether unfortunate episode which meant us having to rearrange the studio and appoint other members of staff. At the same time it was also decided to close the silkscreen facility and to specialise only in lithography.

In making the studio more efficient we decided to look for another mechanised offset printing machine – a formidable task as these cost many thousands of pounds, even second-hand. I knew the type we needed, but this would take a lot of searching and time to find. I then had an incredible stroke of luck! Unexpectedly, news came from a friend that a printing firm in Cambridge had been taken over by the Burlington Press, with the result that the exact machine we required was for sale. Built by the Swiss company FAG, it had a refrigerated bed and computerised controls, and for weeks we wondered about its price, which would surely be way above what we could afford. We had a minute budget of £4,000, which we guessed was about one tenth of what it was worth. In trepidation we went to see its owners. The Managing Director, Barry Canning, listened to our story with apparent interest and sympathy. 'It's running perfectly – what can you offer?' he said. We quoted our figure and prepared to leave. His reply astonished both Sam Alper and myself. 'Yes, that's fine if you can get it off the premises by the end of the month.' I could not believe my ears.

It was during this time that Michael Adams became a member of the studio staff. Having had much experience in the world of public relations, he was to prove invaluable as an organiser, establishing contacts with artists, exhibitions and publishing houses. His sympathy with the aims of the studio, which may have begun in his early days at art school, has grown over the years, to the extent that he has proved to be an important figure in its current development. A family link with Sir Edward Poynter in earlier days added to his background interest in the fine art world. Another member of staff to join at this time was the printer Richard Metcalfe, who was able to bring experience in the practical matters of photo-process and offset printing, which were very useful at a time when these skills were taking on a new importance in the studio.

By 1995 the broad base of lithography that we could offer printmakers was quite considerable, and this was fully exploited by three artists: Kim Lim, Anna Maria Pacheco and Richard Deacon. Beginning in 1993, they were selected by the Henry Moore Foundation in successive years to spend time in the studio on experimental lithographic work. All benefited from this opportunity, choosing to explore the medium in different ways. It was interesting that Richard Deacon, who was new to the process, became fascinated by the possibilities of

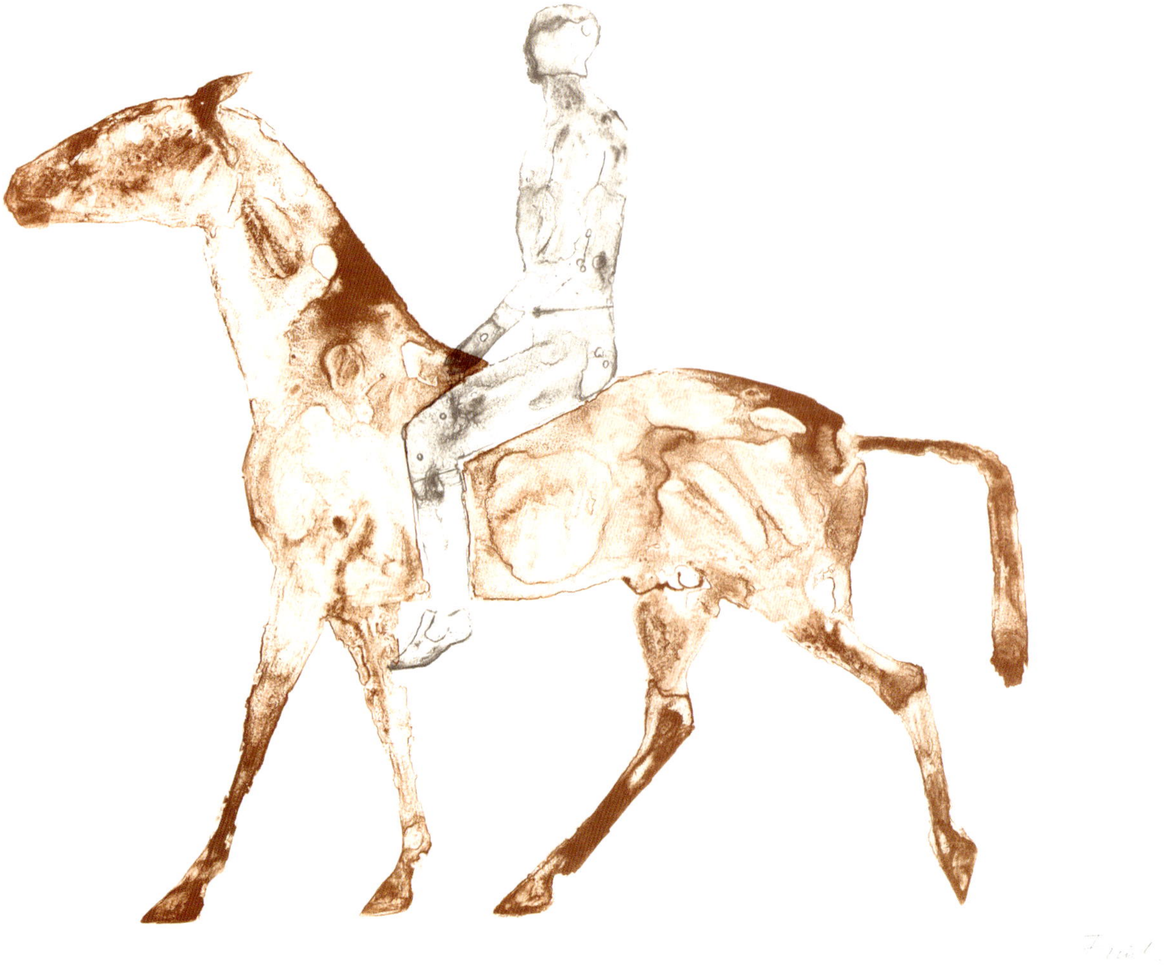

Elisabeth Frink, *The Grey Rider*, lithograph on zinc. Publisher: Leslie Waddington Prints Ltd., 1970.

lithographic stone and not, as might have been expected, the latest photopolymer technologies.

In pursuing my own work, annual journeys to Shropshire had enabled me to collect material for my next exhibition at the Curwen Gallery, in 1997. This was well received, being a development in technique and colour from previous one-man shows. Over many years of repeated summer visits I had formed an affinity with the character of the locality around southwest Shropshire, particularly Bishop's Castle, where we had made many friends. There were pressures on us from local friends and acquaintances to spend more time in that remarkable landscape, but on reflection we decided to remain in London, primarily to help the activity of the Curwen Studio. Somehow this made our annual trips there even more important in the years that followed. Another event that occurred at this time was my retirement from teaching at the Slade, after some forty years. It had been a formative activity, most of the time concerned with postgraduate students, many of whom had come from abroad each year and were anxious to make the most of their opportunities at the Slade. Bartolomeu dos Santos, Peter Daglish, David Leverett and myself (with assistants) had built up the reputation of the department to the extent that in the art world it had a status that owed much to the perceived quality of its students. I was the last of my generation to leave. However, due to changes of college policy, questions of space requirements and departmental costs, it was decided to turn the department into a 'mixed media' area. With the nature of the

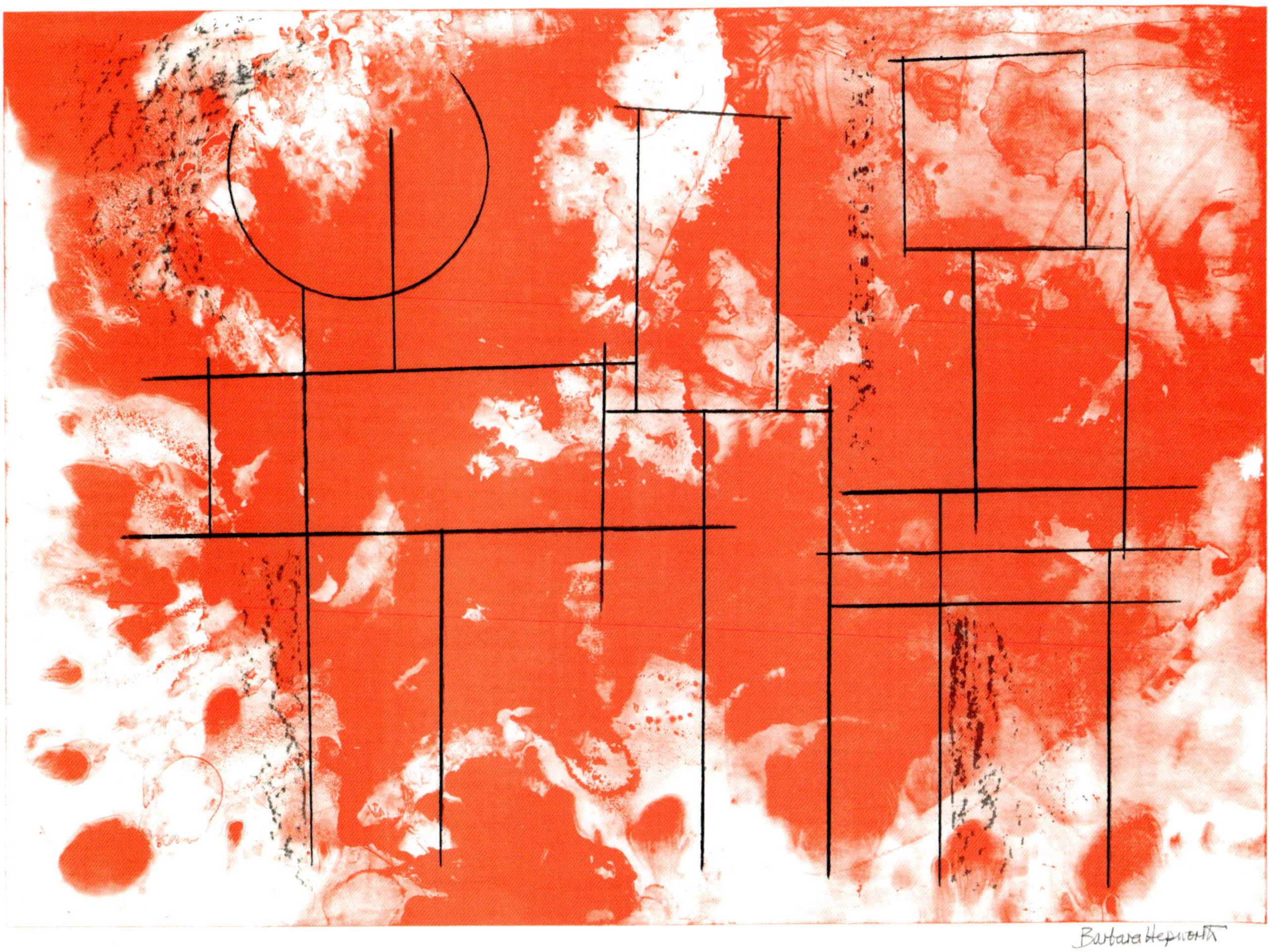

Barbara Hepworth, *Idea*. Published by Curwen Prints Ltd, 1971.

staff changing, so did its philosophy, and slowly most of the equipment was replaced by photo- and computer-origination devices and a minimum quantity of equipment (etching presses and a lithographic press) preserved for hand-drawn purposes. There is still throughout the world a body of artists whose careers stem from this former department, and I maintain contact with many of them.

In 1998, John and Jill Hutchings and I organised an exhibition in the Curwen Gallery to celebrate 40 years of the Curwen Studio, to feature a representative group of artists. Patrick Heron agreed to make a special print which involved a journey with Jill to his home in Zennor in Cornwall. On a memorable September afternoon we sat in the garden of the Eagle's Nest with all the equipment, while Patrick drew the separations and enthusiastically discussed the colour possibilities of the image. The permutations of the eight colours were what held his and our interest. A few weeks later, when he arrived in London for the opening of his retrospective at Tate Britain (then still known as the Tate Gallery), we selected one from among 60 different variations. After much consideration, agreement was reached and the print was editioned in time for the Curwen Gallery's exhibition. The catalogue (bearing his print on its cover) was an affirmation of the studio's continuing purpose throughout its 40-year history.

Other aspects of the studio's work were now developing, and in the following year, 1999, we embarked on a special project with Josef Herman – an artist's book embodying his philosophy of life, to be called *The Song of the Migrant Bird*. Josef had set his heart on the making of this work, so for most of that year a lot of our efforts went into developing those images: I spent many long hours with him and Nini, his wife, in the basement studio at Edith Road. He wished to express in graphic terms some of the deep emotions embedded in his life. At this point his health was declining, so it became imperative that we complete the work, which was so important to his ideals and life as an artist. Finally it was finished, and the following year it was shown at the Royal Academy to a very appreciative public. It was Josef's last major work.

During the course of 1999, Sam Alper had become strongly linked with the work of the studio and was using his influence wherever possible to further its aims. Often he and I disagreed over policy and practical matters, but such differing of opinion was inevitable and usually ended, eventually, with understanding on both sides. Then, in the summer of that year, my wife Jenny and I journeyed to Winchester with other members of our family so that I could receive an Honorary Doctorate of Letters from Southampton University. This was an unexpected but enjoyable outing for all concerned – despite the sweltering heat that June day.

Curiously, a month or so later at a gallery opening in Ipswich, by accident I met Robert Simon's daughter Jenny, and during the course of our conversation found out that she was looking for another job that was more interesting than her current one in Hove. We were looking for managerial staff at the time, so I asked her to come and talk to Sam Alper. After much discussion, we finally arranged that she should move to Linton with her family and start work as soon as possible. With Jenny's arrival Sam was able to leave much of the administration in her hands. She now plays a crucial role in the company on many levels, dealing on a daily basis with the studio's activities.

Thus a remarkable reconnection of the Simon family with Curwen had come to pass. By this time, too, the studio staff were fully settled after the upheaval of the move from Tottenham Court Road – my colleague Tom Martin has been working with us since 1997, and his skill and experience has grown year by year, so that he is now an important member of our staff, both as artist and printmaker.

The promotion of the studio's work became increasingly important. With Sales Director Michael Adams's help and cooperation we approached the Royal Academy with a view to showing the prints made by academicians over the previous 40 years. This idea was well received and, in 2000, an exhibition was staged called *Forty Years in Print*, with a catalogue illustrating the work of some 70 artists who had worked in the studio. The exhibition proved, despite unexpected problems with one of the sponsors, Barrington Fleming, to be a very successful example of lithography's versatility in being able to accommodate such a diverse range of artists. It was undeniably a milestone in our relationship with the Royal Academy.

The Curwen Print Study Centre

The millennium year was to be significant for us in another way, in the formation of a print study centre housed in unused premises next to the studio. For us this was not a new idea. I had suggested its possibility to Sam when I'd left the Slade, sensing that recent developments in art schools were pointing to the need for preserving the traditional printmaking methods. Such a project would

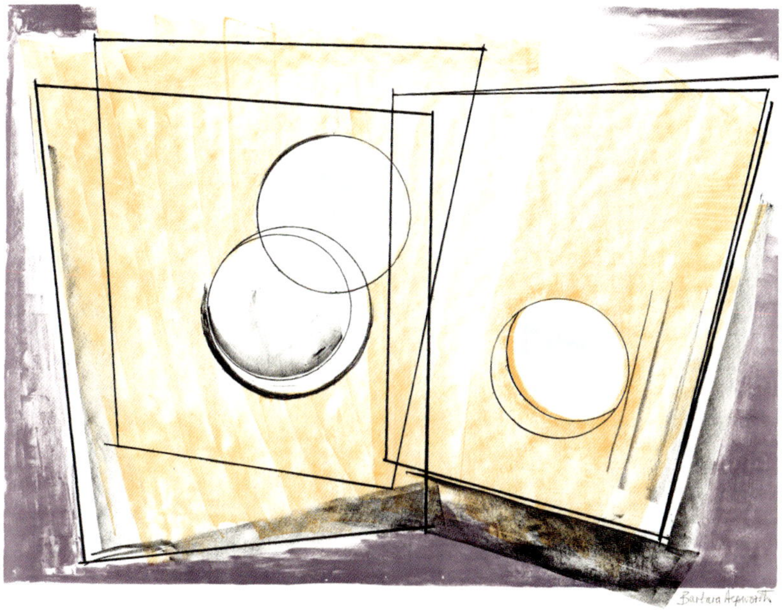

Barbara Hepworth, *Oblique Forms*, lithograph.
Published by Curwen Prints Ltd, 1969.

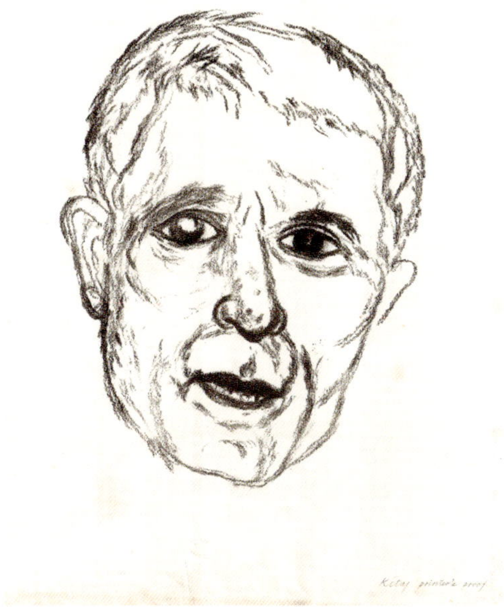

R. B. Kitaj, *Self Portrait*, transfer lithograph.
Published by Marlborough Fine Art, 1991.

have to be separate from the Curwen Studio, but would also benefit being associated with it. The new centre, which would operate as a charity, would demonstrate not only lithography but etching, screenprinting, computer and intaglio processes. A staff led by an administrator would deal with the broad range of visitors, from classes of seven-year-old children to mature artists and those teachers who wished to have refresher courses. This was the broad outline. Maybe it sounded overambitious at the time but we were keen to try and make it a reality. It was the start of an adventure involving the search for finance, suitable trustees and machinery, and appropriate staff. Because of my involvement with the studio, it fell to Sam Alper to devote the time needed to bring this into being. I helped when I could, particularly in the early stages, such as during the calamitous dealings with the local Arts Council, which would have involved huge legal expenses if we had continued down that line. However, after many months of attempted negotiations, we decided to withdraw our application and apply for private sources of funding, which proved to be a wiser course of action. Encouraged by the enthusiasm of people from varied walks of life who helped in every which way with the practicalities of providing materials such as paper and printing machines, it took us considerable time to assemble what is now a thriving facility for students of all kinds who are keen to learn printmaking. One of the most encouraging events was a successful appeal for an educational grant from Brussels, which also led to connections with similar projects abroad. It has been a difficult journey, with constant financial and logistical problems, but we have been particularly fortunate to have Lorraine Chitson as our Administrator. She has guided the centre's growth over the past nine years, together with her assistant Susan Jones and the other staff, establishing a resource for the future use of artists and students alike which already has a high reputation. I think John Curwen would have approved.

In the meantime, the Curwen Studio had been continuing in its unceasing work with printmakers. Stephen Conroy, Basil Beattie, Mary Fedden and John Bellany were some of the artists occupying the studio's time with hand drawn work. However, I was keen to give professional photographers the opportunity to explore the process of continuous-tone lithography – so that such image makers could see its possibilities in the studio. Michael Adams suggested we approach his friend Mike McCartney, who had become an established

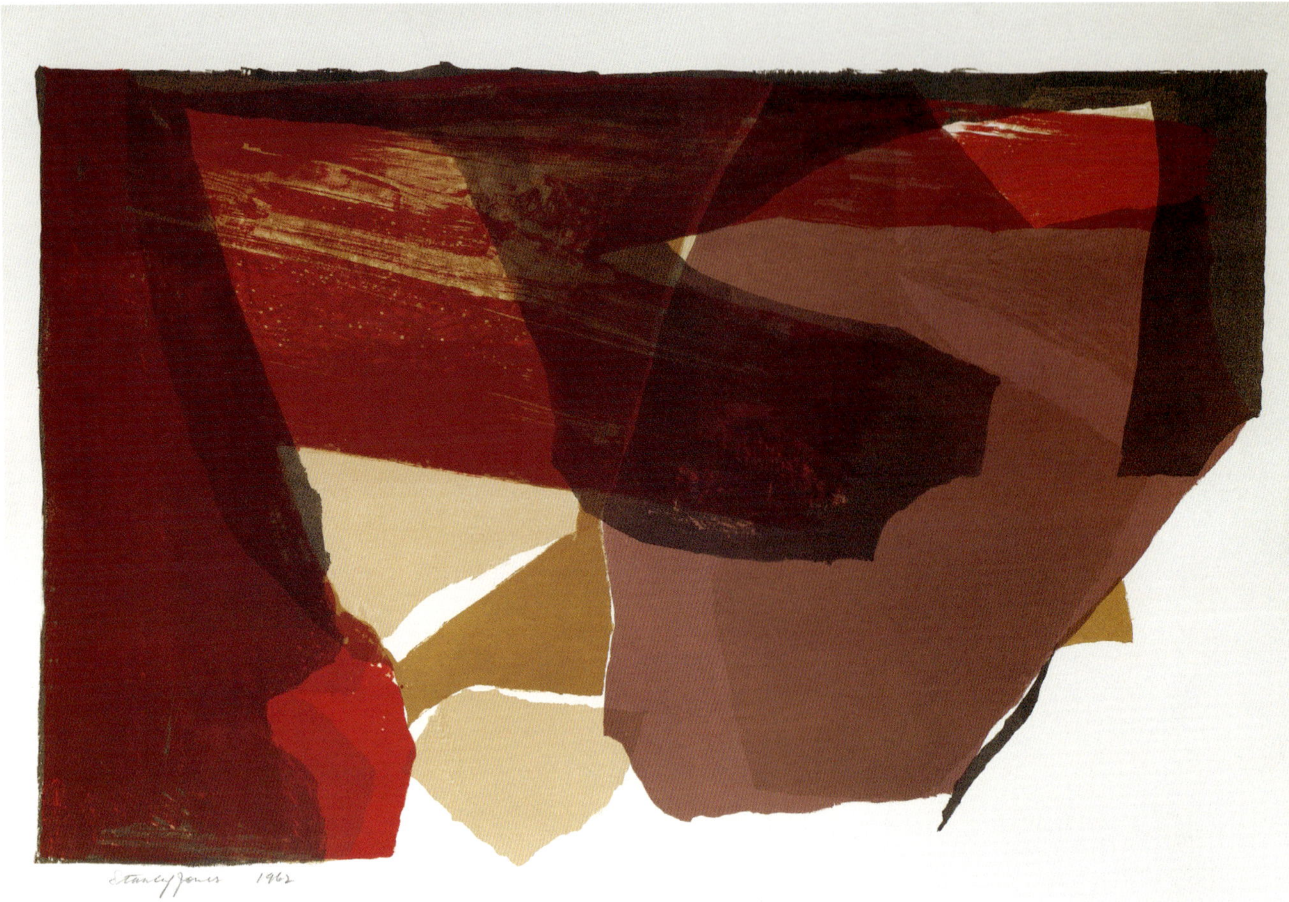

Stanley Jones, *Essex Landscape*, lithograph, 1963. Publisher: Editions Alecto.

photographer in Liverpool. Mike was keen to try out the idea and duly appeared in the studio to watch and comment, often wryly, on the two early monochrome 35mm negatives taken in the Cavern Club in the early 1960s. We were able to produce much-improved versions of the two original negatives on the printing press. He was able to clarify detail and tone in the proofing and was somewhat surprised at the possibilities obtainable through the process. Putting a glass on the print meant no distorting dots or pixels were present – he was fascinated by the clarity and richness of the printed image. We then pulled the editions on archival paper to be signed by him as lithographic prints, giving these images a much life longer than their bromide counterparts. Such a process is now an established technique within the studio for hand drawn and purely photographic work.

Artists vary considerably in the way they are introduced to lithographic printmaking: aside from art-school contact, it could be through publishers, through galleries, through following their own curiosity or by way of a fellow artist. This last example was the case with Kyffyn Williams, who first appeared in the studio with Elisabeth Frink in 1974, when he produced his work *Pontllyfni in Snow.* Some 28 years later Kyffyn was keen to explore hand-drawn lithography again with plans for making limited edition prints and I was able to introduce him to Michael Adams. We were duly invited to visit him on Anglesey at his cottage on the shore facing the Menai Strait. Seeing us trudging through the autumn mud he appeared at his door and welcomed us inside. We entered a sombrely lit and low-ceilinged house full of Kyffyn's work and memorabilia – from paintings and drawings to prints and book illustrations.

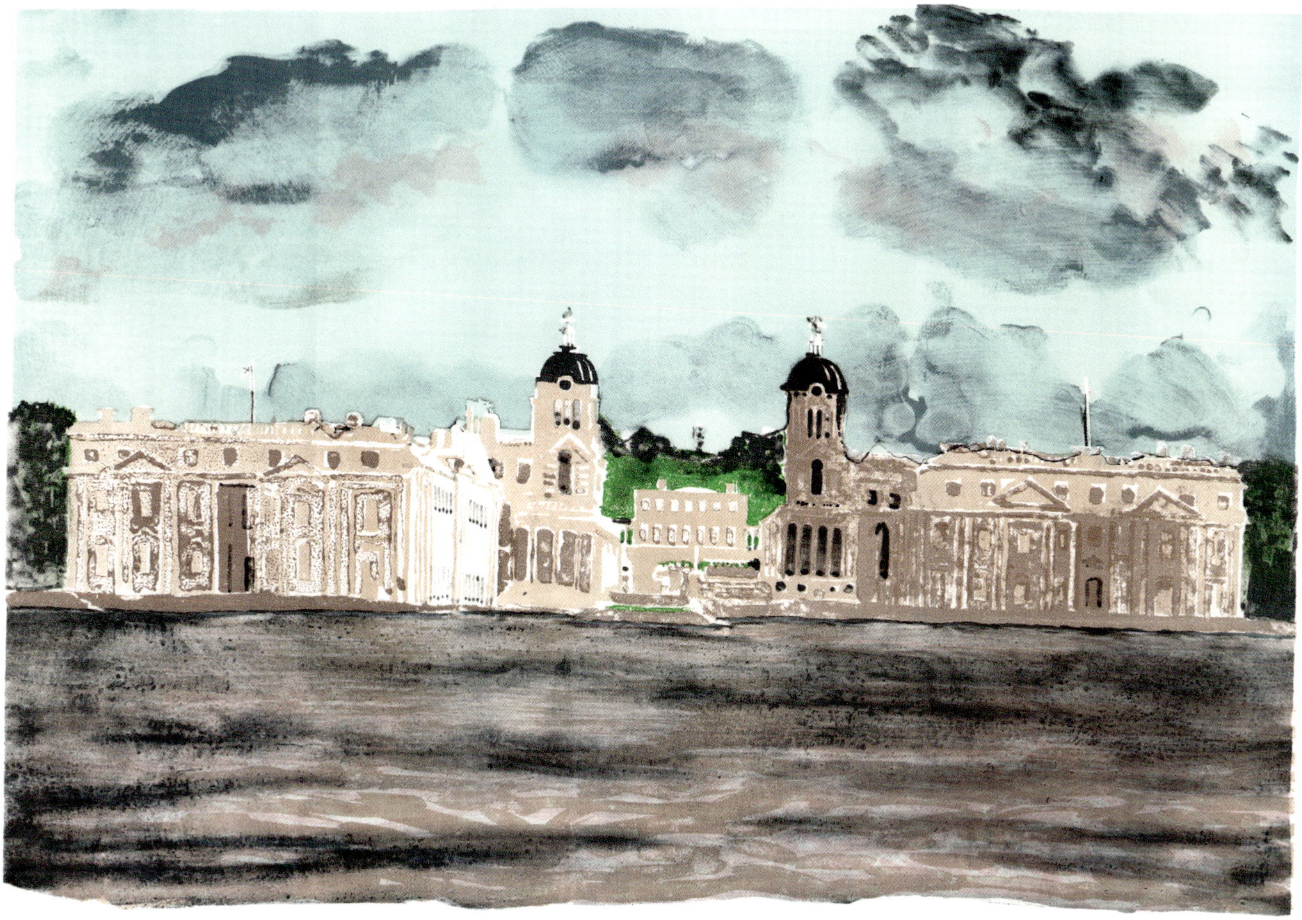

Patrick Proctor, *Greenwich Observatory*, lithograph, 1989. Publisher: Redfern Gallery.

He had been working there alone for many years, having achieved a remarkable status in the Welsh artistic community, where his character and influence have remained over a long period. Michael began to act as intermediary for the Studio, travelling regularly from his home in Cheshire to Kyffyn's studio where we had an open invitation to visit him and discuss the work. For four years Kyffyn worked constantly on printmaking, dedicated to the idea of making his work available to the general public. It also helped to produce funds for the construction of a space representing his work, his memorial gallery – the Oriel Ynys Môn Gallery on the Isle of Anglesey.

The contact developed into a firm friendship and soon Kyffyn was keen to explore hand-drawn printmaking again. He had decided to make original prints so that the public could potentially have access to his work. It was the renewal of this old acquaintance with the Studio which helped him produce a body of work.

By 2001 the Print Study Centre was beginning to establish itself and attract a wide interest. Unfortunately at this time, Sam's health began to decline and there were difficulties in daily communications with him. We had to accept the situation and make preparations accordingly. The diagnosis of cancer, which he refused to accept, had complicated matters, but gradually his presence in the studio diminished to nothing as he became more invalided. It was difficult to appreciate that such a multi-faceted individual, whose business acumen and creative interests had governed his life for so long, would not be around in the studio much longer. Amongst many other activities, the Chilford Hall complex of businesses was his creation, together with the establishment of the vineyard. His collecting of painting and sculpture had given him a constant interest in fine art and sparked his interest in the Curwen Studio, which he worked so hard to re-establish. We have so much for which to be to grateful to him and, despite our differences over the years, fundamentally we always agreed on the studio's aims and purpose.

Sam died in October 2002 and was buried in the grounds of Chilford Hall. Fiona, his wife, and his son Simon now represent the family's involvement in the studio's day-to-day activities and help in the general introduction of artists and their work into the facilities of the Studio, or the Print Studies Centre.

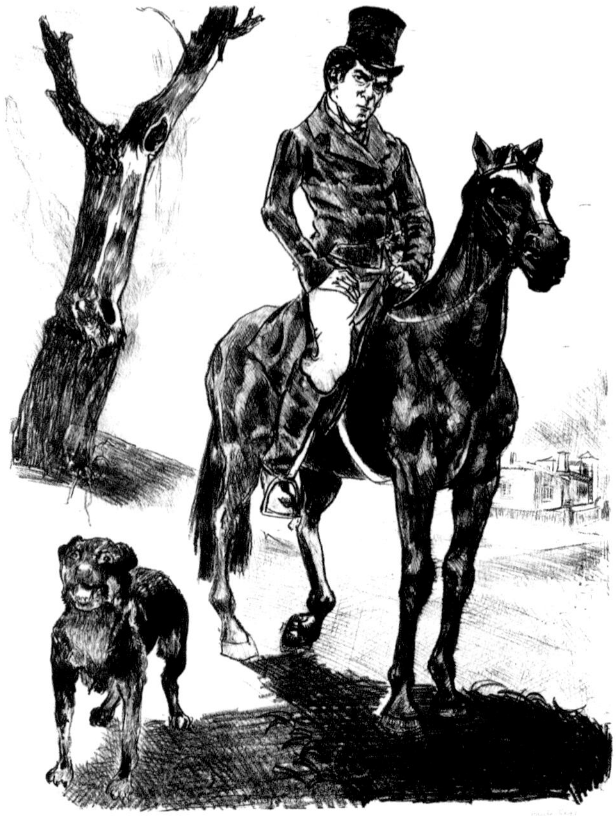

Paula Rego, *Mr Rochester*, lithograph, 2003.

Paula Rego

Towards the end of November 2001, in Dover Street, just around the corner from the old Midford Place premises, I had met an acquaintance from my Slade days, Paula Rego, who I had not seen for several years. During the course of our conversation she told me that she had been trying to make some lithographic prints – but for various reasons she was not satisfied with them. 'Why not come to the Curwen Studio for a day and see if we can help?' I suggested. 'Where are you now?' she asked. 'Near Cambridge,' I replied. 'Not far, really.' But I could tell by her response – not enthusiastic – that the idea did not appeal to her at this point. However, before we parted she asked for the studio number – perhaps she would come after all. I had almost forgotten about this meeting when a few weeks later Paula phoned to arrange a visit. This was the beginning of a two-year project with the studio.

The Brontë sisters and the enigmatic characters portrayed in their novels had fascinated Paula for some time; she now had the opportunity to explore her ideas and link them with a process that would offer a freedom close to her painting and drawing methods. It was Charlotte Brontë's novel *Jane Eyre* which Paula chose to form the basis of a series of prints totalling 25 published images, to be shared between the Marlborough Gallery and herself. Having started them off in her own studio she would then bring the material for translation into lithography. At first there was the experimental stage, where technical possibilities were examined; occasionally they took her interest off into an entirely new area, where her imagination could expand and develop. She wanted to try all forms of lithography – working on stone, zinc and aluminium plate, traditional transfer paper and grained film, and even combining some processes together. Always, though, the embodiment of the idea was inextricably bound up with whatever form of lithography she chose.

This took considerable thought and practice, particularly in her use of colour in relation to a chosen idea. She seemed to know which subjects were suitable for the sensuality of stone, and would spend many hours in concentration with lithographic crayons and ink, poring over the evolution of the image and its components. Choosing colours on some images was also a prolonged process, on each one representing many hours of fine balancing at proofing stage. The works on transfer paper were different, as these gave her the opportunity of working in her own studio on the specially prepared paper. She could draw from her models, as is her normal practice, and bring the results to the studio for transferring to plate. This practice suited her thinking admirably – helping in the interpretation of her nightmare-ridden dreamland. Should the drawing not be satisfactory, she could then throw it away and start again.

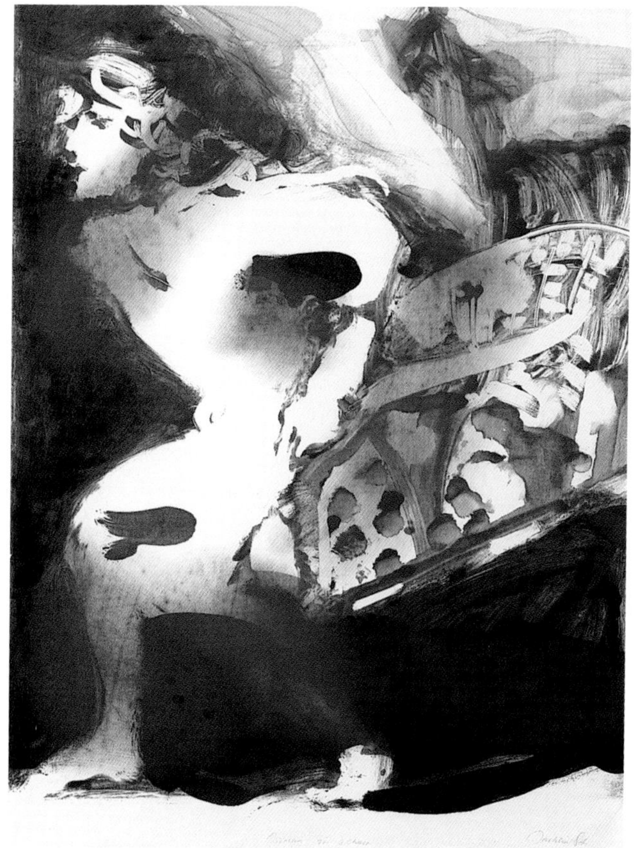

Bill Jacklin, *Woman in Chair*, monoprint, 1984.
Marlborough Fine Art Publishers.

After almost two years' combined effort, in October 2003 the prints were shown at the Marlborough Gallery to general acclaim, before touring worldwide to the same chorus of appreciation. At the same time, other artists were using the studio for their own purposes. Two large projects, one with Kyffyn Williams for the Oriel Ynys Món Gallery, were completed in the autumn of 2004, as was the printing work for Albert Houthuesen (drawn images posthumously inherited by Richard Nathanson, his dealer and publisher). At this time John Claridge, the photographer, had started a special series of prints in which he worked extensively on the negatives before proofing them with Tom and his assistants, who were now trained in continuous-tone techniques. I mention this development because by arrangement I had decided to spend a little more time at home with my own work (and my wife Jenny), travelling to the studio only one day or so each week – a practice I still maintain. Modern communication systems have now made this feasible, and I certainly do not regret reducing my daily hundred-mile drive to one day a week. Naturally at this stage it meant altering the staff structures so that progressively they could take on new responsibilities and interests. Tom Martin would now be in daily charge of the studio staff. It was a timely change, because I was then preparing for another one-man show of paintings at the Curwen Gallery, with the source material again related to the landscape around Wenlock Edge.

During the spring of 2005 I spent much time talking to Linda Sandino at the British Library for the *Artists' Lives* series of recordings. This was not an easy task to begin with: reliving experiences in retrospect demands much concentration. However, with Linda's co-operation, we managed by conversation over many hours to navigate our way through my life as an artist. Much of what we discussed naturally involved the development of the Curwen Studio and the times through which it

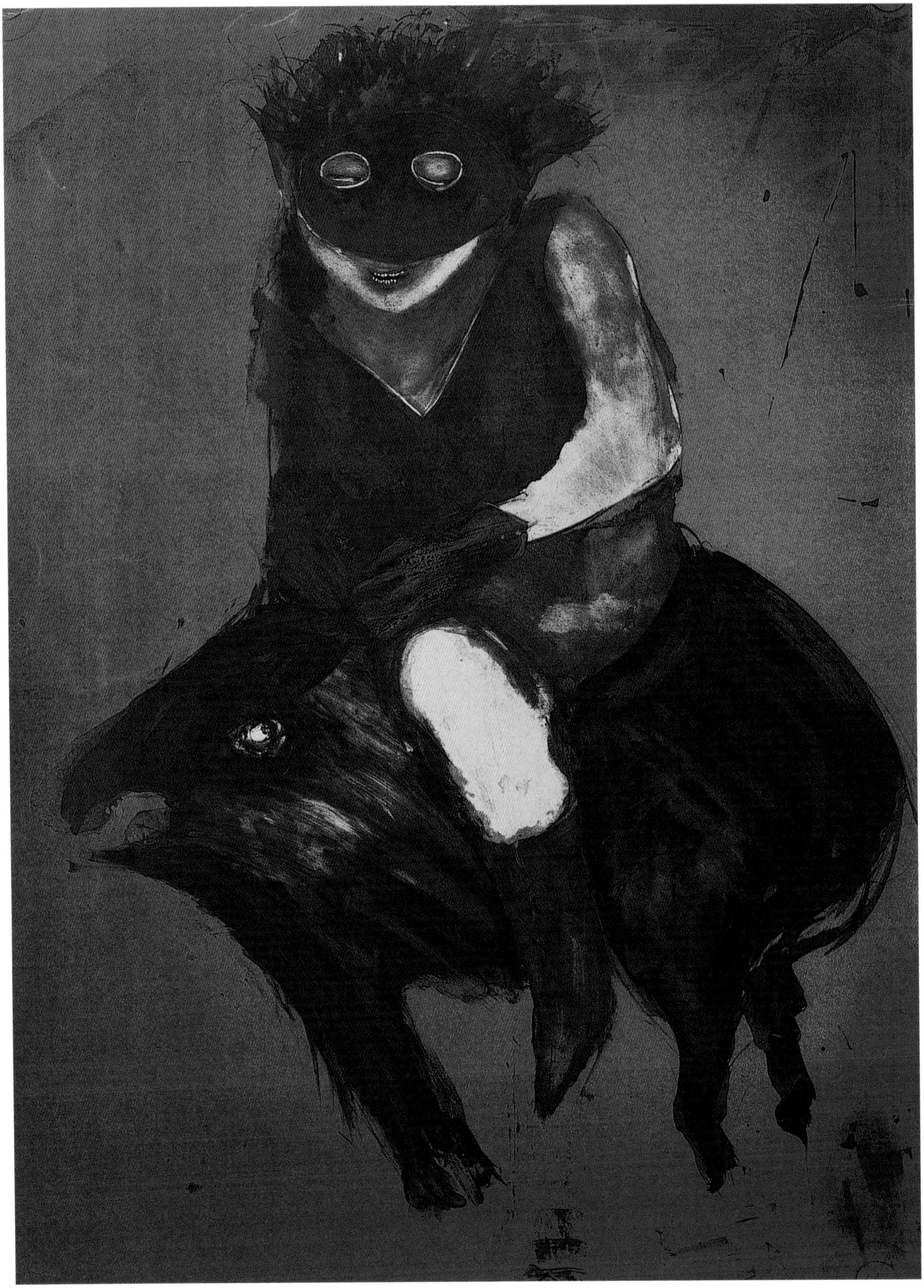

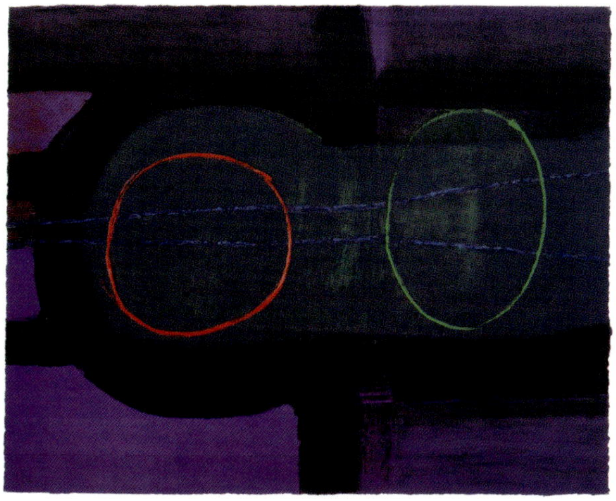

Above: Wilhelmina Barns-Graham, *Two Circles on Purple* lithograph. Published by the artist, 1991.

Left: Anna Maria Pacheco, *Woman and tapir*, monoprint, 1992. Experimental print.

had lived, as well as my own relationship with it – hence the idea for this book. A specialist facility, the studio has nevertheless needed re-forming, depending on the demands of the time; this has often involved taking bold decisions while at the same time managing to protect its essential character. Holding to the principle of making artists' original work, in this case using lithography, has required our staff to be both technically skilled and also flexible and sympathetic to the artist's ideas. Artists working at the Curwen studio for a time become part of the team. For most of them it is an unusual experience, as the creation of a painting or sculpture is normally a solitary occupation.

Of course, commercial printing processes have advanced enormously, revolutionising the industry in ways which would have been unimaginable 50 years ago. Most of the technical problems which worried the developing commercial lithographic industry in the 1920s and '30s have disappeared. As in every other field, scientific research is constantly pushing back the boundaries of what's possible, with lasers, the making of inks with micro-particles (nano-inspired technology) and further developments in computer technology all making a difference to our work. However, artists are experimenters and creators in many directions, and printmakers are no exception, attracted to risk factors that will lead to special results. This has been one of the attractions of the studio during its lifetime – that it provided a chance to push at the boundaries of old as well as new technologies.

50th anniversary celebrations: 2008

During our 50th anniversary year we were fortunate to be offered the Goodison Room at Tate Britain, to stage a retrospective of the studio's work, which also included the book *Art and Print: The Curwen Story*, written by Alan Powers. Robert Upstone was in charge of organising the exhibits plus the making of a studio film featuring Paula Rego creating a print, which formed part of the exhibition. Other events were organised, such as an evening discussion at the Tate in October, chaired by Robert Upstone, in which Alan Powers gave a commendable talk about the significance of Curwen and the artists who have worked there. It was very well attended, with Paula and I at the end answering questions from a very attentive audience. There were also other studio exhibitions and celebrations throughout the year. Jenny Roland organised one event to include friends and associates of the studio in reception rooms next to Tate Britain. People wrote magazine articles, there was a sale of work at Bloomsbury Auctions, and a special evening at the Art Workers' Guild, where Jenny and I exhibited artists' work and talked about the studio.

It was a significant year in so many ways; for me, a point in time appropriate in gathering together for the purposes of record some of the experiences which have guided the studio's progress since 1958. Bound by an unwavering respect for imagination and craftsmanship, it is the artists, printmakers and staff who have been the

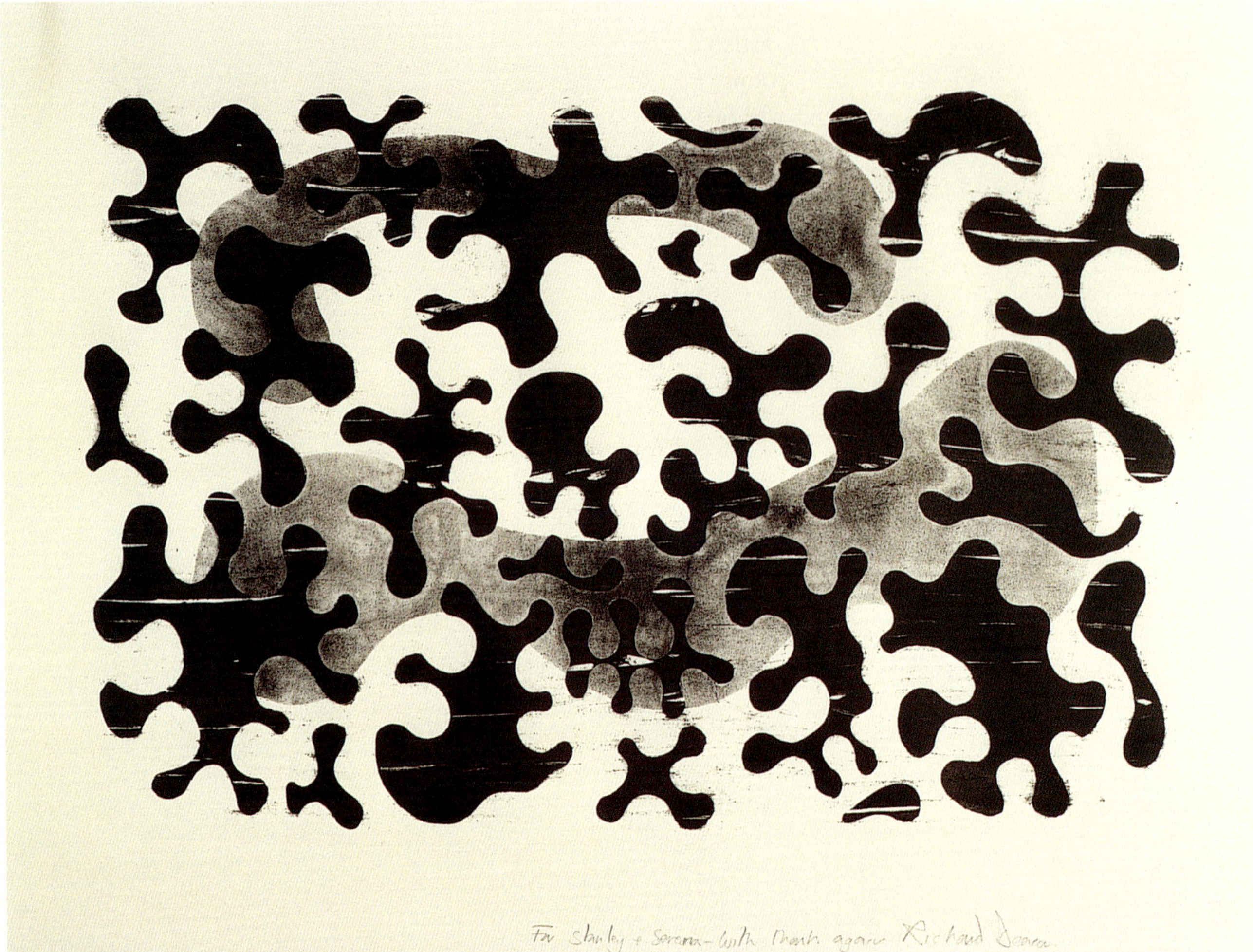

Richard Deacon, *Tomorrow*, experimental proof. Curwen Gallery, 1995.

formative element in the studio's continuing development. Writing as a witness to this series of events, I hope to have conveyed something of the flavour of the Curwen Studio, its unique spirit of adventure in dealing with painters or sculptors and their printed images. After all that has happened, we can only be intrigued by what lies ahead.

INDEX

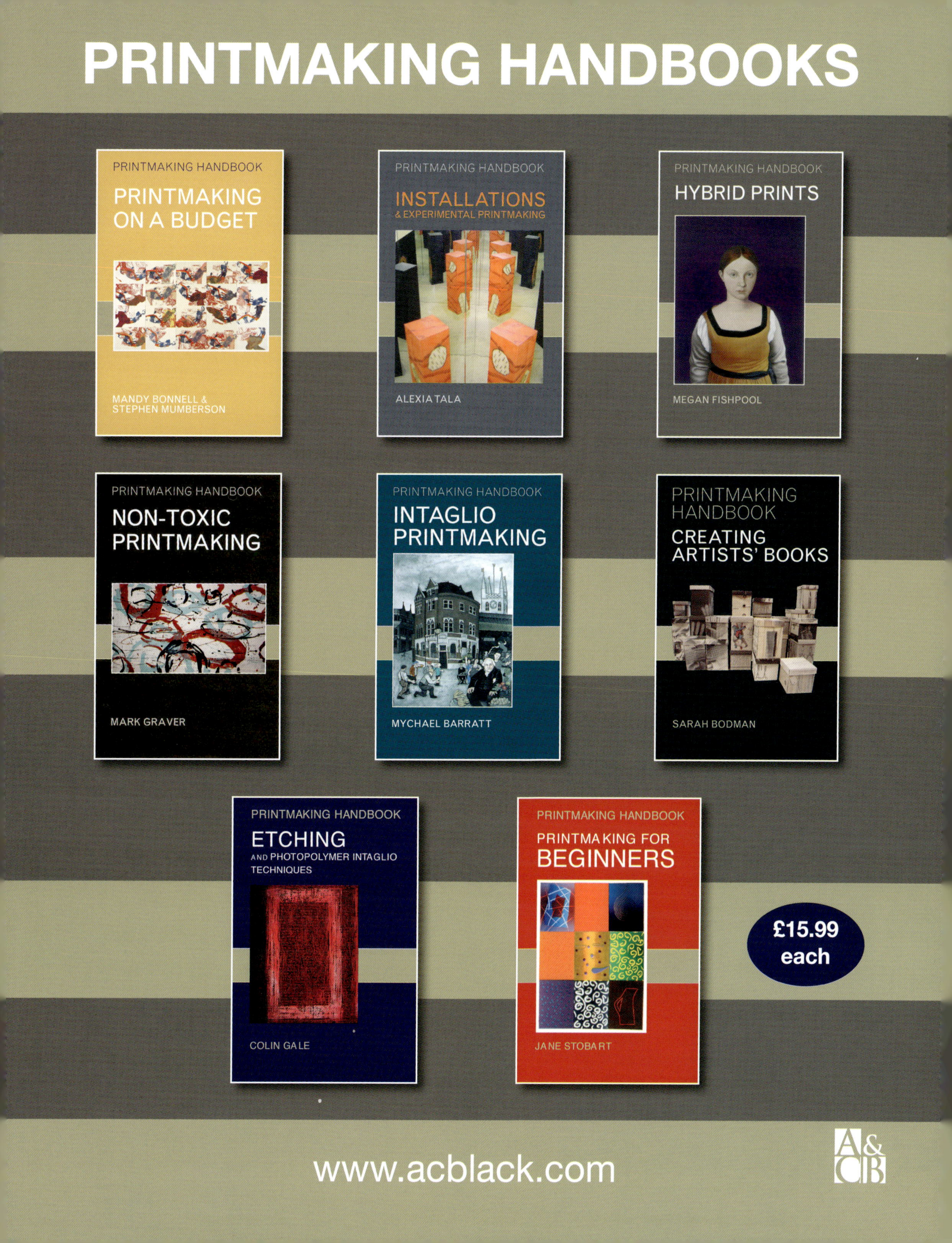
PRINTMAKING HANDBOOKS
PRINTMAKING HANDBOOK
PRINTMAKING ON A BUDGET
MANDY BONNELL & STEPHEN MUMBERSON
PRINTMAKING HANDBOOK
INSTALLATIONS & EXPERIMENTAL PRINTMAKING
ALEXIA TALA
PRINTMAKING HANDBOOK
HYBRID PRINTS
MEGAN FISHPOOL
PRINTMAKING HANDBOOK
NON-TOXIC PRINTMAKING
MARK GRAVER
PRINTMAKING HANDBOOK
INTAGLIO PRINTMAKING
MYCHAEL BARRATT
PRINTMAKING HANDBOOK
CREATING ARTISTS' BOOKS
SARAH BODMAN
PRINTMAKING HANDBOOK
ETCHING AND PHOTOPOLYMER INTAGLIO TECHNIQUES
COLIN GALE
PRINTMAKING HANDBOOK
PRINTMAKING FOR BEGINNERS
JANE STOBART
£15.99 each
www.acblack.com
A&CB

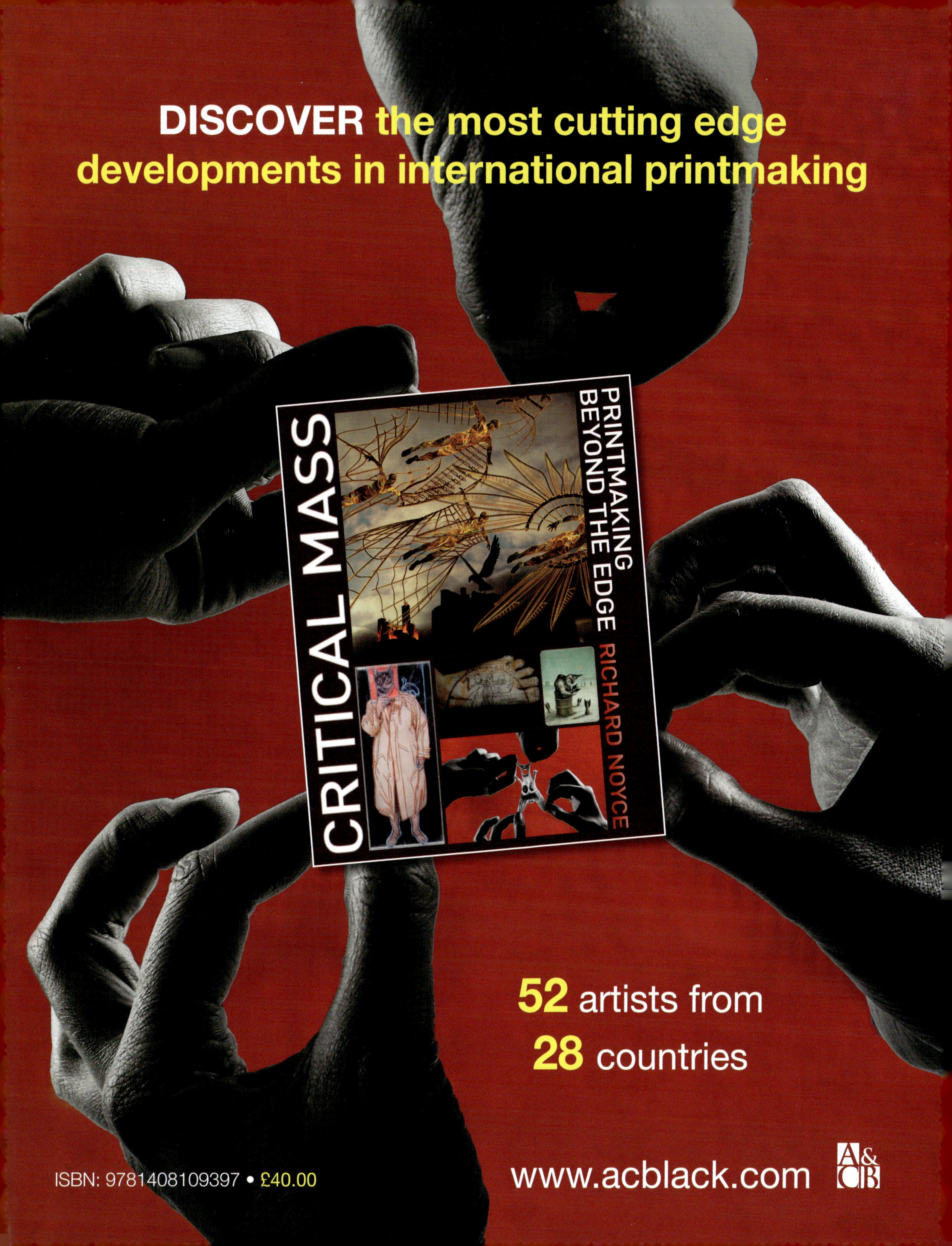
DISCOVER the most cutting edge developments in international printmaking
CRITICAL MASS
PRINTMAKING BEYOND THE EDGE
RICHARD NOYCE
52 artists from 28 countries
ISBN: 9781408109397 • £40.00
www.acblack.com

PRINTMAKING AT THE EDGE by RICHARD NOYCE

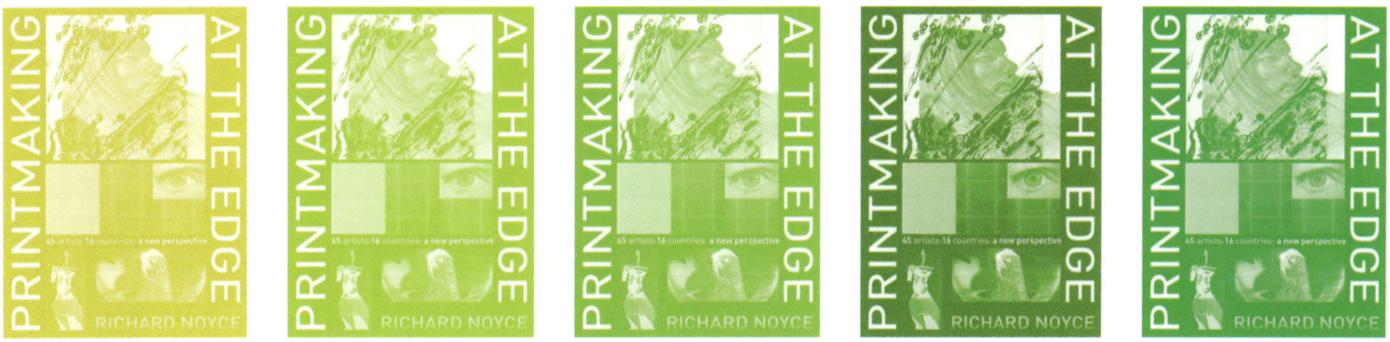

Explore the innovative techniques used by printmakers today

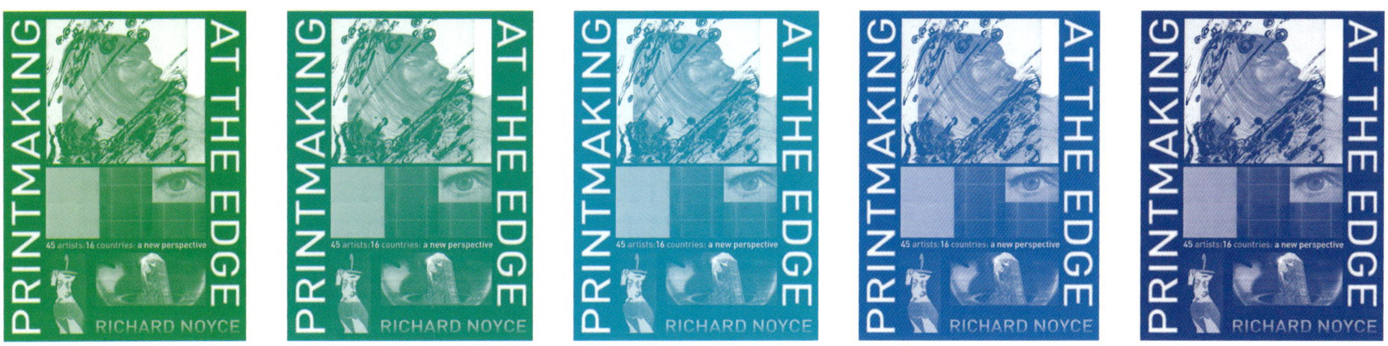

45 artists from 16 countries

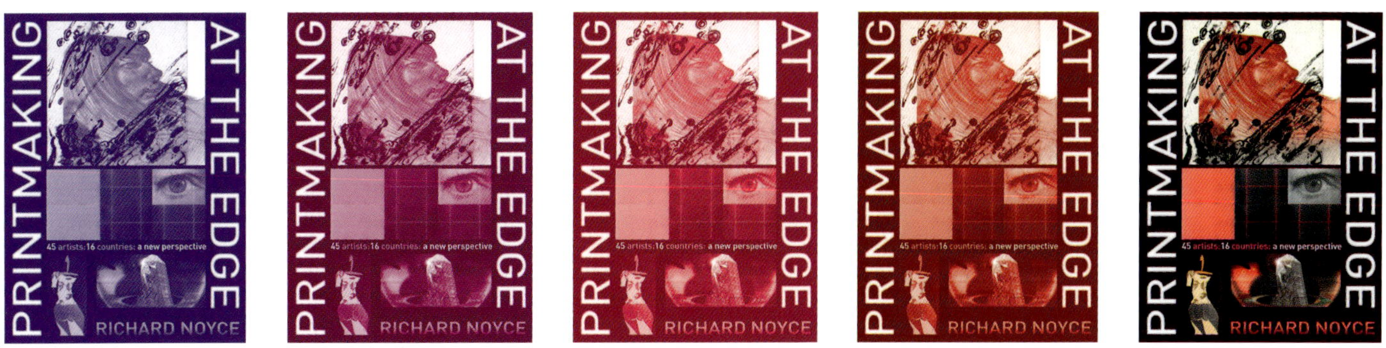

ISBN: 9780713667844 • £35.00

www.acblack.com

A&C B